SECOND EDITION

What
SUCCESSFUL
Teachers Do

SECOND EDITION

What
SUCCESSFUL
Teachers Do

101 **Research-Based Classroom Strategies for New and Veteran Teachers**

Neal A. Glasgow ◉ Cathy D. Hicks

CORWIN PRESS
A SAGE Company

For information:

Corwin Press
A SAGE Company
2455 Teller Road
Thousand Oaks, California 91320
www.corwinpress.com

SAGE Ltd.
1 Oliver's Yard
55 City Road
London, EC1Y 1SP
United Kingdom

SAGE India Pvt. Ltd.
B 1/I 1 Mohan Cooperative
    Industrial Area
Mathura Road, New Delhi 110 044
India

SAGE Asia-Pacific Pte. Ltd
33 Pekin Street #02-01
Far East Square
Singapore 048763

Printed in the United States of America

Library of Congress Cataloging-in-Publication Data

Glasgow, Neal A.
 What successful teachers do : 101 research-based classroom strategies for new and veteran teachers / Neal A. Glasgow, Cathy D. Hicks. – 2nd ed.
     p. cm.
 Includes bibliographical references and index.
 ISBN 978-1-4129-6618-4 (cloth) — ISBN 978-1-4129-6619-1 (pbk.)
 1. Effective teaching. 2. Motivation in education. I. Hicks, Cathy D.
 II. Title.
 LB1025.3.G5163 2009
 371.102–dc22

                         2008030592

This book is printed on acid-free paper.

09 10 11 12 13 10 9 8 7 6 5 4 3 2 1

Acquisitions Editor: Carol Chambers Collins
Editorial Assistant: Brett Ory
Production Editor: Appingo Publishing Services
Cover Designer: Michael Dubowe

Contents

Foreword

The interesting thing about successful teachers is that they never stop learning. I said that five years ago in my foreword to the first edition of *What Successful Teachers Do.* Perhaps that original statement is more relevant and more important today than it was then, because we are leaving too many of our kids behind today. In fact, many of the original predictions have become validated by the publication of this update. This new edition will help teachers teach the kids of today and tomorrow.

The new revised book has some of the best strategies from the first book, along with many new strategies based on the latest educational research.

More and more states are struggling with teacher retention problems, and this book may serve as a helpful resource for teacher induction programs to assist new teachers on their journey toward classroom effectiveness. Veteran teachers will also find new strategies to kick-start their classrooms.

This book, by Neal Glasgow and Cathy Hicks, both veteran and master teachers, makes it easy to keep on learning. The format reads like a well-thought-out lesson plan. The Strategy, Research, Classroom Applications, Precautions and Possible Pitfalls, and Sources provide the teacher with the confidence needed to apply the Strategy in tomorrow's lesson. It offers solid research to develop real strategies in a brain-based, learning-friendly way.

After teaching for more than 30 years, I am still constantly striving to be a better teacher. However, I prefer to work smarter, not harder. This book cuts to the chase. The nine chapters arrange the Strategies in categories which are useful for both beginning and seasoned teachers.

When I first looked at the book, I was instantly hooked. Since my life has been a search to become a more effective teacher, I was pulled in by the title, *What Successful Teachers Do.* After 30 years of teaching, however, I have learned to be wary of books that carry messages such as "believe and you can achieve." I want proven methods and materials, not feel-good promises. This book delivers with 101 research-based classroom strategies for teachers in the real world.

The Strategies cover a wide spectrum of important topics for investigation for successful teachers, from working with students, colleagues, and families to managing classroom, curriculum, assessment, teaching style, and self.

Perhaps most important to me is that the authors have written with the underlying belief that students don't care what you teach if you don't teach that you care. Strategies deal with test anxiety and the use of humor to help put students at ease, to gain attention, and to let students know that the teacher is indeed an empathetic, caring human being. Successful teachers take time to talk to and listen to their students.

Strategies that encourage peer coaching are invaluable. I am amazed that even today, as I travel the world providing teacher training, many teachers do not realize the wealth of knowledge and experience in their own buildings. Teachers do not need to suffer in the silence of isolation. They need to talk, share, and grow with their colleagues. A worthwhile caveat is to surround oneself with mentors who are positive and to avoid the teacher who is negative.

This book addresses the timely issues of technology, diversity, students with special needs, and professionalism, which are paramount for today's educators. It helps a teacher deal with integrating technology and diversity in the classroom. It offers time-saving classroom management skills as well as suggestions on how teacher support Web sites can help you avoid inventing the wheel with existing classroom methods and materials. And the ideas on becoming a professional, like dress for success and join professional organizations, are priceless because many teachers find out about these secrets only after years of experience.

The authors also explore an important area that needs more attention for both students and teachers. It seems as if almost everyone involved with education today is stressing proficiency and standards testing. These are important concerns, but what about reality testing? Do you know about youth culture and how it relates to student health, to school safety, and to learning? Is your classroom youth-culture friendly? And what about you as a teacher? Are you eating a well-balanced diet, getting a good night's sleep, and exercising? Teaching is a stressful occupation. Teachers need to keep themselves safe and healthy because safe and healthy teachers do make better teachers and teach more effectively.

An intriguing thing about these Strategies is that their effectiveness may vary from teacher to teacher, class to class, school to school, and year to year. But becoming a successful teacher is not a destination; it is a never-ending, wonderful journey. And successful teachers continually reflect on their classroom experiences along the way.

No matter where you are in your teaching career, this book will take you places you have been, will be, and wish to be. In fact, I have found some strategies that I can't wait to try!

Dr. Stephen Sroka
www.DrStephenSroka.com

Preface

In the five years since this book was first published, it has sold close to 25,000 copies and has been a prominent resource for many induction and mentor programs throughout the United States. Clearly the need for useful research-based strategies is stronger than ever before. Beginning and veteran teachers have provided positive feedback regarding the ease of access to current educational research that this book allows. In addition, many teachers have commented anecdotally on our easy-to-read format and the utility of the information we've included.

When we wrote the first edition of this book, the teaching profession faced a dilemma of monumental proportions. In 2003 it was estimated that 2 million new teachers would be needed nationwide. Research predicted that 50% of new teachers would not continue after three to five years in the profession. Seventeen percent were not expected to last even one year. Little has changed since then. Research also indicates that teachers don't really learn their craft until they have been teaching at least five to six years. It takes that long for beginning teachers to experiment with and adapt the rules and procedures they must employ in their classroom, to develop and refine lesson plans, and to embrace a sense of community and camaraderie with their students and colleagues. Further, we know that good teachers continually strive to improve their own professional growth by attending conferences and inservices, collaborating with colleagues, and keeping up with the latest professional journals. Bridging the gap between the crucial need for teachers yet expecting excellence in teaching is the challenge facing educators, school districts, and institutes of higher education. We hope this book will serve as a resource for beginning teachers and veterans alike, as they develop and polish the skills that will define them as educators throughout their professional careers.

While many new and veteran teachers receive advice and support from mentors, veteran colleagues, and induction programs, this book's intent is to bring the reader methodologies based on educational research findings. This book is not meant to be read as one would read a novel, but rather used as one would refer to an information guide. Our objective is to focus on useful and practical educational research that translates into a range of choices and solutions to individual teaching and learning problems. Within these chapters we present a wide range of instructional strategies and suggestions based on educational, psychological, and sociological studies. The strategies are based on research done with preservice, student, beginning, and experienced teachers.

Strategies within the chapters are structured in the following user-friendly format:

- *The Strategy*—a simple, concise, or crisp statement of an instructional strategy
- *What the Research Says*—a brief discussion of the research that led to the strategy providing the reader with a deeper understanding of the principle(s) discussed
- *Classroom Applications*—a description of how this teaching strategy can be used in instructional settings
- *Precautions and Possible Pitfalls*—caveats intended to help teachers avoid common difficulties before they occur
- *Sources*—provided so the reader may refer to the original research

We feel teachers may benefit from the practical classroom applications based on the research findings. Our hope is that our work can provide advice and support regarding many facets of teaching that can be especially troublesome. The strategies provide reality-based suggestions to strengthen and support classroom theory and practical application.

It is our hope that if beginning teachers accept some of these ideas, maybe they can avoid the "baptism by fire" that many teachers experience when they first start teaching. Veteran teachers can also benefit from the knowledge gained from recent research. Given the critical need for teachers now and in the future, we, as a profession, cannot afford to have potentially good teachers leaving the profession because they don't feel supported, they're too overwhelmed, or they suffer from burnout.

If you are a beginning teacher reading this book for the first time, there may be strategies that don't apply. As in any new endeavor, as a beginning teacher, you might "not know what you don't know." We ask that you come back and revisit this book from time to time throughout the year. What may not be applicable the first time you read it may be of help at a later date. Veteran teachers can refresh their teaching toolbox by scanning the range of strategies presented in the book to apply to their own teaching environment.

Teaching, and education in general, has never been more exciting or more challenging. Expectations for teachers, students, and schools continue to rise. The more resources teachers have at their fingertips to assist students along the educational journey, the better the outcome. Hopefully, teachers will find this book useful and practical in defining and enhancing their teaching skills.

Acknowledgments

In a completely rational society, the best of us would be teachers and the rest of us would have to settle for something less, because passing civilization along from one generation to the next ought to be the highest honor and the highest responsibility anyone could have.

—Lee Iacocca

W e are grateful to the people at Corwin Press for their complete collaboration and support. We are also thankful to the thousands of students who have been in our classes over the past 30 years and have helped remind us that we teach students, not just subjects. They inspire us to continually want to grow and develop as educators.

Neal Glasgow would like to thank his coauthor, Cathy D. Hicks, and his collaborator, Sarah J. McNary. He always appreciates the high standards and expectations they bring to their writing projects. He would also like to thank his editor, Carol Collins, for seeing the need for a second edition and for her support; he would like to again thank his editor on the first book, Faye Zucker, for recognizing how helpful research-based teaching strategies can be. His wife, Dr. Peg Just, continues to be an inspiration, and she provides a model for what dedication to quality work looks like.

Cathy Hicks would like to thank her coauthor, Neal Glasgow. She is also thankful and deeply indebted to the many exemplary teachers and colleagues she has worked with and learned from along her own educational journey. Their influence, dedication, and professionalism have helped remind her of the pivotal role that a teacher's relationships with student, subject, and staff play in the quest for true excellence in the classroom.

Heartfelt thanks to Ms. Terry King, Associate Superintendent of San Dieguito Union High School district. Terry's belief in and support of new teacher induction as a critical component of new teacher success has impacted the lives of thousands of students attending the San Dieguito district. There is not a finer administrator or education advocate to be found anywhere.

Corwin Press acknowledges the important contributions of the following reviewers:

Dara Feldman
Director of Education Initiatives
Virtues Project International
Kensington, MD

Mary Ann Hartwick
Coordinator, LESD/ASU
Litchfield Elementary School District
Verrado, MS

Renee Peoples, NBPTS
Teacher/Math Coach
West Elementary School
Bryson City, NC

Brigitte Tennis
Headmistress and Seventh-Grade Teacher
Stella Schola Middle School
Redmond, WA

About the Authors

Neal A. Glasgow has been involved in education on many levels for many years. His experience includes serving as a secondary school science and art teacher both in California and New York, as a university biotechnology teaching laboratory director and laboratory technician, and as an educational consultant and frequent speaker on many educational topics. He is the author or coauthor of ten books on educational topics: *What Successful Schools Do to Involve Families: 55 Partnership Strategies* (2008); *What Successful Literacy Teachers Do: 70 Research-Based Strategies for Teachers, Reading Coaches, and Instructional Planners* (2007); *What Successful Teachers Do in Diverse Classrooms: 71 Research-Based Strategies for New and Veteran Teachers* (2006); *What Successful Teachers Do in Inclusive Classrooms: 60 Research-Based Strategies That Help Special Learners* (2005); *What Successful Mentors Do: 81 Research-Based Strategies for New Teacher Induction, Training, and Support* (2004); *What Successful Teachers Do: 91 Research-Based Strategies for New and Veteran Teachers* (2003); *Tips for Science Teachers: Research-Based Strategies to Help Students Learn* (2001); *New Curriculum for New Times: A Guide to Student-Centered, Problem-Based Learning* (1997); *Doing Science: Innovative Curriculum Beyond the Textbook for the Life Sciences* (1997); and *Taking the Classroom to the Community: A Guidebook* (1996).

Cathy D. Hicks is currently the Beginning Teacher Support and Assessment (BTSA) Induction Coordinator for the San Dieguito Union High School District in Southern California. She oversees an induction program supporting beginning teachers. She serves on the executive board of the California Association of School Health Educators (CASHE) and is an adjunct faculty of California State University San Marcos. She is the coauthor of four books: *What Successful Teachers Do: 91 Research-Based Strategies for New and Veteran Teachers* (2003); *What Successful Mentors Do: 81 Research-Based Strategies*

for New Teacher Induction, Training, and Support (2004); *What Successful Teachers Do in Inclusive Classrooms: 60 Research-Based Strategies That Help Special Learners* (2005); and *What Successful Teachers Do in Diverse Classrooms: 71 Research-Based Strategies for New and Veteran Teachers* (2006). She is a frequent presenter on educational topics at both the state and national level. She taught physical education and health at both the middle and high school level for more than 25 years. During that time she was involved in the California State Mentor Teacher Program and mentored new teachers in her district for more than 17 years. Her energy, enthusiasm, and passion for teaching and supporting new teachers reinforce the career path she chose in elementary school. She believes the most effective teachers are the ones who never settle for "good enough," but continue to grow, stretch, reflect, create, collaborate, and take risks throughout their teaching careers.

1

Interacting and Collaborating With Students

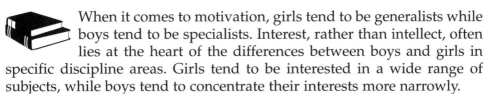

Strategy 1: Use different motivational strategies for girls and boys.

What the Research Says

When it comes to motivation, girls tend to be generalists while boys tend to be specialists. Interest, rather than intellect, often lies at the heart of the differences between boys and girls in specific discipline areas. Girls tend to be interested in a wide range of subjects, while boys tend to concentrate their interests more narrowly.

A study was conducted with 457 students; 338 students attended special mathematics- and science-oriented schools while 119 students attended regular schools but had excellent grades in mathematics, physics, and chemistry. At the beginning of the two-year study, students were asked to rate their interest in later studying science. Several times over a period of two years, teachers were asked to rank their students' interests in science. The ranking of the girls worsened over time.

Girls and boys were asked to rate how much they liked doing a variety of mathematical-physical and linguistic-literary tasks. Mathematical-physical tasks included finding variations of solutions to problems, solving especially difficult tasks, creating tasks by oneself, doing puzzles, and playing chess. Linguistic-literary tasks included making puns; following dialogues in literature, drama, or a radio play; having discussions with intellectuals; and finding contradictions or inconsistencies in texts. The results showed that girls are interested in a variety of areas and that they tend to concentrate their studying in all subjects or content areas rather than investing in one at the expense of the others, as boys tend to do. Over time, girls' interests expanded while boys' interests narrowed.

Classroom Applications

On average girls often seem not to be as motivated in science and math as boys while achievement or grades might be equal to or better than boys as a group. This phenomenon does not happen because girls have less talent in science than boys. It is because of their greater interest in a wide range of other topics. Consequently, girls will be more easily motivated if science and math concepts touch a wider range of subjects. A greater context and relevance helps students develop a better framework in which to place content-specific facts and concepts.

Most specific curricular content does not exist without a more general context or relevance that touches a range of related issues. For example, try going beyond the book facts to make these connections.

- Relate the structure of the atom or radioactivity to Madame Curie and women's issues she may have experienced during her life.
- Link creativity, discovery, and imagination in arts to creativity in science and other areas where this type of thinking is important.
- Connect creative writing to surrealist painting and the beginnings of psychoanalytical thought and brain research during the same time period.
- Relate the development of technology to sociology or human history. What role did technology play within the social and cultural constructs at specific times in history? Have students work on projects that correspond with their interests and write papers or reports.

Precautions and Possible Pitfalls

Don't be disappointed if efforts to motivate girls do not produce observable desired effects. For older girls, entrenched identities tend to have been set in the younger grades. Continue to give all girls the opportunity to demonstrate their abilities to achieve in science. Try narrowing efforts to a few promising and less resistant girls. A little positive reinforcement and recognition can help. Identify quality work done by girls and have it acknowledged beyond the classroom in the school paper, science fair, or student competitions, and so on. These efforts might plant seeds that will blossom in later years.

Sources

Brickhouse, N., Lowery, P., & Schultz, K. (2000). What kind of girl does science? The construction of school science identities. *Journal of Research in Science Teaching, 37*(5), 441–458.

Pollmer, K. (1991). Was behindert hochbegabte Mädchen, Erfolg im Mathematikunterricht zu erreichen? [What handicaps highly talented girls in being successful in mathematics?]. *Psychologie in Erziehung und Unterricht, 38*, 28–36.

 ## *Strategy 2: Add humor to student interactions.*

What the Research Says

 When students are asked to describe exemplary teachers, one of the main characteristics they choose is a sense of humor. Students frequently recall that their favorite teachers made them laugh and, more important, made learning fun. Glasser (1986) included fun in his list of the five primary needs of humans, along with survival, belonging, power, and freedom. He further asserted that all behavior is a constant attempt to satisfy one or more of those needs.

It is no secret that teachers who engage students have found the use of humor as a positive way of putting students at ease, gaining attention, and showing students that the teacher is indeed human. According to Quina (1989), if teachers and students can laugh together, they can most likely work together as well. In these days of standards and high-stakes accountability, if students are comfortable and enjoy the learning process, they are more likely to remember more of the material presented.

Csikszentmihalyi and McCormack (1995) indicated that only after a student has learned to love learning does education truly begin. What student doesn't reflect fondly on a teacher who used stories, analogies, or amusing anecdotes to enhance learning and aid in the retention of knowledge?

Classroom Applications

Humor does not simply mean telling jokes. Humor involves putting a positive spin on reality. Negative humor deals with sarcasm and cynicism, which is never appropriate in the classroom. The teacher who uses humor in a positive way models for students a better way to deal with everyday adverse situations, teaches students not to take small crises and assignments too seriously, and creates a more welcoming atmosphere.

In addition, humor helps a student deal with stress, can enhance his or her self-image, and counteracts unhappiness, depression, and anxiety. It can stimulate creative and flexible thinking, facilitate learning, and improve interest and attention in the classroom.

Humor can be an extremely useful tool in building rapport. A teacher who can laugh at himself or herself, and can laugh with (but never at) students, can help establish a positive, inviting classroom climate.

The use of humor can do a lot to generate interest and grab a reluctant student's attention. The teacher who dresses up as Lincoln to deliver the Gettysburg Address, or who has students write and perform a rap song to learn the endocrine system and its functions, will make the information presented memorable for the students.

One of the many characteristics of a good teacher is to aid students as they become active learners. A goal of many teachers is to have students enjoy not only the class, but also the subject matter. Humor can help achieve this goal.

Precautions and Possible Pitfalls

The teacher must be careful not to use inappropriate humor that could be offensive or sarcastic or that makes references to ethnic, racial, religious, or gender differences. This type of humor is totally inappropriate in the classroom and is almost always at the expense of students. The teacher must also be sensitive to cultural differences as well as age-appropriate humor. It is important for each teacher to find a distinct style of humor. If teachers are not comfortable using humor, they can start off slowly by reading a funny quip or quote. One veteran teacher, knowing her lesson would involve extensive lecturing that day, used an overhead cartoon when students complained they had been sitting for a long time. The text stated, "The mind can hold only what the seat can endure."

Sources

Csikszentmihalyi, M., & McCormack, J. (1995). The influence of teachers. In K. Ryan & J. Cooper (Eds.), *Kaleidoscope: Readings in education* (pp. 2–8). Boston: Houghton Mifflin.

Glasser, W. (1986). *Control theory in the classroom.* New York: Harper & Row.

Quina, J. (1989). *Effective secondary teaching: Going beyond the bell curve.* New York: Harper & Row.

Strategy 3: Be sensitive to possible gender and ethnic differences.

What the Research Says

Historically, girls and certain ethnic minority groups have underachieved in schools. This is especially true in science and math classes. Research suggests that girls and boys may have different science preferences and self-perceptions depending on the specific area of science. Fourth-grade girls were found to prefer biological science while boys preferred physical sciences (Kahle & Damnjanovic, 1994; 1997). This may impose obstacles to success for students inside and outside the classroom. Stereotypes often convey incorrect explanatory information about specific groups, such as Blacks are lazy, girls are bad at science and math, and so forth, that may be used as negative attributions for performance by adults and the children themselves.

One study identified three underlying attributional structures of all stereotypes.

1. Stereotypes that, when used, become internal controllable attributions and explanations for controllable behaviors or states of affairs and imply internal, stable, controllable causes. Examples: Whites are bigoted, certain girls are promiscuous, Mexicans are lazy, and so on.
2. Stereotypes that suggest a trait, attribute, or behavior that is beyond the person's control. Examples: jocks are dumb, old people are senile, women are weak, Irish are lucky, and so on.
3. Stereotypes that imply external causes that lie outside the individual being stereotyped and remove responsibility and place it on factors outside the student's control. Examples: believing some groups are underprivileged by a racist society or believing African Americans and Latinos (as a group) are not as successful as Whites because they are lazy or inept.

It was found that each one of these attributional signatures has specific effects on judgments of responsibility. Recognizing that stereotypes are vehicles for attribution judgments, educators can better prepare themselves to deal with the effects that stereotypes may have on students and their perceptions. Then they are better able to counteract or diminish them.

Classroom Applications

Classrooms are increasingly characterized by ethnic diversity, and this trend will continue to become even stronger. Teachers often have unconscious stereotypes of students based on their ethnicity and gender. It is very important for teachers to treat each student as an individual and to tune in to and understand each student's thoughts and feelings about learning each discipline.

Precautions and Possible Pitfalls

 Beware of stereotyping students based on gender or ethnicity! Although there are general trends for girls versus boys (e.g., preferring biology to physics) and for students from different ethnic groups, teachers should not assume their students have any predisposed characteristics. Teachers can subtly communicate a self-fulfilling bias or expectation for their students. Keep expectations high for all students.

Sources

Kahle, J. B., & Damnjanovic, A. (1994). The effects of inquiry activities on elementary students' enjoyment, ease and confidence in doing science: An analysis by sex and race. *Journal of Women and Minorities in Science and Engineering, 1,* 17–28.

Kahle, J. B., & Damnjanovic, A. (1997). How research helps address gender equity. *Research Matters to the Science Teacher, 9703,* 1–5. Retrieved November 18, 2008, from http://www.narst.org/publications/research/gender2.cfm

Reyna, C. (2000). Lazy, dumb, or industrious: When stereotypes convey attributions information in the classroom. *Educational Psychology Review, 12*(1), 85–110.

 Strategy 4: Look at homework through the eyes of students.

What the Research Says

In their book, Etta Kralovec and John Buell (2000) presented a unique view of the homework concept and questioned the value of the practice itself. Few studies have been conducted on the subject, and while the book offers perspectives from both sides of the debate, it is clear that the homework concept needs to be examined more closely. For example, Kralovec and Buell cited homework as a great discriminator because children, once leaving school for the day, encounter a range of parental supports, challenging home environments, afterschool jobs and sports, and a mix of resources available to some and not to others. Clearly opportunities are not equal. Tired parents are held captive by the demands of their children's school, unable to develop their own priorities for family life.

Kralovec and Buell (2000) also provided examples of communities that have tried to formalize homework policy as the communities tried to balance the demands of homework with extracurricular activities and the need for family time. They also pointed out the aspects of inequity inherent in the fact that many students lack the resources at home to compete on equal footing with those peers who have computers, Internet access, highly educated parents, and unlimited funds and other resources for homework requirements.

They also pointed out that homework persists despite the lack of any solid evidence that it achieves its much-touted gains. Homework is one of our most entrenched institutional practices, yet one of the least investigated.

The questions their research and discourse explore are: With single-parent households becoming more common or with both parents working, is it reasonable to accept the homework concept, as it is now practiced, as useful and valid considering the trade-offs families need to make? How does homework contribute to family dynamics in negative or positive ways? Does it unnecessarily stifle other important opportunities or create an uneven or unequal playing field for some students?

Classroom Applications

 Consider the inequalities that may exist within the range of students in classes regarding their ability to complete homework assignments. Certain students may be excluded from opportunities for support and other resources. Consider the following questions:

- What is homework?
- How much homework is too much?
- What are or what should be the purposes of homework?
- Can different assignments be given to different students in the same class?
- Do all students have equal opportunity to successfully complete the homework?
- Who is responsible for homework, the students or the parents?
- Do all students have the same capacity to self-regulate?
- How are other school activities or family-based responsibilities factored in?
- What is the best and most equitable way to deal with overachievers?
- Is the homework load balanced between teachers?

Precautions and Possible Pitfalls

Traditionally homework has been seen as a solution rather than the cause of educational problems. It takes a little bit of time to acclimate to the homework concept and to look at it with new eyes. However, the value of homework in providing opportunities for students to deepen their general knowledge should not be ignored. This is especially important for students in the United States whose achievement lags behind students from other countries that have longer school days and years. Beware of the politics involved in any discourse regarding the homework concept.

Source

Kralovec, E., & Buell, J. (2000). *The end of homework: How homework disrupts families, overburdens children, and limits learning.* Boston: Beacon Press.

Strategy 5: Use the jigsaw technique as an effective cooperative learning strategy.

What the Research Says

Contrary to some beliefs about cooperative learning having only social benefits, research shows that the jigsaw method helps students learn and apply academic content as well. An experimental study was conducted with seven classes of students in Grades 7 and 8. The 141 students were separated into four experimental classes and three control classes. The experimental classes were taught with the jigsaw technique, while the three control classes received regular instruction through lectures. The experiment lasted about four weeks, with one double lesson per week. This study examined the social, personal, and academic benefits of jigsaw and traditional instruction. The social and personal benefits observed to result from the jigsaw method are growth of self-control, self-management, ambition, independence, and social interaction.

Jigsaw also was found to reduce intimidation in the classroom, which inhibits learning and leads to introverted student behavior. The academic benefits of jigsaw include improved reading abilities, systematic reproduction of knowledge, ability to make conclusions, and summarizing.

When compared with students in traditional classes, students in the jigsaw classrooms demonstrated improved knowledge as well as an ability to apply that knowledge. Students were not afraid to ask questions or to scrutinize presented information when they were able to ask for and receive an explanation from a peer.

Examining another jigsaw educational model, the Williams (2004) article suggested that schools can improve intergroup relations on campus by implementing a cooperative learning technique known as the jigsaw classroom. Williams argued that the use of the jigsaw classroom would facilitate a recategorization process by which members of racial-ethnic groups other than one's own ("them") will begin to be seen as being members of a more inclusive "we." Williams also examined on-campus discrimination and ways in which the jigsaw classroom has the potential to reduce this discrimination.

Classroom Applications

 This example of the jigsaw technique takes place in a physics class and is meant to explore theory and application in an authentic context. The jigsaw technique operates in six steps.

1. Separate a new part of the curriculum into five major sections.
2. Split a class of 25 students into five groups of five students each. These groups are the base groups. (The groups should be heterogeneous in terms of gender, cultural background, and achievement levels.)
3. Every member of the base group selects or is assigned one of the major sections. For example, one member might focus on the section on the physics of light, another might focus on the section on energy conversion for photosynthesis, while another focuses on the section on vision, neurons, and sight, and so forth. If the number of group members exceeds the number of sections, two students can focus on the same section.
4. The base groups temporarily divide up so each student can join a new group in order to become an "expert" in his or her topic. All the students focusing on the physics of light will be in one group, all the students focusing on energy conversion in photosynthesis will be in another group, and so on. These students work together in temporary groups called expert groups. There they learn about their topic and discuss how to teach it to students in their base groups.
5. Students return to their base groups and serve as the experts for their topics. Everyone then takes a turn teaching what he or she learned about his or her topic to members of the base group.
6. A written test is given to the entire class.

In steps 4 and 5, students have an opportunity to discuss and exchange knowledge. Step 6 gives the teacher an opportunity to check the quality of students' work and to see what and how much they learned from each other. One of the advantages of this method of cooperative learning is that in jigsaw there is always active learning going on and students do not become bored while passively listening to reports from other groups, as sometimes happens with the Johnson and Johnson (1975) learning together method.

The Williams (2004) model of the jigsaw classroom was designed to produce classroom conditions that would be more conducive to improving intergroup relationships. In this version of the jigsaw classroom, students are put in situations where competition among individuals is incompatible with success; individual outcomes are dependent on positive, nonsuperficial interactions with others.

Students in the jigsaw classroom are first divided into small groups of students, each of which is composed of individuals from different racial and/or ethnic backgrounds. The groups are each given assigned content material that is to be learned by the whole group. The content is then broken into sections, and each section is distributed to an individual group member who is responsible for learning it and teaching it to the other group members.

Each group member then breaks out of their group to meet and form an expert group made up of others with the same assigned content material. Expert groups review the assigned material and ensure that all group members are clear on the material. They then discuss ways in which the material can be presented to their jigsaw group. In this situation high-ability students are able to tutor lower-ability students and reinforce their capability to present the material to their group. Therefore, when they return to their group they can be true "experts."

Members of all groups rely on each other for learning, and each can be considered an important group member. In this case, assessment is done on an individual basis. In the jigsaw classroom, members of all racial and ethnic groups come together and begin to look at each other more favorably, because the jigsaw classroom originally was designed to reduce intergroup prejudice. This is accomplished through cooperative interracial interactions, individualized contacts, and the support of authority figures (teachers, parents, administrators). According to Williams (2004), there are other benefits that include greater student self-esteem and reduced individual competitiveness.

Precautions and Possible Pitfalls

Cooperative learning simply does not work in all classes. Each class comes with its individual social mix that can make or break cooperative learning attempts. It is also suggested that teachers wait until they have class discipline and management plans in place and working before attempting cooperative learning strategies.

While students teach members of their base groups in step 5, teachers are frequently tempted to join in the discussions and advise students regarding the best way to teach the subject to their base group. This type of teacher intervention prevents the social and intellectual benefits of jigsaw. Although a teacher has to monitor group work in order to intervene when there are substantial mistakes in understanding the academic content, the teacher should not interfere with how students decide to teach this content to their peers.

Williams (2004) stated that the jigsaw classroom works best when groups are assigned text-based material. Also, it was important to note that the jigsaw classroom appears to reduce prejudice only toward groups whose members were included in the jigsaw group. Positive attitudes will extend beyond jigsaw group members to their racial-ethnic groups, but the results will not extend to all racial-ethnic groups.

Sources

Aronson, E., Blaney, N., Stephan, C., Sikes, J., & Snapp, M. (1978). *The jigsaw classroom*. Beverly Hills, CA: Sage.

Eppler, R., & Huber, G. L. (1990). Wissenswert im Team: Empirische Untersuchung von Effekten des Gruppen-Puzzles [Acquisition of knowledge in teams: An empirical study of effects of the jigsaw techniques]. *Psychologie in Erziehung und Unterricht, 37*, 172–178.

Johnson, D., & Johnson, R. (1975). *Learning together and alone: Cooperation, competition, and individualization*. Englewood Cliffs, NJ: Prentice Hall.

Williams, D. (2004). Improving race relations in higher education: The jigsaw classroom as a missing piece to the puzzle. *Urban Education, 39*(3), 316–344.

Strategy 6: Manage student-controlled peer interaction within a cooperative framework.

What the Research Says

 Schools are expected to give students insight into content knowledge, learning techniques, reasoning, and logic, while learning a variety of specific processes and applications. In addition, it is expected that class activity will be conducted in a manner that gives all students equal opportunities for learning and personal development. The focus of this study centered on the activity between students and their peers and between students and the teacher, within the arenas of science teaching and learning.

The study centered on the observation of two eighth-grade girls within a science class from very different social and academic backgrounds. The researchers found the dynamics of student interactions in the specific lessons analyzed did not give all students the same opportunity for learning, and the two girls seemed to be at two different ends of the learning scale. The researchers' conclusions found a very clear "unofficial" classroom arena of discourse and dialogue. This discourse was very much controlled by the students, and it seemed to result in a student-controlled differentiation in the integrated classroom. In very subtle ways, teachers and students construct opportunities and limitations for each other through their actions.

Looking at student interactions beyond the traditional variables of gender, class, or ethnicity can deepen analysis of the learning environment during science lessons. The study points out that discovery learning and group work may not lead to a discovery of science concepts. Rather it leads to a student's social creativity and to opportunities for identity construction within groups. These constructs can detract from rather than enhance a student's opportunity to learn. In an integrated setting, strategies that are supposed to equalize differences between students can create inequities. A second study identified the components of a successful approach and framework for the inclusion of social planning into academic experiences.

Classroom Applications

One cannot analyze a lesson as if it were one lesson for a number of similar students. Rather, one has to look at the subtexts in the classroom—at the varying aspects of life in the social beehive of a school class. Most studies see the classroom dominated by teacher discourse. The classroom also provides an arena for a number of less formal student-dominated discourses. Without more in-depth consideration, the lessons may not provide the same opportunities for all the students.

To begin, be sure to consciously try to deal with the nonintegrative consequences of free choice of seating by assigning students to desk partners who are at different levels of ability and from different backgrounds. Be aware of and discuss with students the potential imbalances in opportunities for classroom participation that could also lessen the quality in which students experience instruction. Discuss the ways the domination of the social constructs by certain students limit other students' opportunities for learning and participation.

In spite of the potential problems group dynamics present, unofficial dialogue, small-group work, and peer learning offer opportunities for learning that whole-class teaching cannot. Interactive patterns of small-group work enable contributions from a larger number of students.

The carefully crafted, situated nature of learning in which the social aspects of the classroom and beyond are taken into consideration play an essential role in student learning. Many recent studies are framed by the notion that students and teachers create discourse communities in which learning social aspects regarding the construction of content knowledge needs to be a significant part of curricular planning. Carefully orchestrating interdependency in small-group work, public sharing, collaboration with experts, and a redefinition of responsibility in learning and teaching transform students into active learners.

However, the organization of such relationships needs to be routinely considered along with content and assessment. Research suggests that paying attention to the following themes in collaborative curriculum development can serve as a framework:

- Tasks related to real-world questions generate more instructional support than topic-bound tasks; embed content coverage in motivating questions.
- Collaborative interactions in groups increases when tasks are student initiated.
- Providing instructional support for students contributes to group decision making.
- Group productivity increases when students gain ownership.
- Student dialogue centers on the procedural aspects of the activity when completing teacher-designed activities.
- When student dialogue centers on their own experiences, students are more cognitively engaged.
- Interactions with outside resource people increase student investment in the project.

Precautions and Possible Pitfalls

New teachers should be aware of how easy it is to fall into a comfortable pattern of classroom organization. Discipline management often takes precedence over teaching and learning management. Classroom social and academic organizations that yield class control and discipline may not always provide the less restrictive and most beneficial learning environment for the greatest number of students. Teachers may have to accept a few less-mature students falling through the cracks so that others can benefit from different learning and teaching arrangements.

Reorganizing academic social arrangements is not always popular with students and may cause friction. Often informal social and peer group arrangements affect learning more than a teacher's more formal strategies. Keep the bigger picture in mind and maximize the benefits of effective strategies for the greatest number of students.

Sources

Crawford, B. A., Krajcik, J. S., & Marx, R. W. (1999). Elements of a community of learners in a middle school science classroom. *Science Education, 83*(6), 701–723.

Sahlstrom, F., & Lindblad, S. (1998). Subtexts in the science classroom—and exploration of the social construction of science lessons and school careers. *Learning and Instruction, 8*(3), 195–214.

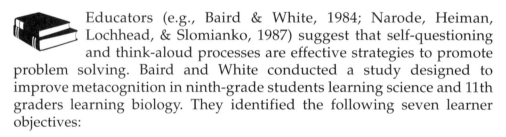

Strategy 7: Teach students to use self-questioning and think-aloud techniques.

What the Research Says

Educators (e.g., Baird & White, 1984; Narode, Heiman, Lochhead, & Slomianko, 1987) suggest that self-questioning and think-aloud processes are effective strategies to promote problem solving. Baird and White conducted a study designed to improve metacognition in ninth-grade students learning science and 11th graders learning biology. They identified the following seven learner objectives:

1. Increased knowledge of metacognition
2. Enhanced awareness of their learning styles
3. Greater awareness of the purposes and natures of tasks
4. More control over learning through better decision making
5. More positive attitudes toward learning
6. Higher standards for understanding and performance set by the students themselves and more precise self-evaluation of their achievements
7. Greater effectiveness as independent learners, planning thoughtfully, diagnosing learning difficulties and overcoming them, and using time more productively

Instructional materials included a question-asking checklist, evaluation of learning behaviors and outcomes, a notebook, and a techniques workbook where students tried concept mapping. This extensive study went through four phases and involved 15 methods of collecting data, including videotapes and audiotapes, classroom observations, questionnaires, and tests. The results showed increased student control over learning and understanding content.

In more recent research, Roscoe and Chi (2007) found that peer tutors in cooperative learning arrangements tend to utilize a pervasive "knowledge-telling" bias. Peer tutors in cooperative relationships, even when trained, focus more on delivering knowledge rather than developing it through questioning and think-aloud strategies. As a result, Roscoe and Chi felt the true potential for tutor and cooperative learning arrangements may rarely be achieved.

Classroom Applications

How do professionals in any career think and reason, conduct their work, and keep learning and being creative? Are the career skills required similar? How do problem solvers and creative people in any discipline create an intellectually rich and fertile mental environment? Some thinking and reasoning strategies are more conducive to making discoveries and bringing clarity of understanding.

Self-questioning and think-aloud techniques are routinely practiced within the context of research laboratory and office team meetings everywhere. Original and creative processing has gone from an individual process to more of a group enterprise as reasoning and knowledge are distributed among many stakeholders within a specific laboratory, office, company, or agency. The more diverse the group, the more beneficial shared reasoning and knowledge become. The following are a few basic suggestions to focus on while using these types of instructional strategies.

- Use self-questioning and think-aloud techniques within cooperative groups to distribute reasoning and knowledge within the group. This is especially important within the context of inquiry-based learning activities.
- Have students follow up on surprising results or ideas. Pay attention to unexpected findings in the control conditions because these results can lead to other fruitful learning and teaching pathways.
- Have students engage in analytical reasoning in both formulating and asking good questions, hypothesizing, solving research or investigative problems, and synthesizing new ideas along the way. Think out loud using distant analogies as an explanatory device. Have students refer back to other experiences where similar

thinking frameworks were used. Make frequent use of analogies as explanations (a common way professionals converse).

- During self-questioning and thinking out loud activities, make sure the students' current goals are not blocking them from considering alternative theories or ways of looking at content and other learning activities.

Some examples of more universal self-questions are

Planning

- How can I design situations to test my ideas?
- What are all the critical elements that need to be considered?
- What elements of learning or knowledge bases need to be addressed or acquired?
- How can I show that learning and understanding have taken place?

Monitoring

- Does the initial plan meet my needs, or does it need adjusting?
- Should I try a different approach?
- Am I processing all my work and effort accurately?
- Am I covering, observing, and recording everything I'm supposed to?

Evaluating

- How effective was my self-reflection of my work?
- To what degree were my conclusions or final results justified by research materials or gathered information?
- What useful feedback did I get from others?
- How could I improve as a consumer of information?

Precautions and Possible Pitfalls

 Given classroom peer pressures, students critiquing each other's questions may be a challenge for the teacher. Avoid embarrassing students who ask ineffective questions by not calling attention to them in a whole-class setting.

Group work presents many pitfalls. Not all students will feel comfortable using these techniques or buy into the strategies. Teachers will have to decide how involved they want students to become in this type of instructional strategy.

Based on the work of Roscoe and Chi (2007), teachers may need to guide students, in tutoring or cooperative learning situations, to develop questioning and think-aloud strategies when interacting with one another. In this way students won't be memorizing facts and knowledge but creating personal meaning by exploring prior knowledge, delving into understanding, or applying the knowledge in new situations and contexts.

Cooperative or tutor learning is a meaningful strategy when coupled with questioning and think-aloud strategies and is a worthwhile educational intervention. Commonplace tutoring activities, such as explaining and questioning, provide many opportunities for tutors to engage in reflective knowledge building. Unfortunately, students in groups do not always take advantage of these opportunities. By analyzing cooperative peer tutors' actual behaviors and their connection to learning outcomes, teachers may further extend the impact and effectiveness of cooperative learning and tutoring programs. This knowledge can then be used to further fine-tune peer relationships that target such interactions. Careful observation of this type may lead to immediate and exciting applications for teachers and students.

Hopefully the process will not become too contrived and lose its effectiveness. Closely monitor groups. The more routine this type of discourse becomes and the more practiced the students, the more their comfort level will rise. To begin, consider having each group engage in these strategies while the others watch as a way to maintain control, guide, and reinforce positive behaviors.

Teachers who attempt this suggestion for implementation must be aware that it is meant to be an enhancement for the instructional program and not a deterrent. If one technique doesn't seem to work with a particular class, it ought to be replaced with a more effective approach.

Sources

Baird, J., & White, R. (1984). *Improving learning through enhanced metacognition: A classroom study.* Paper presented at the annual meeting of the American Educational Research Association, New Orleans, LA.

Brown, G. A., & Edmondson, R. (1984). Asking questions. In E. C. Wragg (Ed.), *Classroom teaching skills: The research findings of the Teacher Education Project* (pp. 97–120). Beckenham, UK: Croom Helm.

Dunbar, K. (2000). How scientists think in the real world. *Journal of Applied Developmental Psychology, 21*(1), 49–58.

Narode, R., Heiman, M., Lochhead, J., & Slomianko, J. (1987). *Teaching thinking skills: Science.* Washington, DC: National Educational Association.

Roscoe, R. D., & Chi, M. T. H. (2007). Understanding tutor-learning: Knowledge-building and knowledge-telling in peer tutors' explanations and questions. *Review of Educational Research, 77*(4), 534–574.

Strategy 8: Lighten the load by training students to be tutors.

What the Research Says

A classroom of students helping other students has been found to be an efficient and effective method of enhancing achievement. Twenty teachers participated in a study of classwide peer tutoring with 40 classrooms in elementary and middle schools. Half of the schools implemented classwide peer tutoring programs and half did not. Both urban and suburban schools participated in the study. Students came from diverse backgrounds, both culturally and linguistically. There were three different categories of students: average achievers, low achievers without learning disabilities, and low achievers with learning disabilities. The peer tutoring programs were conducted three days a week, 35 minutes a day, for 15 weeks. Stronger students were paired with weaker students. Teachers reviewed each pair to ensure they were socially compatible. In all pairs, students took turns serving in the roles of tutor and student. Student pairs worked together for four weeks; then teachers arranged new pairings. Teachers received instruction on how to train their students to be tutors. Tutor training included teaching students how to correct each other's errors. Achievement tests were administered before and after the peer-tutoring program. Regardless of whether students were average achievers or low achievers, with or without learning disabilities, students in the peer tutoring classrooms achieved higher levels than those in the classrooms without classwide peer tutoring.

Classroom Applications

There are many areas in all content classes that lend themselves to a peer-tutoring program. When there is a skill to be learned and all one needs is experience with success (i.e., drill with immediate feedback), then peer tutoring could provide an efficient way to monitor and support a student trying to master the skill. Say a student has difficulty identifying an unknown chemical, an anion, or a cation. Individual students within groups can specialize as peer tutors in specific chemical tests or flame tests, or a general peer tutor (under the guidance of a teacher) can be quite beneficial. There are many tests at which peer tutors can become expert and then share their expertise with individual students. A student who has difficulty doing these tests could find that a peer tutor is a genuine asset.

Foreign-language classes are a natural for tutoring. Advanced students can routinely help less-skilled language students. Rather than waiting for an opportunity to talk with the teacher, a student has access to the peer tutor, saving everyone time. Additionally, in explaining the methodology to the student, the tutor is also provided with an opportunity to strengthen his or her own understanding of the concept of test reactions or a specific element of language (a higher-order thinking skill). Thus, there is often a mutual benefit to a peer-tutoring program.

Precautions and Possible Pitfalls

Not every student makes a good tutor. Some are not mature enough to manage the responsibility. A tutor-training program offered by the teacher can precede peer tutoring. Some kids are natural tutors while others must be given some instruction on how to conduct the specific concepts or sessions, what sorts of difficulties to look for on the part of the tutee, and what points to stress in the sessions (based on the teacher's assessment of the class). Any individual difficulties on the part of the tutees should be mentioned to the tutor prior to the sessions.

Tutors should be taught to guide student learning and not merely solve problems for students. Students with severe learning disabilities may not be receptive to tutoring or benefit from classwide peer tutoring unless the tutors first receive individualized instruction from learning disability specialists.

Finally, there may be classes in which a tutoring system simply doesn't fit. Classes with discipline problems or classes with homogeneous learners may not provide the best setting to begin a tutoring program. In some cases managing tutors in tough classes can be more trouble than it is worth. The teacher should carefully consider the class before committing to this method.

Source

Fuchs, D., Fuchs, L., Mathes, P. G., & Simmons, D. (1997). Peer-assisted learning strategies: Making classrooms more responsive to diversity. *American Educational Research Journal, 34*(1), 174–206.

Strategy 9: Address gender issues in the classroom.

What the Research Says

Research from a study by Good and Brophy (1987) found that teachers give male students greater opportunities to expand ideas and be animated than they do females. In addition, teachers tend to reinforce males for general responses more than they do females. Beginning teachers need to be cognizant of the tendency to give more and better feedback to males than to females (Sadker & Sadker, 1994). Previous studies by Fennema and Peterson (1987) stated that although female students learn best cooperatively and males learn more easily through competition, it is noteworthy for teachers to give all students opportunities to participate in both learning modes.

Weaver-Hightower (2003) stated that beginning roughly in the mid-1990s, a specific and developing shift toward examining boys' education occurred internationally in research on gender and schooling. He went on to say that in many industrialized countries, particularly England and Australia, media furor, parental pressure, practitioner efforts, policy attention, and a great deal of research all have come to focus on the state of boys in schools. He called this shift in gender and education research the "boy turn." Weaver-Hightower felt the phrase is a convenient double entendre, encapsulating two opinions—perhaps falsely dichotomous—about the shift to boys.

Weaver-Hightower (2003) went on to explain that although distressing to many people, particularly feminist and pro-feminist researchers, there has been a trend away from concern about girls. Weaver-Hightower saw this boy turn in research as having some positive impact on our understanding of gender and schooling. He felt that such work has produced the necessary complement to the research on girls, increasing our recognition that gender inequity is not a deficiency in girls but rather is caused by problematic masculinities and femininities. The boy turn, however, still has many other contributions to make, including sometimes identifying problems that might place boys at a disadvantage—not overall, but in particular ways.

Classroom Applications

Spend some time examining gender issues in the primary research and you will find that until recently, most policy, practice, and research on gender and education focused on girls and girls' issues. Most, if not all, educators feel this is as it should be, for in every society women as a group relative to men are disadvantaged educationally, socially, culturally, politically, and economically. In early interventions in education, particularly by liberal feminists and some radical feminists, schools were seen as significant causes of inequality for women and, more important, as an environment through which such inequalities could be addressed.

According to Weaver-Hightower (2003), in the United States, such discussions of gender arguably hit their zenith in the early 1990s with the publication of a number of reports and popular books about girls and their educational disadvantages. The American Association of University Women (AAUW) garnered the largest media splash with the publication of *How Schools Shortchange Girls* (1992). In the report, the AAUW argued that math and science curriculum and pedagogy, biased standardized tests, and environments that do not account for girls' special concerns are educationally depriving girls. Other books of the period, such as Sadker and Sadker's *Failing at Fairness* (1994), Peggy Orenstein's *School Girls* (1994), and Mary Pipher's *Reviving Ophelia* (1994), presented girls as suffering tremendous psychological damage and educational neglect. According to these authors, girls, as compared with boys, display more eating disorders, depression, self-esteem drops, and even self-mutilation; girls are called on less often by teachers, show score and enrollment gaps in math and science, and receive fewer and lower-quality comments from teachers. Widespread attention to these issues has led to great strides in understanding the function of gender in educational contexts, from the processes that affect female entry into and success in math, science, and technology.

Weaver-Hightower's (2003) concept of gender issues included an admonition that researchers still have many contributions to make, including sometimes identifying problems that might place boys at a disadvantage—not overall, but in particular ways. Part of the responsibility of researchers and educators, especially those whose goal is a more equitable society in terms of gender, is to gauge the true impact of such disadvantages and then, rather than weighing them against a hierarchy of disadvantage, find ways to fix them without hurting groups of people who have other problems.

Before looking further into gender issues, beginning (and veteran) teachers need to be familiar with Title IX of the 1972 Education Amendments. Title IX forbids discrimination or segregation of students by gender in school programs, courses, or activities. Most people familiar with Title IX think of its legislative implications as specifically to support equal opportunities for girls in sports. The reality is that the law provides equal opportunities for girls and boys at school.

Videotaping a lesson might help a teacher practice and polish new instructional strategies. One way to provide opportunities for success is to provide learning strategies for all students. For example, to make sure every student has equal opportunities to answer questions in class, the teacher could have 3" × 5" cards with a student's name printed on each card. During a question and answer session, the teacher can shuffle the cards and choose one. The teacher then calls on the student named on that card to answer the question. Once the student answers the question or verbally participates in a discussion, the teacher can make a mark on the card to record that student's participation. This same system can be used to assign students to cooperative learning groups as well as to assign specific roles within that group (investigator, recorder, etc.).

Teachers should find guest speakers from both genders and from diverse populations. Females and males in nontraditional roles can become role models for students as well as help them see themselves in those careers in the future.

Teachers need to experiment with and implement those strategies that are sensitive to the caliber and equality of interaction with each student, provide occasions for every student to participate actively in his or her own learning, and build opportunities for all students to take leadership roles.

Precautions and Possible Pitfalls

 Teachers need to examine their own biases with regard to gender differences and the ways this attitude might affect their teaching. Having a colleague observe class while keeping track of the number of times female students versus male students are called on, whether the interaction is different with boys than with girls, and what types of questions and instructional strategies are used with girls as compared to boys are all helpful ways to bring biases to the forefront and to find ways to improve.

Sources

American Association of University Women. (1992). *How schools shortchange girls.* New York: Marlowe.

Fennema, E., & Peterson, P. (1987). Effective teaching for girls and boys: The same or different. In D. C. Berliner & B. V. Rosenshine (Eds.), *Talks to teachers* (pp. 111–125). New York: Random House.

Good, T. L., & Brophy, J. E. (1987). *Looking in classrooms.* New York: Harper & Row.

Orenstein, P. (1994). *School girls: Young women, self-esteem, and the confidence gap.* New York: Anchor Books.

Pipher, M. (1994). *Reviving Ophelia: Saving the selves of adolescent girls.* New York: Grosset/Putnam.

Sadker, M., & Sadker, D. (1994). *Failing at fairness: How America's schools cheat girls.* New York: Scribner.

Weaver-Hightower, M. (2003). The "boy turn" in research on gender and education. *Review of Educational Research, 73*(4), 471–498.

 Strategy 10: Reduce the emotional distances between teachers and students.

What the Research Says

This research describes the conceptual framework, methodology, results, and ideas from a project on the "Emotions of Teaching and Educational Change" (Hargreaves, 2000). Drawing upon interviews with 53 teachers in 15 schools, Hargreaves described key differences in the emotional closeness and levels of interaction between elementary and secondary teaching.

The study found that secondary school teaching is characterized by greater professional and physical distance from students, leading teachers to often treat emotions and emotional involvement as intrusions into the classroom and teacher-student relationships. As a result, teachers and students rarely share emotional goals or develop emotional bonds or connections. This means, according to the researchers, that secondary teachers may not feel that they are known by their students as moral, emotional, and caring people. Teachers are then stereotyped, and emotional misunderstandings develop. Students see teachers without a real-life context or personality.

Teachers often are responsive to students' emotions only when these emotions might interfere with students' learning. In most classrooms, emotions are noticed only when they force a departure from what is developmentally and academically "normal." This notion is often in conflict with the elementary teaching and learning environment where emotional connections are more the norm. These situations are often exasperated by high school and middle school students who have four or more teachers a day and the same number of content or subject areas. Teachers are more concerned about fending off and managing negative emotions that threaten to intrude from the outside rather than developing positive emotions in their own right. A secondary teacher often will develop and build more meaningful relationships with students outside the classes in extracurricular activities. Outside the class they built a more solid base of understanding on which successful teaching can be attained.

The study also found that the many current forms of curricular reform reinforce fragmented interactions between teachers and their students because cognitive content coverage is the focus. Standardized testing contributes to this. This makes personal understanding and personal knowledge and acknowledgment difficult to achieve. The study concluded with the statement that if we are serious about standards, we must become serious about emotions too. We must look again at the organizational conditions and professional expectations that can increase emotional understanding between teachers and students. Hargreaves (2000) argued that emotional connections contribute to educational goals and student achievement and should be included in curriculum reform and pedagogical strategies.

Classroom Applications

Most secondary school teachers see more than 150 students a day and are expected to try to meet all their needs. Content curricular goals are the focus, and emotional and personal connections with students often take a backseat. However, if teachers look at their own careers as students, they will find that the teachers they remember most are those who formed some personal, emotional bond with their students. The students found themselves working harder for that teacher. Teachers need to take time to know their students, which can seem risky for new teachers when coverage of subject matter seems so important. Focusing on or emphasizing content or subject matter alone can limit the effectiveness of a good teacher. First, coverage doesn't ensure that learning has taken place. Second, curricular coverage only works if students care about what the teacher has to say. There has to be buy-in and engagement. It is true that to teach students, teachers must first reach them.

Consider the following argument for nurturing a more collegial, emotionally friendly learning environment. Today some reform philosophies compare the act of athletic coaching to classroom teaching pedagogy. Coaches generally know their players to a greater degree than most teachers know their students. They are aware of individual and team mood swings. They know when to motivate and when to back off. The coaches read the needs of their teams and players and design pathways and strategies to properly train team members. Coverage doesn't work here when or if players need more specific help.

By taking more of a coaching perspective, teachers will see their students in a more personal, caring style. They will form a more collegial teaching and learning environment and create opportunities for closer emotional connections.

Additionally, extracurricular activities are increasingly coached or led by "walk-ons" or people from the community. Teacher-coaches are becoming rarer. A new teacher should try working with students outside the formal classroom. Students will begin to know the teacher better, and the teacher's reputation as a "person" will filter through the student body. If teachers have a passion for a sport or other activity, they should think about sharing that enthusiasm with their students.

Another way to better connect to students, especially students who present unique problems, is to network with other teachers who share them. Often other teachers can provide insight into a student's performance. As new teachers learn more about what their students' interests are, they will gain a more informed perspective with regard to how to deal with them. Teachers can also share strategies and reinforce each other's efforts.

Precautions and Possible Pitfalls

Just as teachers have expectations for their students, students have expectations for their teachers. Some students have come to expect a less personal connection and simply aren't interested in forming more complex relationships with their teachers. They like remaining academically anonymous. The beginning teacher will have to learn when to accept this and when to back off. This holds true for parent relationships also. Some parents want to be involved and others don't. The new teacher shouldn't take a lack of involvement personally.

Also, the teacher should be careful about coming across in a too-contrived manner. The new teacher should be sincere in his or her efforts and should try to work within his or her own personality, rather than trying to develop a new one just for teaching.

Source

Hargreaves, A. (2000). Mixed emotions: Teachers' perceptions of their interactions with students. *Teaching and Education, 16*, 811–826.

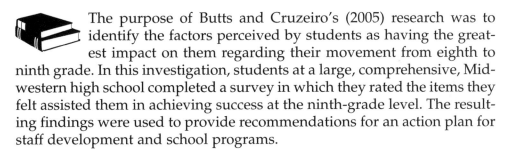

Strategy 11: Help students make an effective transition from eighth to ninth grade.

What the Research Says

 The purpose of Butts and Cruzeiro's (2005) research was to identify the factors perceived by students as having the greatest impact on them regarding their movement from eighth to ninth grade. In this investigation, students at a large, comprehensive, Midwestern high school completed a survey in which they rated the items they felt assisted them in achieving success at the ninth-grade level. The resulting findings were used to provide recommendations for an action plan for staff development and school programs.

Classroom Applications

 Here are the top eight student responses to the survey items used to identify the important qualities students felt helped or really helped them make the transition to ninth grade.

- Teachers who explained well
- Going to class every day
- Having friends in class
- Interesting classes
- Teachers who were easy to talk to
- Avoiding negative influences
- Getting homework done at school
- Understanding class expectations

Also high on the students' response list were

- Students and teachers cooperate
- Good class behavior
- Confidence to do work
- Structured environment

The survey items reflected two general categories: items over which teachers had full or some control in the ninth-grade student's daily life and items that fell more under administration or school control. Most of the top items deemed helpful or really helpful fell under some or total control of the teachers.

Middle schools, junior high schools, and elementary schools tend to be more comfortable for students as they usually are smaller and students are known well within the smaller, more personal academic environments. First-time high school students need the support of teachers who care, explain things well, and are easy to talk to. Teachers who explain their expectations and standards, teach using a variety of methods for curricular delivery, and are able to structure a warm and welcoming small internal academic environment or community within the background of the larger school would rate well. Student–teacher and student–student relationships are enhanced in such a setting because there is usually more time to form supportive relationships. When students feel comfortable in a class and are engaged in interesting activities with friends, they may not feel the need for other support, such as mentors or tutors. A sense of belonging needs to be developed, and new peer relationships need to be facilitated by the teachers.

Precautions and Possible Pitfalls

Recommendations from this study are limited by its small sample size and its limited, narrow demographic and should not be generalized for all high schools. Responses to surveys may vary in other settings. Further research may reinforce the current conclusions or provide further insights so that all ninth graders engage in successful transitions. While the ideas presented may have merit, the scale of the research limits it validity. However, anecdotally, teachers should look at the data and look for opportunities to modify their practices to help students find the peace of mind to perform at their maximum levels.

Source

Butts, M. J., & Cruzeiro, P. A. (2005). Student perceptions of factors leading to an effective transition from eighth to ninth grade. *American Secondary Education*, 34(1), 70–82.

2

Managing the Classroom Environment, Time, and Discipline

> ☑ *Strategy 12: Post an agenda before the start of class.*

What the Research Says

 Using an agenda of the day's lesson makes learning more relevant to students and takes the mystery out of what is going to be covered in class that day. An agenda also helps keep the teacher organized with regard to the information to be learned. An agenda that includes the lesson outline on the board or an overhead transparency can arouse students' thinking about the various topics and help them connect to prior knowledge about those topics. A connection between existing knowledge and new knowledge is a critical component of meaningful learning.

Based on Ausubel's (1960) theory of how knowledge is structured, the most meaningful learning is dependent upon a lesson's material being organized in a way that "connects" and makes it meaningful to the learner. The student needs to be able to connect the information being taught with ideas, concepts, and examples that are already present in the learner's cognitive structure. According to Ausubel, the framework of a pre-organized agenda provides a stable sequential structure that students can use as a framework to build upon the objective of the lesson. It prepares students in advance for what is to come, tells students how the teacher has organized the material, and makes the material to be received more meaningful. This process is what Ausubel calls *meaningful reception learning*.

In a more current twist on agendas, Scott and Compton (2007) pointed out that many students, especially those with disabilities, have difficulty in middle and high school with assignment organization and completion. Their article presented a learning strategy to assist students in keeping a calendar or agenda book. The strategy presented for students cues to specific actions they must take in order to remember assignments, study for tests, complete projects, and organize their materials.

Classroom Applications

Who remembers being in a class and having no idea what was going to be covered that day, whether a test was imminent, or if the teacher would assign a hefty homework packet over a holiday weekend? Most students have had this experience more than once. Using the board or an overhead transparency to cover the day's agenda can serve a number of purposes. The agenda should be posted at the beginning of class, preferably as students are entering the room. Students then know what is to come. It can also cut down or eliminate the number of "What are we going to do today?" questions teachers frequently encounter. There are no surprises about an upcoming assignment, a concept being taught that day, test due dates, or homework assignments.

In addition, using an agenda places the onus of responsibility on the students for keeping a record of what material is to be covered, not only for themselves but for students who are absent. Schools that use block scheduling, where students attend class every other day, can benefit even more by not having to wait two days before catching up. The student can instead call a homework buddy, who checks the agenda written down that day. The use of an agenda can alleviate miscommunication problems ("I didn't know we were having a test today") and can reduce the academic stress some students feel while trying to juggle and organize homework, projects, tests, and so on. A sample agenda might include the following information: standard(s) addressed, homework due, review from previous lesson, new material, next test or project due, and new homework. The teacher can easily create these agendas as a computer presentation software slide (e.g., using PowerPoint), and a record is then kept for future planning.

Using this type of agenda helps keep the teacher focused on the lesson and leaves no secrets for the student about what will be covered that day. By using an overhead transparency, teachers who are assigned to multiple classrooms (not uncommon for a new teacher) are able to take the agenda with them and not waste valuable time rewriting the day's activities in each room. After a lesson, the teacher can use the agenda to make notes about pacing, transitions, and lesson evaluations to be used in the future.

The Scott and Compton (2007) model focused on an agenda book. The authors felt that students, especially those with disabilities, are challenged by the necessity to organize and complete assignments within a specific time frame. An agenda book typically consists of a list of classes and a place to write down homework assignments and notes within a framework of a calendar or schedule. This allows students to keep important information within a date matrix, and often teachers ask that students have their parents sign the agenda book nightly. There may also be a place in the book for teacher and parent notes. Depending on the ability level of the students, teachers will often need to teach the agenda book to their students. Some students may use the agenda book totally independently, while others will wait for teachers to tell them what to put in the book.

Teachers will need to scaffold the creation and use of the agenda book. Scott and Compton (2007) suggested that, at some point during class, teachers use a TRICK BAG. It's important to realize this can and should be modified for the age and academic maturity of the students in the classroom. The TRICK BAG is summarized as follows:

T—Take the book out and discuss what is important to insert for that day.

R—Record the assignment in the correct place. Show examples of agenda entries and monitor the student's work. Teachers can model this with an overhead projector or similar technology.

I—Insert the important details. Model a way of choosing what is important and what might be missing in specific entries. Brainstorm what the important details are.

C—Circle the materials needed. List the materials students need to complete the assignments and circle them.

K—Keep materials in the homework folder. If students have a separate homework folder, help them organize it and identify what should go in it.

B—Be sure to read it. Have students write down agenda entries in a variety of ways. Have students critique the agenda book for usefulness and practicality.

A—Ask a partner to check it. Discuss appropriate times and ways to ask a partner to check another's agenda book.

G—Make sure it gets into a backpack and on its way home.

This strategy can also be modified for electronic date books or computer organizational programs. The goal is that students will become better at task organization and rely less on teachers and parents for assistance. These small organizational successes can really help increase a student's feelings of overall success and lead to improved academic achievement.

Precautions and Possible Pitfalls

The agenda should not be a detailed outline of each facet of the lesson, but rather a general outline of the day's activities. When students begin copying detailed agendas into notes, their focus turns to note taking, and the teacher risks losing their attention. In addition, agendas should include enough information to pique the student's interest about the day's lesson, but not be so detailed that they become meaningless notes. Copying the agenda should take the student no more than two to three minutes at the beginning of class (allowing the teacher to take attendance, speak with a student, etc.).

Sources

Ausubel, D. (1960). The use of advance organizers in the learning and retention of meaningful verbal learning. *Journal of Educational Psychology, 51*, 267–272.

Scott, V. G., & Compton, L. (2007). A new trick for the trade: A strategy for keeping an agenda book for secondary students. *Intervention in School and Clinic, 42*, 280–284.

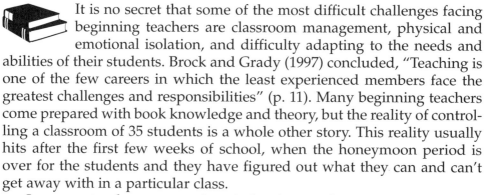

Strategy 13: Become knowledgeable about youth culture.

What the Research Says

It is no secret that some of the most difficult challenges facing beginning teachers are classroom management, physical and emotional isolation, and difficulty adapting to the needs and abilities of their students. Brock and Grady (1997) concluded, "Teaching is one of the few careers in which the least experienced members face the greatest challenges and responsibilities" (p. 11). Many beginning teachers come prepared with book knowledge and theory, but the reality of controlling a classroom of 35 students is a whole other story. This reality usually hits after the first few weeks of school, when the honeymoon period is over for the students and they have figured out what they can and can't get away with in a particular class.

In many teacher preparation, induction, and mentoring programs across the nation, these issues are being addressed with concrete solutions and qualified mentors. Connecting with exemplary veteran teachers who have experience and rapport with adolescents can also be a big help. New teachers at the secondary level report that their teacher colleagues have a positive influence in helping them understand the challenges of adolescents. Conversely, elementary teachers felt their principals were extremely helpful in providing support and encouragement.

Classroom Applications

No longer can we tolerate a "sink or swim" attitude. In California, the BTSA (Beginning Teacher Support and Assessment) induction program focuses on the beginning teacher learning as much as possible about the students in their classrooms. Knowing which languages are spoken at home, previous student test scores, the community in which these students live, and the students' cultural and socioeconomic background all help the novice teacher understand and adapt to the needs of the students they teach. Teachers should check literature, music, clothing trends, and so on. Spend time looking over popular magazines, check on students' favorite films and television shows, and, most important, take time to talk to and listen to kids.

Precautions and Possible Pitfalls

With the social climate today and students coming to class with a myriad of challenges and concerns, it is more important than ever for teachers to be aware of the problems and challenges of adolescent culture. What may seem trivial to an adult can be monumental to an adolescent. Students would rather be considered "bad" in front of their peers than "stupid." Yet many times a novice teacher will put students in the position of acting out because they don't know the answer to a question. Be careful not to judge students based on what other teachers say. All students deserve teachers who have not made up their minds on what the students are capable of in the classroom. However, be careful of becoming too much of a "buddy" or "friend"—not retaining adult status or modeling adult ideas and behavior. The more a teacher can invest in understanding the students, where they are coming from, and what is important to them, the more successful the teacher can be in implementing classroom management procedures.

Sources

Brock, B. L., & Grady, M. L. (1997). *From first-year to first-rate: Principals guiding beginning teachers*. Thousand Oaks, CA: Corwin Press.

Lortie, D. C. (1975). *Schoolteacher: A sociological study*. Chicago: University of Chicago.

Strategy 14: Utilize the most successful strategies for preventing and managing classroom discipline problems.

What the Research Says

The purpose of Zuckerman (2007) was to identify strategies for preventing and managing classroom discipline problems that most teachers, especially new teachers, can use successfully right away with no experience. Sixty-eight science teachers, during their first weeks of student teaching, reported their class management successes were well-remembered events. They used one or a combination of 18 different proactive and reactive discipline and management strategies adapted from Levin and Nolan (2003).

Zuckerman (2007) found that three strategies appeared to produce the desired results with these teachers' classes. They are (1) changing the pace of the activity of lesson, (2) using the least disruptive or intrusive discipline intervention utilizing a sequence of nonverbal to verbal strategies, and (3) conferencing and conferring privately with a chronically disruptive student.

Classroom Applications

Much like any consumer product rating system, Zuckerman (2007) tested a series of discipline and class management practices with student teachers. What makes Zuckerman's work so interesting is that students were tested by student teachers, not veterans. Veterans have a library of prior knowledge and history within the school that gives them an advantage with any behavior management strategy. Their experience gives them much more experience in behavioral pattern recognition. Basically, they see potential problems earlier and use that information more effectively to manage the learning and teaching environment. Students usually come into their classroom knowing what to expect from veteran teachers. Students are not as likely to "test" the boundaries of a veteran teacher's tolerances. Also, it is likely that veteran teachers know some of their students' histories before instruction begins. The purpose of Zuckerman's research was to identify a few successful strategies that work for novice teachers and those working with them.

An overriding theme emerged from the research, which held the philosophy that it's a teacher job to help students manage their own behavior rather than the teacher's responsibility to control it. Zuckerman (2007) broke the seven best strategies into three categories: strategies for prevention, strategies for managing common disciplinary problems, and strategies for managing chronically disruptive students.

In the first category, lesson planning, preparation, and execution were cited as important proactive considerations. Lessons featured motivating, novel, brains-on, minds-on, or hands-on activities that were usually limited to a brief and definite period of time. Directions were provided both in written and verbal form. Questioning focused on high-level thinking skills and open-ended questions, not just "factoid" or "right" answer questions. Lessons appealed to a wide range of learners, and the teachers were always prepared with backup plans should the lesson not go as planned.

Classroom rules and norms were well defined and communicated clearly to the class, and teachers solicited oral "buy-in." Teachers could also list the rules and expectations and have the students sign them, acknowledging the existence of the rules and that they understand them. The better rule lists extended to standards for classroom discourse, respect for the learning environment, and a homework and assignment contract. Teachers offered detailed explanations for the rationale for their expectations and standards. Finally, proactive seating arrangements and strategies helped. Depending on the setting, alternating boys and girls helped separate friends to assist students avoid potential distractions.

The second category looked at strategies for managing common disciplinary problems. Changing the pace of a lesson, giving nonpunitive time-outs, individually motivating the interest of students beginning to show signs of off-task activity, or refocusing off-task behavior all are strategies to keep in mind during lessons. Setting or modifying a deadline can motivate students to pick up the pace and/or to not be as easily distracted by others. Simply sitting everyone down and asking for individual or group progress reports can help. Use the resulting dialogue as a "teachable" moment to clarify the details of the lesson and expectations and to reinforce the standards for performance.

More reactive strategies for limiting, stopping, or punishing a break in class protocol are based on degree of emphasis. Beginning with nonverbal reactive strategies, teachers can communicate dissatisfaction and refocus the desired behavior with looks or eye contact, increased proximity to the disrupting student or students, or gestures such as pointing to a book or tapping a desk.

The next steps included talking to or moving the student. Using a single rhetorical question like, "Why is this not working?" or more direct appeals or requests to stop the behavior can then follow. Giving students choices regarding the consequences of continuing bad behavior can also be an option. Some teachers go so far as to take the student to a quiet area and call their parent right then and there. Usually teachers only need to do that once, and word quickly gets out to the class that teachers will follow through with consequences. Whatever strategies teachers choose, they need to be firm and consistent in setting and maintaining the high standards established by the class rules and other guidelines. Finally, if student behavioral changes are positive, be sure to find opportunities to reinforce and acknowledge their efforts.

The third category of suggestions focuses on managing chronically disruptive students. In the realm of proactive strategies, the general idea is to help chronically disruptive students develop their social intelligence, especially self-control. Relationship building topped one student teacher's strategy list, while another worked on breaking the discouragement cycle. The *discouragement cycle* is described as a vicious cycle of a student's unfilled need for self-esteem that drives inappropriate behaviors. Building self-esteem increases the student's feeling of significance and tops the list of strategies.

Reactive strategies included changing a student's seat and reviewing the student's behavior in a discussion. Others worked with the student privately to try to get the student to commit to modifying his or her behavior. Rewards and positive reinforcement also played a part in mitigating student behavior. Students who exhibited changed behavior were able to return to their original seats.

All 68 student teachers in this study (Zuckerman, 2007) were able to adopt and utilize successfully specific proactive and reactive strategies to mitigate and manage classroom behavior and discipline problems. Several of the strategies showed greater promise for novice teachers. Changing the pace of a lesson, using the least intrusive interventions sequencing from nonverbal to verbal, and conferring privately with chronically disruptive students are strategies that are more likely to garner desired behavior changes. Teachers using these strategies promoted and taught self-control techniques, showed a greater willingness to cooperate with students, and tended to create a more motivating learning environment.

Precautions and Possible Pitfalls

Somewhat minimized within the ideas of Levin and Nolan (2003) is the focus on individual student–teacher relationships and the role student–teacher relationships have in developing positive and effective discipline in the classroom. Social and emotional literacy theory relies on teachers forming these types of relationships. Teachers are becoming more aware of and in tune with educators such as Glasser (1998) and Rogers (1998), who see relationships as central to teaching and behavior management.

Glasser (1998) reported that by the end of primary school, more than 50% of students believe that teachers and principals are their adversaries. The implication here is not that teachers should be striving to get students to like them, although this would be the ideal, but to foster and maintain relationships that are generally warm, positive, and respectful. The challenge for teachers here is to "like" students whom they find challenging or offensive. That sounds tough, but it is exactly what is needed if teachers want to create a classroom environment where respect and cooperation are fostered.

Walsh (2006) offered his personal insight and reflection regarding middle school students who don't seem to care about school or learning. Walsh proposed the following positive engagement principles to address the challenges teachers face with reluctant learners:

- Get to know students so they can experience an informed and interested role model.
- Take time to talk to students, even as they push you away.
- Don't take student antagonism and inaction personally by taking a step back; instead, build trust and use positive regard.

Sources

Glasser, W. (1998). *The quality school teacher.* New York: HarperCollins.

Levin, J., & Nolan, J. F. (2003). *What every teacher should know about classroom management.* New York: Holt, Rinehart & Winston.

Rogers, W. (1998). *You know the fair rule.* Melbourne: ACER.

Walsh, F. (2006). A middle school dilemma: Dealing with "I don't care." *American Secondary Education, 35*(1), 5–15.

Zuckerman, J. T. (2007). Classroom management in secondary schools: A study of student teachers' successful strategies. *American Secondary Education, 35*(2), 4–16.

Strategy 15: Recognize how peer influence determines the quality of classroom engagement, interaction, and discourse.

What the Research Says

Pierce (2005) examined and discussed how life in high school classrooms, from a student perspective, is managed and often dictated by student peer influence. Pierce stated that students are tangled in webs of subtle peer influence that can encourage, constrict, poison, and otherwise determine students' classroom interaction. Students exhibit both academic and social poses not only for the teacher but also for their peers, who create classrooms that can be comfortable, indifferent, or intolerable. Pierce went on to describe students as working hard to follow tacit and subtle codes of appropriate behavior within the assembled classroom peer groups.

Pierce (2005) worked one-on-one with six high school students to gather data from interviews, group discussions, and individual writing. These relationships centered on the case study approach to data collection. The Pierce study revealed a network of social compromise that students make in class that interfered with authentic engaged learning. Pierce felt that teachers can reclaim and reform classrooms from sites of student accommodation to sites of engaged, active, and enjoyable accomplishment.

Classroom Applications

Student culture varies in each class as students adopt and engage in their peer relationships within the context of the class and the academic agenda. The temporary culture of the each class can change as different mixes of students come and go from period to period. The social compromise that students make or are forced to make in response to their peers can hinder learning and impair a teacher's ability to work with a class. Often constricted in the web of peer relationships are the individual needs of students and their personal desires, goals, and aspirations. Students learn to play a game of managing the individual cultural variations within each of their classes while also maintaining compliant behavior playing the school's game. This type of posturing can hide students' individual feelings and needs. Students often act one way toward a teacher and the class but feel another. Students continually maintain their classroom appearances for their peers within classrooms. They perform for both their peers and their teachers. Their behaviors, roles, and duties change with each class and are continually mediated and renegotiated with new teachers and in other settings.

Individual teachers need to recognize that students move with their peers from grade level to grade level and from class to class. Peer relationships are maintained for long periods of time and often maintain a higher priority in the lives of students than teaching and learning. Sometimes maintaining important relationships is harder than the coursework students encounter. School-related stress can pale next to the daily responsibility students feel for peer interactions. Throw a student into a classroom with a teacher, peers, and subject matter, and students will usually strike a pose reflecting their relationship to their peers or keeping up appearances above all other factors. The bottom line here is that peer relationships and the social structure of the school dominate many students' views of school and classroom life. Classroom routines are often something to tolerate and usually fail to offer interesting academic intellectual challenges.

Participants in the Pierce (2005) study expressly valued opportunities for learning they considered "real life." They felt that classroom and school situations were artificial and had little immediate value compared to real-life issues, challenges, and opportunities. Often students will exhibit very different behaviors at school than they would at their after-school workplace.

Teachers need to accommodate students in classrooms in ways required to manage them, the curriculum, and the subject matter. Teachers have the power to engage students in more authentic and meaningful work and curriculum rather than just overpower their social agenda by force of will or coercion. If teachers want students to do more in class than just work on their social and peer relationships, they must reexamine and adopt different roles for both students and teachers. Students will continue to be focused on each other until teachers provide experiences that cause them to reorganize their own priorities. Peer influence, or the results of peer influence during the school day, is felt by both the student and the teacher. Pierce (2005) commented that this influence is constricting rather than liberating. However, some classes thrive based on motivated and engaged peers setting the tone and agenda for learning in a positive way.

Pierce also went on to explain that cooperative learning arrangements, when carefully structured, offer alternative classroom arrangements to the more traditional teacher as transmitter of knowledge model. Cooperative learning arrangements promote a style of teaching and learning that is more like real life than typical school life. Products of academic processes become the equal of workplace production.

Students are conditioned by traditional and mundane patterns of classroom routine and busy themselves maintaining appropriate appearances for both their teachers and their peers, balancing the agendas of both teachers and classmates. If curriculum and pedagogy are not motivating and interesting, the student's peer social agenda will always take priority. Make lessons relevant and meaningful in the lives of students. Make the real-world connections to capture their attention.

Acknowledging that students and teachers have different priorities and agendas is a valuable first step in managing teacher efforts and the efforts of students. Identifying the intersection of the competing agendas is a way for teachers and students to begin to work together to a more equal balance in the teaching and learning environment.

Precautions and Possible Pitfalls

When lessons are not motivating or interesting to students, some will push through, plotting a way through the boredom to get the best grade possible with as little effort as necessary. Teachers shouldn't make the mistake of thinking that learning is taking place just because students are going through the motions. Teachers may get a compliant student but not an engaged student. They also may get a false sense of security that learning has taken place.

Producing dynamic lessons and teaching relevant to all students is a difficult task. Some students have such a strong social agenda that the best teaching strategies will fail to get them to change their priorities. However, given the strength and value of peer influence, it makes sense to harness it in a positive way, not just hoping for increased involvement with the curriculum but with each other in academic discourse. There are many forms of cooperative learning arrangements—too many to review here—yet some form of cooperative learning offers the most promise in channeling peer influence.

Source

Pierce, K. M. (2005). Posing, pretending, waiting for the bell: Life in high school classrooms. *High School Journal, 89*(2), 1–15.

 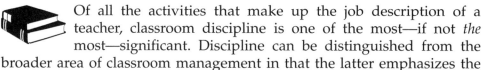

Strategy 16: Share discipline-related problems with a colleague.

What the Research Says

Of all the activities that make up the job description of a teacher, classroom discipline is one of the most—if not *the* most—significant. Discipline can be distinguished from the broader area of classroom management in that the latter emphasizes the provision of quality instruction as a means of limiting disruption in instruction whereas discipline is generally represented as what teachers do in response to students' misbehavior. It is the gap that exists between the discipline procedures used by the teacher and his or her idea of the best or better practice. This research looks at the tensions that arise from a teacher's desire to use educationally justifiable models of discipline while still quickly gaining and maintaining order in the classroom. It examines the resulting stress that arises when teachers are unable to discipline the students as they would ideally prefer. The results indicate that teachers who report more stress are those most interested in empowering their students in the decision-making process. The most concerned teachers indicated a greater range of worry, self-blame, tension, wishful thinking, and self-isolation. There was also an indication of a greater tendency for these teachers to get sick as a result of the stress.

Institutional pressure also contributes to a teacher's choice of a discipline plan that they might not make for themselves. This can be especially true for new teachers. Many times, a beginning teacher is forced to employ a variety of coping strategies, both public and personal. Tensions can and do exist between personal philosophy and institutionally preferred teacher–student interaction. Beginning teachers often seek the privacy and isolation of their rooms to negotiate a management role that works for them. Their results sometimes remain minimally acceptable from an institutional perspective.

In this case (Lewis, 1999), a survey was conducted to assess teachers' level of concern about discipline. Questionnaires were administered to half of all teachers in a sample of 15 government-regulated secondary schools in Melbourne, Australia.

Lewis (1999) found and suggested that teachers generally cope productively with the stress of being unable to produce self-defined best practices in the area of classroom discipline. It was also clear that those teachers who are most stressed are more likely to include in their coping management skills maladaptive strategies which contribute to and help maintain high levels of stress. This may be happening because the dysfunctional strategies undermine or negate the benefits that accrue from the use of more adaptive strategies such as setting clear expectations and creating a less confrontational focus. Most important, the results stress that teachers experiencing the greatest amounts of discipline problems make matters worse by not letting others know about their concerns and suffering in silence.

Classroom Applications

To begin, it can be argued that even when student misbehavior disrupts a teacher's attempt to instruct students, the teacher's level of stress is reduced and coping mechanisms are enhanced when the teacher feels part of a professional school community. New teachers tend to suffer in silence for fear of appearing weak or unable to control their classes. Both experienced teachers and teachers in a school new to them face problems site-established teachers don't.

The students predisposed to misbehaving will test the teacher and the teacher's management and discipline policies to an extent greater than colleagues established at the site. Some students will attempt to transfer responsibility for their grades or failures to the teacher, and they will tell their parents it is the teacher's fault. This is not to say that students are always wrong and the teacher is always right. A teacher's policies very well might be out of that school's paradigm of acceptable practice and what the students are familiar with. Chances are the teacher is not too far off, but not knowing what colleagues are doing may make a new teacher feel insecure. However, if a teacher is having problems with specific classes or students, he or she should

- Avoid new-teacher management and discipline problems by networking with site-experienced teachers before school starts. Adjust personal policies as necessary to fit the situation and specific student groups.

- Share classroom management and discipline policies with the students early. Adjust and fine-tune them after receiving student input. Have students sign the rules, thereby acknowledging their existence and their understanding of them. Collect them and file these signed documents. Students are more reluctant to break rules when they have signed and formally acknowledged them. This procedure also begins a discipline paper trail.
- Listen to students' concerns. Try not to argue points in front of the class unless there is an already-established relationship of trust with the students. Work with individuals privately so as not to provide misbehaving students with an audience.
- Bounce the situation off a colleague, counselor, or administrator. Take advice and be ready to mitigate, litigate, or compromise. Teachers may find that the students have valid points. Reduce the tension of the situation by negotiation. Teachers may also need to acknowledge a student's concerns and stand his or her ground. Focus on the problems, not the emotional part of the situation.
- Prepare a backup plan. What is the next step to be taken? If it is to present the issue to counselors or administrators, talk to them early and let them know the problem is coming. If they know the students and the parents, they can often suggest strategies for home communication. Again, listen to their suggestions.
- Teachers need to be prepared to learn from their mistakes and fine-tune management and discipline policies for the next class or school year.
- Don't suffer in isolation! New teachers often see management problems as personal weaknesses that they want to hide from evaluators and others. A willingness to adjust, adapt, and listen and learn from others helps alleviate the feeling of isolation. A clearly visible relationship with other professionals on campus tells students that the new teacher is in the loop and is supported by other established educators. Have counselors, exemplary colleagues, or administrators visit classes. Get comfortable working while in the proximity of colleagues.

Precautions and Possible Pitfalls

Most schools have discipline management policies that are designed to leave a paper trail. Most of the time, classroom management and discipline policies work and never need documentation. However, every so often, a student doesn't respond, and the teacher will need to document the disciplinary process taken. Sometimes teachers wait too long, hoping the student will come around before starting the paper trail. Knowing when to formally document discipline and bring others into the mix is something a new teacher learns with experience. However, there is usually a point where the system fails to remedy a discipline problem. The system may work for 95% of the students, but some just don't respond. At that point, it is a good time to bring in support and be ready to document what teachers have done up to that point.

Sources

Bullough, R. V. (1994). Digging at the roots: Discipline, management and metaphor. *Action in Teacher Education, 16*(1), 1–10.

Lewis, R. (1999). Teachers coping with the stress of classroom discipline. *Social Psychology of Education, 3*, 155–171.

 ### *Strategy 17: Save voice by engaging students in curricular conversations.*

What the Research Says

 Several recent studies suggest that teachers experience a higher frequency of voice-strain symptoms (67%) compared to non-teachers (33%), regardless of their age (Smith, Gray, Dove, Kirchner, & Heras, 1997). On average, a teacher talks for 6.3 hours during a typical school day (Siebert, 1999). In another study of more than 1,000 teachers, it was found that almost 21% had a pathological voice condition (Urrutikoetzea, Ispizua, & Matellanes, 1995).

Classroom Applications

With teachers using their voices all day, lecturing, answering questions, giving instructions, and sometimes even yelling, the constant strain on their vocal cords can lead to an increase in teacher absenteeism. New teachers frequently raise their voices as a way of compensating for noisy or disruptive students. When students are talking in competition with the teacher, the first thing a novice teacher might do is raise his or her voice to either get students' attention or to drown out student raucousness. Add classrooms with loud ventilation systems, poor insulation between classrooms, and outside sources such as automobile traffic and aircraft overhead, and it's no wonder teachers' voices become strained.

A resolution to this is the paradox "less is more." One of the most effective classroom management techniques in dealing with noisy or disruptive students is to actually reduce the volume of the teacher's voice to almost a whisper. This technique forces the student(s) to stop talking to be able to hear the teacher speaking. Often teachers fall into the trap of raising their voices, sometimes to the point of yelling—a technique not generally considered effective in the long run. Many new teachers believe a louder voice will restore order. This tactic may work in the short term, but soon students will just tune out. A far more effective method is for the teacher to stop talking completely until the students or class is quiet. The obvious statement from beginning teachers is, "If I stop talking and teaching every time a student is talking out of turn, I'll never get the lesson taught." This is simply not the case. If a student or the class is talking or disruptive, they aren't listening to what the teacher is saying anyway. Teachers end up repeating instructions multiple times, losing valuable classroom time. Students will quickly learn that instruction stops when students aren't attentive. The key is for the teacher to resist the urge to shush students or to immediately return to talking once the noise begins to abate. Students need to learn early that instruction will stop and the focus of the lesson will not continue until everyone is quiet and paying attention. For the teacher, this refrain from talking may seem like minutes, but in actuality, it's usually only 15 to 20 seconds of wait time before the class is quiet.

Teachers often think that if they aren't talking, then they aren't teaching. Beginning teachers should explore ways in which to give directions without using verbal instructions. Teachers can write directions on the chalkboard or put them on an overhead transparency. Another way to prevent voice strain is to establish procedures such as an agenda that is posted (to stop the 20 "What are we going to do today?" questions). Teachers should have procedures in place for turning in homework, passing papers, asking a question, or getting into groups; such procedures don't require their voice. With younger students, hand signals or a bell might signal it's time to get into groups.

Precautions and Possible Pitfalls

When it comes to teaching, we need to remember the axiom "work smarter, not harder." Frequently, new teachers forget that there are other ways of delivering the lesson besides direct instruction. With the short attention spans of students of all ages, teachers need to explore alternative methods of instruction. A teacher's voice is an important instrument in teaching, and care should be taken to preserve it.

Sources

Siebert, M. (1999, February 7). Educators often struck by voice ailments. *The Des Moines Register*, p. 4.

Smith, E., Gray, S. D., Dove, H., Kirchner, L., & Heras, H. (1997). Frequency and effects of teachers' voice problems. *Journal of Voice, 11*(1), 81–87.

Urrutikoetzea, A., Ispizua, A., & Matellanes, F. (1995). Vocal pathology in teachers: A video-laryngostroboscopic study of 1,046 teachers. *Rev Laryngology, Otology, Rhinology, 116*(4), 255–262.

Strategy 18: Recruit a teaching partner as a peer coach.

What the Research Says

In this study (Kohler, Crilley, Shearer, & Good, 1997), the effects of peer coaching procedures were analyzed. In this case, reciprocal peer coaching was described as teachers observing one another and exchanging support, companionship, feedback, and assistance in a coequal or nonthreatening fashion. Peer coaching is designed to foster a teacher's development and acclimation during periods of development and introduction of new instructional practices in the classroom. This is in contrast to the traditional methods of staff development that rely on one-shot inservice training. Districts that inaugurate fundamental changes in the ways that teachers work, learn, and interact are also presumed to be more effective in addressing students' learning needs and capacities (Firestone & Bader, 1992; Little, 1990).

In this case (Kohler et al., 1997), four teachers planned and conducted instructional innovation during the study on peer coaching relationships. They mixed and matched, completing the instructional planning and tasks both independently and with peer coaching. Outcomes measured the focus of teachers' collaboration with a peer coach, each teacher's procedural practices and refinements, a variety of student and teacher processes, and the teachers' ongoing concerns and satisfaction with the innovation. They found the following:

- Three stages of different levels of need were identified as distinctive. Not surprisingly, they occur in a longitudinal fashion in Year 1 through Year 3. The first stage is described as survival, where teachers question their competence and desire to become teachers. Assistance takes the form of reassurance and specific skills almost on a daily basis as new teachers adapt to the transition into schools. In the second year, teachers have entered into a consolidation stage that focuses on instruction and the needs of individual students. In the third stage of renewal, teachers have become competent. Previously adopted activities and patterns have become routine and, in some cases, are not very challenging. In this stage, teachers are looking for new ideas in their specialization.

- Teachers working independently make few changes or refinements to their innovations. They made more changes and procedural refinements during peer coaching.
- Many of the changes were sustained and reinforced in peer tutoring arrangements.
- In a related study (Sparks & Bruder, 1987), it was found that 70% of the teachers who participated in coaching felt that their newly developed peer coaching techniques produced marked improvement in students' academic skills and competencies.
- Some educators have suggested that peer coaching and reciprocal learning help avoid isolation and foster communication, trust, and support, which helps alleviate potential burnout.
- Peer coaching provided promising solutions, enabling teachers to develop and tailor innovations to fit their personal teaching styles and needs at their site.

From a minority perspective, some teachers felt it was a violation of traditional norms of autonomy, privacy, and equality in schools. Overall, the findings of the study support peer coaching strategies and suggest further refinement to help with some of the concerns voiced during the study (Kohler et al., 1997).

Classroom Applications

Peer coaching works. If it has not been a part of a teacher education program, teachers should arrange their own relationships. There is ample academic and professional literature on many versions of the technique. There are also many versions of these arrangements that can evolve into team teaching or integrated or cooperative learning when teachers from different content areas share the same students and a similar curriculum or pedagogy.

Students involved in such relationships often feel much less isolated as teachers begin to know them well. It shrinks the size of the school as teachers team together and share students and support each other's curriculum and instructional practices.

Many of these relationships begin informally; new teachers need to be open to these opportunities. Occasionally they are mandated. Effective collaboration can take practice and acclimation. New teachers may need to put their nervousness aside and go into these relationships feeling a little uncomfortable. Consider teaming with another new teacher. A little background research can also help teachers find new ways to use peer coaching as teachers see how others use it in their settings.

Precautions and Possible Pitfalls

 Peer coaching can take time. Instead of doing grades or a million other things, the new teacher will need to be available to observe and plan with others. If this is a problem, consider peer relationships for a single unit or lesson and then move on. Teachers don't need to sustain peer coaching beyond its usefulness. Come together only when it is logical and practical.

Sources

Firestone, W. A., & Bader, B. D. (1992). *Redesigning teaching: Professionalism or bureaucracy?* Albany: State University of New York.

Kohler, F. W., Crilley, K. M., Shearer, D. D., & Good, G. (1997). Effects of peer coaching on teacher and student outcomes. *Journal of Educational Research, 90*(4), 240–250.

Little, J. W. (1990). Norms of collegiality and experimentation: Workplace conditions of school success. *American Education Research Journal, 19*, 325–340.

Sparks, G., & Bruder, S. (1987). Before and after peer coaching. *Educational Leadership, 3*, 54–57.

 Strategy 19: Manage the special challenges within block scheduling.

What the Research Says

The purpose of this study (Zepeda & Mayers, 2001) was to examine the experiences of new teachers as they negotiated the beginning of their career in less traditional schedules. In this case, a new teacher was described as a teacher less than three months out of his or her teacher preparation program. The study lasted one calendar year and included 31 first-year teachers. Data was collected from these teachers in three urban school districts that had high schools offering a 4 × 4 block schedule. Data was also collected from the first-year teachers only and did not include administrators, master teachers, and other support staff.

Three areas emerged as problematic: adjusting instruction to extended class period formats, transitioning learning activities, and assessing student progress.

In the adjustment category, the problems identified included managing class time, varying instruction throughout the class period, running out of materials or activities before the end of class, and relying on only a single instructional method. Many fell into patterns of worksheets or end-of-chapter questions, long lectures, or letting students do homework to keep them quiet until the bell. First-year teachers were not prepared to vary instructional strategies or make transitions. Some resorted to college-type teaching, heavy on notes and lecture.

Transition periods from one activity to another, using a variety of instructional strategies that are desirable in a block format, became a sticking point for new teachers. Maintaining a learning environment and climate became difficult, and students "messed around too much" or saw it as a time to misbehave. Because of this, new teachers often avoided transition periods and used only limited numbers of instructional strategies. Teachers in the study often reported being very uncomfortable with students out of their seats or moving around. "Losing control" became a very limiting fear in the creation of learning environments.

This fear also limited assessment strategies and tactics. Many new teachers found that pencil-and-paper tests could not adequately assess gains in student learning. Yet performance assessments were rare, again because of the fear of losing control. Thus "seat work" became the norm. Socratic seminars, cooperative learning strategies, simulations, role-playing, and laboratory or workstation strategies presented management problems that most new teachers were not equipped to deal with. New teachers often had problems knowing how much value or weight to place on more authentic assessments and "doing" types of activities. They did not realize that alternative forms of assessment could be quantified by criteria matched to learning objectives through rubrics.

Longer class periods require careful, structured planning; use of a variety of instructional methods; and diverse assessment practices to maximize the potential they offer. New teachers on the block and especially first-year teachers had problems fully developing skills in these areas. The study also found that if the staff development opportunities were beyond the range of the first-year teachers, learning advanced techniques created frustration for the teachers that transferred to the classroom.

Classroom Applications

If a new or preservice teacher anticipates teaching in a block schedule format, he or she should consider the results of this study. Most, if not all, schools that use a block or modified block schedule also favor a student-centered curricular approach to student learning or pedagogy. It is also clear that new teachers often encounter discipline and management problems when students leave their seats. Unfortunately, experience is often the best teacher. For new teachers, their student-teaching experience might have been very different from what they may be facing in their first teaching position. So what can a teacher do?

There are many terms within educational jargon that describe teaching and learning arrangements better suited for the longer time frames typical of block schedules. The concepts of problem-based, theme-based, student-centered, or activity and discovery learning ask students to take a more active role in their own learning. Teachers facilitate or orchestrate learning rather than dictate it. Brown University's Ted Sizer's Coalition of Essential Schools philosophy sees the student as a worker and the teacher as a facilitator. The point here is that students are required to take a more proactive role in their own learning: when they need to know things and what they need to know. These types of teaching and learning arrangements also require the students to learn a new role. Many students have not learned to self-regulate in classrooms that teach in a student-centered manner.

Successful student-centered classroom environments in block formats often look chaotic but are actually highly planned and organized chaos. The most important idea to keep in mind is to teach students to learn in these new settings. Most kids coming from the "stand-and-deliver" experience are not equipped to deal with the new expectations in longer classes. Between a teacher's inexperience and the students' inexperience, it will require time, usually a semester to a year, for both teachers and students to adjust.

Teachers can help themselves by learning all they can about how to create, manage, assess, and evaluate activity-based classes (typical of block schedules) and activities. Every activity and expected student or curricular outcome needs to be broken down into smaller, manageable units with built-in student accountability at each step along the way. How small the teacher makes these subunits depends on the maturity and educational needs of the students being managed. The pace of instruction needs to be flexible, and the teacher needs to expect to make adjustments on the fly as the students give clues that they're not getting it or as the teacher encounters curricular roadblocks. Every student moves at a different pace.

When administrators come into a class, the teacher needs to be accountable. Teachers should be prepared to tout their latest student-based activity and show the administrator how they manage the learning that is taking place. Have an administrator shadow an activity or a student through that activity. Any administrator in a block schedule–type school knows what the teacher is up against and can often offer help or direct the new teacher to another teacher who could be helpful.

Precautions and Possible Pitfalls

Student-centered learning and block scheduling do not mean a teacher needs to abandon all stand-and-deliver or other more traditional techniques. To completely abandon techniques a teacher is experienced with or has learned and add a whole new set of methods is a ticket for frustration and potential disaster. Teachers should plan to step out of their comfort zone, but not completely. Planning short-term units, using unfamiliar strategies, acclimating slowly, and tinkering and modifying along the way may be more effective with a new teacher. Eventually new teaching and learning methods will take over or blend with the teacher's existing methods. Again, teachers are learning on their feet, and this takes time.

If new teachers are trying another teacher's strategy or activity, they should expect to modify it to fit their own comfort zone. Stepping into a new position needs to be seen as a work in progress. A teacher should expect a full acclimation to be a two- or three-year experience.

Source

Zepeda, S. J., & Mayers, R. S. (2001, April/May). New kids on the block: Beginning teachers face challenges. *High School Journal, 84*(4), 1–11.

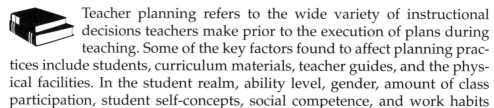

Strategy 20: Become a classroom manager before becoming a content specialist.

What the Research Says

Teacher planning refers to the wide variety of instructional decisions teachers make prior to the execution of plans during teaching. Some of the key factors found to affect planning practices include students, curriculum materials, teacher guides, and the physical facilities. In the student realm, ability level, gender, amount of class participation, student self-concepts, social competence, and work habits contribute to many other planning considerations.

Curriculum materials influence decisions based on the quality or quantity of textbooks and support materials. The physical facilities include room size and a variety of other related school characteristics that include the all-important school schedule. The goals of the administration, site administrators, and school and department policies also add to the many considerations teachers face. To these external forces add the teacher's own interests, subject matter specialty, and experience.

This study (Sardo-Brown, 1996) looked into the literature and found few studies that viewed novice teacher planning. Sardo-Brown's study looked at how two teachers planned their first and second years of teaching and compared and contrasted the differences between the years. The two teachers in the study were selected based on their competency within their graduating education classes and because both had obtained employment in secondary schools right out of teacher education.

Some of the most noticeable findings between first- and second-year planning include

- A clear trend with the idea that they did not plan to emphasize content during the early weeks of school, but considered management issues a higher priority.
- Both second-year novices dedicated much more time to how to set up and teach rules, procedures, and class structure, along with how to develop early rapport with their students.
- The teachers moved farther away in time and reference from their student-teaching experiences where rules were "routinized" and planning was rule-bound.
- In the second year, they were more receptive to new ideas and inservicing.
- Both planned major adjustments to their methods of assessment.
- Both sought out more time-efficient strategies and planned to use more high-level assessment strategies as learning devices.
- Both novices in this study married between their first and second years and looked for new ways to get more leisure time. Both credited their marriages for growing confidence in themselves as teachers and both felt "older."
- In the second year, they tried to do more of their planning at school.
- Both viewed the area of assessment as a major concern and planned numerous changes in their second year. They felt they were not prepared to successfully tackle assessment in their first year.
- Both felt more comfortable planning in their second year.
- Both continued to struggle with the problem of reconciling their own beliefs about their teaching with the incongruent beliefs of the principal and other colleagues.
- They both had a greater awareness of the cognitive and emotional needs of their students.

Classroom Applications

It is clear from the research that preservice teachers move from content specialists and borrowers of instructional tactics to educators and instructional strategists their second year and thereafter. First-year teachers often "don't know what they don't know," until experience becomes their teacher. The tactic derived from the research is being able to learn from what teachers see in front of them rather than from what someone tells them.

New teachers should develop their own analytical skills as they implement a "best guess" instructional plan. Teachers need to do the "science" it takes to determine what happens when real students meet a teacher's management and instructional strategy. Seeing everything a new teacher does as a work in progress will be comforting. Keep in mind that a teaching style is something new teachers will find in themselves and not something they learn. The classroom experience is like the game on Friday night; it tells teachers what they need to work on the following week.

Teachers will do well to also remember that they are standing on the shoulders of those who came before and who all went through similar experiences. How beginning teachers view themselves as teachers should not be based solely on early efforts. It should be based on how teachers respond to that effort and reflection and how resilient and adaptive they can be. Teachers need to analyze those problems, adjust, and move on.

Precautions and Possible Pitfalls

Don't panic! It's clear from the research that time on task is a large factor in one's development as a teacher. For most veterans, there are few shortcuts from the first days in class to the beginning of the second year. Holding off on career reflections for the time being and focusing on how students can be helped should be a priority. New teachers will gradually become less concerned with how others see them and, as time passes, more concerned with their students and how teachers can help them.

Source

Sardo-Brown, D. (1996). A longitudinal study of novice secondary teachers' planning: Year two. *Teaching & Teacher Education, 12*(5), 519–530.

Strategy 21: Fill in the time by varying instructional strategies within block scheduling.

What the Research Says

A study by Benton-Kupper (1999) explored the experiences of three high school teachers in their second year of transition from a traditional six-period-per-day schedule (45-minute periods) to a block four-period-per-day schedule (90-minute periods).

Their findings suggested that the block schedule provided more opportunities than the traditional six-period day for instructional strategies that actively engage the students in learning. The additional time provided in a double period allows teachers to provide more depth of content within their classroom through discussion, projects, and instructional materials.

Classroom Applications

For middle and secondary schools across the nation using some type of block scheduling (four 90-minute periods per day or three 120-minute periods per day, classes meeting every other day), the opportunities abound for teachers to provide time to work individually with students, go deeply into the content, and assess the students' individual learning styles. Teachers at schools where the block schedule has been implemented for many years report that the block increases their ability to know where students are in terms of learning the content. The result of this knowledge allows the teacher to plan and instruct lessons that will lead to student success (Buckman, King, & Ryan, 1995).

In a block period, there is a tendency for the flow of the lesson to be less disjointed than in a traditional format. Having extended time in a block gives teachers the opportunity to construct a full lesson, introduce a topic or concept, discuss it, and bring that topic to closure, all within one class period. Teachers may also find more time in the block schedule to develop difficult key concepts.

In a Southern California high school that has had block scheduling (120-minute periods, every other day) for more than 25 years, even new teachers find opportunities within lessons to provide a wide range of instructional strategies that are intended to increase students' interest, knowledge, and success. For example, in one class the teacher was able to review for a test, provide direct instruction, have cooperative learning groups, view a video (including time for class discussion), and begin individual project presentations, all within the same class period. Covering all these instructional strategies in a traditional class period would be impossible.

The extended time frame of block scheduling also allows time for activities implementing multiple intelligences that might be more difficult in a nonblock setting. Teachers report that with block scheduling, there are more opportunities for in-depth reading of literature and class discussions that might not otherwise happen given the relatively short 50-minute period. Without the additional time, more work must be assigned as homework, which does not give students the advantage of having the teacher as a facilitator.

Precautions and Possible Pitfalls

New teachers may, at first, be intimidated by the extended time of block scheduling. Their practice in the planning of lessons may be limited to single periods. Concerns about filling the time with worthwhile activities may abound. If they don't have experience in planning for the block, teachers should consult a trusted colleague or mentor for help in lesson planning. Block scheduling requires a unique perspective. The primary consideration should be to keep students engaged. This can be accomplished by changing activities or focus about every 20 minutes. If students are given the opportunity to experience multiple methods of grasping information, their interest level will be high. The greatest mistake a teacher new to block scheduling can make is to think that lesson planning simply means putting two single-period lessons together. The worst use of the block is for the teacher to present a lecture or lecture-based instruction for the entire class period.

Sources

Benton-Kupper, J. (1999, October). Teaching in the block: Perceptions from within. *High School Journal, 83*(1), 26–34.

Buckman, D., King, B., & Ryan, S. (1995). Block scheduling: A means to improving school climate. *NASSP Bulletin, 79*(571), 9–18.

3

Organizing Curricular Goals, Lesson Plans, and Instructional Delivery

 Strategy 22: Recognize that less is more and streamline the content curriculum.

What the Research Says

Eylon and Linn (1988) reported that, cognitively, students respond better to a systematic, in-depth treatment of a few topics than they do to conventional in-breadth treatment of many topics. Increasingly it is recommended that teachers of all subjects streamline the curriculum and focus more on a limited set of knowledge and skills. Students' misconceptions and lack of understanding of basics reflect limitations of mental processing and memory. Ted Sizer, a well-known progressive educator, identifies "less is more" as one of the major principles to guide educational reform. For more information, see "Less Is More: The Secret of Being Essential" in *Horace* (Cushman, 1994), the online journal of the Coalition of Essential Schools Web site at http://www.essentialschools.org/cs/resources/view/ces_res/88.

Classroom Applications

 Teachers should examine the course(s) preceding theirs that students must take to get the background for their course and examine the courses following theirs for which students are expected to acquire the background. Teachers may then use this knowledge to identify the key information their course must cover. Once these decisions have been made, a teacher can eliminate chapters of the textbook from the course to prevent overload and rote learning.

Precautions and Possible Pitfalls

Don't throw out "diamonds in the rough," potentially interesting learning pathways, or favorite topics. There's a lot to be said for the effects of teacher enthusiasm for specific concepts, topics, and content on student motivation. A wise teacher will use them! The teacher just may have less time to spend on them.

Sources

Cushman, K. (1994, November). Less is more: The secret of being essential. *Horace, 11*(2), 1–4. Retrieved September 18, 2008, from http://www.essentialschools.org/cs/resources/view/ces_res/88

Eylon, B., & Linn, M. (1988). Learning and instruction: An examination of four research perspectives in science education. *Review of Educational Research, 58,* 251–301.

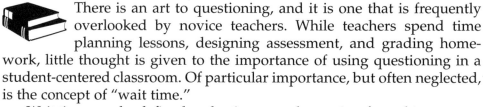

Strategy 23: Master the art of questioning by building in wait time.

What the Research Says

There is an art to questioning, and it is one that is frequently overlooked by novice teachers. While teachers spend time planning lessons, designing assessment, and grading homework, little thought is given to the importance of using questioning in a student-centered classroom. Of particular importance, but often neglected, is the concept of "wait time."

Wait time may be defined as the time a teacher waits after asking a question before talking again (Rowe, 1986). Too often a teacher asks a question and then expects an immediate response. Research shows that the longer the pause (three to five seconds), the more thoughtful the response. The use of wait time is especially useful when asking higher-order questions. A study of preservice teachers who observed middle and high school science classes on the East Coast reported that with little or no wait time, short answers were elicited. When the wait time was increased, the caliber of answers was greater (Freedman, 2000). In this same study, teachers reported that on a typical day they asked about 24 questions in a 40-minute class period. The number of convergent questions was twice that of divergent ones, and they asked the same percentage of lower-order questions (knowledge and comprehension) as higher-order questions (application, analysis, synthesis, and evaluation). When asked what they could do to expand into more desirable questioners, their answer was "more planning."

Classroom Applications

Teachers need to plan and practice the types of questions they will be asking their students. Questioning can be used for many purposes, including checking for understanding, determining students' prior knowledge, beginning a class discussion, or stimulating critical thinking. Questions should be part of the lesson planning process and should be planned just as other parts of the lesson are. The simple counting to oneself (one-thousand one, one-thousand two, etc.) can help remind teachers to wait after asking a question.

Using a mentor or colleague can help a teacher evaluate and improve his or her questioning practice. Having the observer write down the questions asked, while the lesson is being taught, and then reflecting back on that lesson can be useful in assisting new teachers in the improvement of their practice. Another excellent method for reflection is to videotape the teacher while teaching a lesson. The teacher can then see how questions were asked, if they were convergent or divergent, and the amount of wait time that was allowed. All these factors can help novices learn their craft.

Precautions and Possible Pitfalls

Teachers need to be careful not to get caught up in always asking the same type of questions, asking the same students, and expecting a correct answer each time. When asking a question of a specific student, it is important that other students do not shout out the answer if the designated student doesn't answer immediately. Sometimes it is better to ask the question first, and then call on a student. This will help reduce student passivity. In addition, if the teacher asks questions that invite reflection, the learning comes about as a result of a partnership between teacher and student.

Sources

Freedman, R. L. H. (2000). *Questioning strategies in Western New York teachers' science classrooms.* Unpublished raw data.

Rowe, N. B. (1986). Wait-time: Slowing down may be a way of speeding up. *Journal of Teacher Education, 37*(1), 43–50.

> *Strategy 24: Fight boredom by using classroom strategies that stimulate student interest.*

What the Research Says

A study following high school students for three years found that a relationship exists between students' interests and investments in their work at school and their teachers' repertoire of techniques for engaging them (Wasley, Hampel, & Clark, 1997).

Classroom Applications

Although each new school year brings about enthusiasm and optimism for students and teachers, once students encounter instructional routines and procedures that become predictable, their enthusiasm for learning may begin to wane.

By using a range of instructional strategies from one unit to the next, student interest is stimulated. For example, a teacher might have students listen to a speech, discuss it in a group, and then write a paper about the speech. Following this project, the teacher may have students do a group assignment about favorite speeches and the people who gave them. Students could finish up this unit by either delivering their favorite speech or writing one of their own. The instructional model of reading the book, answering the questions at the end of the chapter, listening to a lecture or watching a video, and taking a test does not provide for good instruction. There is no research to support that this method is effective.

Essential to the success of varying instructional strategies is support from school districts in providing professional growth opportunities for teachers by encouraging them to attend workshops or seminars or to network with colleagues about best teaching practices. Also of critical importance is the reflection by the teacher after a lesson is taught. Another powerful strategy is to invite observation by fellow colleagues or mentors. An observation of a novice teacher's lesson and the reflective conversation afterward can be a "mirror" to the novice of what is really going on in the classroom. These mentors can help novice teachers understand that mirroring is essential to their development as professionals.

In many teacher induction programs around the country, districts are now focusing on helping new teachers build a repertoire of techniques, skills, and strategies through ongoing professional development. Districts must allow time for new teachers to attend seminars, conferences, and observations of exemplary teachers to assist these emerging teachers in building a repertoire that is responsive to the students they serve.

Precautions and Possible Pitfalls

 Teachers sometimes fall into a pattern of using a particular strategy (especially if it has been successful) to the detriment of using any others. Although it is important for new teachers to take risks in the classroom, it is just as important to learn what works and what doesn't in a particular classroom setting. Students like consistency and routine to a point; however, if the instructional strategies are never varied, the students become bored and disinterested. Do not be afraid to consult with a veteran teacher on ways to vary strategies, whether it is on the type of assessment being used or using Socratic dialogue to generate student opinions on a piece of literature. It is important to remember that no one technique or strategy works every time with every student.

Source

Wasley, P., Hampel, R., & Clark, R. (1997). *Kids and school reform*. San Francisco: Jossey-Bass.

 Strategy 25: Fit it all in by making realistic time estimates during lesson planning.

What the Research Says

Teachers need to have excellent time-management skills for students to learn effectively. It is sometimes said that "time + energy = learning." Sometimes there's confusion between the time teachers allocate for instruction (e.g., a 50-minute class period) and the time students are actually engaged in learning, which may only be 25 minutes out of the 50 allocated. The concept of engaged time is often referred to as "time on task." Teachers often fail to take into account the off-task time they devote to managing student behavior, managing class-room activities, and dealing with announcements and interruptions.

Teachers may allow a portion of class time for guide practice. How do teachers know when the time they have dedicated to student problem solving or cooperative learning is being utilized most effectively? And once they identify off-task behavior, how do they change the learning environment to allow students to better use the time allotted to them? Chiu (2004) found that teacher intervention initiated during cooperative learning class time helped improve subsequent time on task and problem solving among students who were off task or making little progress. Chiu found that students often did not ask for help when they needed it, so the teachers needed to monitor their work and intervene as necessary. They typically intervened when groups were off task or had shown little problem-solving progress.

Teacher interventions were particularly successful when the teachers evaluated the students' work, provided lower levels of help content, and issued fewer commands. After interventions involving these teacher actions, students were more likely to be on task and to show problem-solving progress. If teachers can accurately evaluate and adapt their interventions to students' needs, students might work together productively to realize the many potential benefits of cooperative learning and better utilize class and instructional time.

Classroom Applications

 Distinguish between time allocated for instruction and engaged learning time when estimating how much time it will take for students to learn a particular set of material. It's the time students actually spend learning that is the key to the amount of achievement.

In the Chiu (2004) study, some teacher actions were more effective than others during teacher interventions, and teacher evaluations explained most of the differences in groups' subsequent time on task and problem solving. During evaluations, the teachers tried to understand the students' work and, hence, diagnose their needs (Chiu, 2001). As a result, they made more informed decisions about the most suitable help needed by the students. In contrast, when a teacher did not evaluate students' work, he or she did not adapt to the students' specific needs. Instead, the teacher might have relied on preconceived ideas about how students should proceed, regardless of their progress.

By working with groups' ideas instead of telling students what to do, these teachers respect and validate students' ideas as worthy of consideration. In this study (Chiu, 2004), such teacher actions might have bolstered students' autonomy and initiative so that they were more likely to be on task and to create new ideas.

Precautions and Possible Pitfalls

Teachers need to be sure to plan time in their lessons for students to digest the material covered, to monitor their comprehension of concepts and tasks, and to engage in clarification as needed. Looking at a lesson only from a teacher's point of view of making sure material is taught or covered, the teacher is likely to underestimate the time students need to understand, record, and remember what they have learned. Teachers should allow sufficient note-taking time to help ensure students have time to take complete notes of the development being done in the lesson, so that they can effectively review for tests at home.

Chiu (2004) stated that teacher actions do not necessarily have uniform effects. Rather, some teacher actions interact with local group contexts to yield different effects. Chiu went on to say that when students already understand the problem situation, teacher commands tend to harm students' subsequent problem solving. However, teacher commands had no effect on groups that did not grasp the problem situation. Perhaps teacher commands were perceived as less threatening to these students' initiative because they had no particular problem-solving approach. Thus, understanding the local group context could be vital to teachers in determining actions that will produce the desired effects.

Sources

Brophy, J. (1988). Research linking teacher behavior to student achievement: Potential implications for instruction of Chapter 1 students. *Educational Psychologist, 23*, 235–286.

Chiu, M. M. (2001). Analyzing group work processes: Towards a conceptual framework and systematic statistical analyses. In F. Columbus (Ed.), *Advances in psychology research* (Vol. 4, pp. 193–222). Huntington, NY: Nova Science.

Chiu, M. M. (2004). Adapting teacher interventions to student needs during cooperative learning: How to improve student problem solving and time on-task. *American Educational Research Journal, 41*(2), 365–399.

Strategy 26: Teach beyond subject or content knowledge.

What the Research Says

Knowing lots of information about or within a subject area will not ensure success as a teacher. This research (Kennedy, 1998) raised questions about what math and science teachers need to know to teach math and science well. The study began by examining reform proposals for K–12 science and math teaching by defining what good teaching practices consist of. It did a literature search to delineate the varieties and types of knowledge that have been associated with this kind of teaching. The focus of the investigation is on subject-matter knowledge, but it continued farther to address the character of the knowledge rather than the content of the knowledge.

The types of knowledge identified by the research include conceptual understanding of the subject, pedagogical content knowledge beliefs about the nature of work in science and math, attitudes toward the subjects, and actual teaching practices with students.

Unfortunately, the literature is incomplete with respect to which types of this knowledge base are relatively more or less important. Reform commentaries include many ideas about the character of knowledge, beliefs, and attitudes that teachers need to teach math and science in a new, less didactic way. Their comments characterize optimal teacher knowledge as

- *Conceptual*—having a sense of size and proportion; understanding the central ideas in the discipline; understanding the relationships among ideas; and being able to reason, analyze, and solve problems in the discipline
- *Pedagogical*—having the ability to generate metaphors and other representations of these ideas based on the knowledge, ability, and experience level of the students
- *Epistemological*—having an understanding of the nature of work in the disciplines
- *Attitudinal*—having respect for, and an appreciation of, the processes by which knowledge is generated through the disciplines

There is one important reason, cited in the research (Kennedy, 1998), for teachers to possess a rich and deep understanding of their subject knowledge. Reformers want them to stop reciting facts to students and start encouraging students to explore the subject for themselves. Teachers confident in their knowledge can orchestrate this self-discovery with carefully designed teaching strategies and learning pathways.

To carry this idea of literacy further, the way teachers come to understand these proposed forms of discipline-based knowledge are appropriate outcomes not just for teachers but also for college-educated citizens. The limits of the study (Kennedy, 1998) are that these characteristics are not clearly understood in the context of actual teaching practices or the way that ideal practice is defined relative to actual practice.

Classroom Applications

 Many individuals new to teaching come with strong content or subject-matter knowledge. Most have majored in a specific area in college or have years of knowledge gathered in the private sector as professionals. Usually after a few years of teaching, teachers find that content knowledge plays a much smaller role in their success or failure as a teacher than they first thought. While content knowledge is important, it rarely defines success or failure as a teacher. A teacher not only controls what students will know about a subject but how they come to know it and the context in which it exists.

The research looks into how content or discipline knowledge exists and is defined. It makes a clear distinction between what there is to know and how that material comes to be known. There is much more to know about subject-matter content than just the facts. Evidence suggests that many teachers present their subjects as vast collections of facts, terms, and procedures with little connection among the components. They also present the facts as if they were self-evident and as though students should accept and remember them without much thought. If teachers are to engage students in high-level thinking skills, teachers themselves must have a grasp of these ideas (the range of understanding knowledge) and must have a healthy respect for the difficulties of developing and justifying knowledge in their field.

Beyond the basics, a teacher should allow the students to use questions and misconceptions in guiding their exploration of subject matter and the nature of knowing. Be prepared to guide students, to clarify confusion, and to ensure that misconceptions are not perpetuated.

Be aware that some questions or hypotheses are beyond either the teacher's or the students' capacities to pursue or generate ideas and will lead the teacher and the lessons astray, down dead-end alleys, or into trivial pursuits. Teachers are not expected to move in any direction the class might want to go. Teachers learn to manage classroom direction by recognizing which questions or comments might be fruitful and which to avoid.

Remember that covering just basic knowledge does not guarantee retention or usefulness. Very often it is *how* a person comes to know something that contributes to long-term retention and usefulness. Students must be motivated to guide the direction (curiosity and interest) in which knowledge is dispersed and acquired.

It also helps to keep in mind that knowledge in any discipline has a past, present, and future. Some learning has a finite shelf life, and students need to understand that, too.

Precautions and Possible Pitfalls

If teachers are having trouble defining the boundaries of content knowledge, they should begin to consider a new term to add to educational jargon: recitational subject-matter knowledge. This refers to the types of knowledge that have traditionally been assessed in achievement tests in the past. Recitational knowledge also covers the ability to recite specific facts on demand, to recognize correct answers on multiple-choice tests, to define terms correctly, and to be good test-takers. Many reformers think that traditional courses and curricula are limited to recitational knowledge. It is their aim to extend the character of discipline knowledge beyond this point.

Keep in mind that *what* to teach is usually more politically loaded than how to teach it or to know it. Also, covering material by incorporating superficial instructional techniques does little for retention. It only provides a false sense of security. Discipline knowledge must include having strategies that the teacher can use to provide context and relevance to recitational knowledge in order to cause true learning to occur.

Sources

American Association for the Advancement of Science. (1989). *Science for all Americans: A Project 2001 report on literacy goals in science, mathematics, and technology.* Washington, DC: Author.

Kennedy, M. (1998). Education reform and subject-matter knowledge. *Journal of Research in Science Teaching, 35*(3), 249–263.

Strategy 27: Use state and national standards to establish benchmarks for assessing students' literacy.

What the Research Says

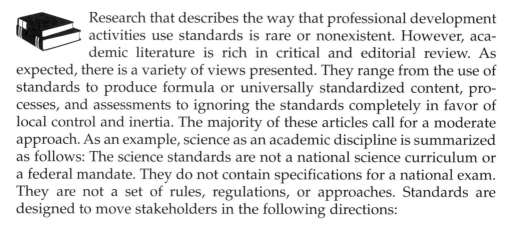

Research that describes the way that professional development activities use standards is rare or nonexistent. However, academic literature is rich in critical and editorial review. As expected, there is a variety of views presented. They range from the use of standards to produce formula or universally standardized content, processes, and assessments to ignoring the standards completely in favor of local control and inertia. The majority of these articles call for a moderate approach. As an example, science as an academic discipline is summarized as follows: The science standards are not a national science curriculum or a federal mandate. They do not contain specifications for a national exam. They are not a set of rules, regulations, or approaches. Standards are designed to move stakeholders in the following directions:

- Teaching the discipline for conceptual change
- Promoting integration of the discipline and other content areas
- Placing students in positions for them to see themselves as potential professionals and critical thinkers using specific content

- Providing a foundation for teachers to create experiences promoting inquiry, wonder, and understanding

Overall, most of the literature calls for the various standards to provide a frame of reference for judging the quality of specific content education that is already provided. In addition, and most important, the standards should be used as a tool that can serve and inspire the teacher.

Classroom Applications

When structuring a semester- or year-long content experience for a class, there are only so many resources that can contribute to content and instructional practices. Some teachers turn to textbooks and their colleagues for concrete help in structuring day-to-day activities. They trust the textbook to cover the mandated content and colleagues to help provide the timeline or pace, choice of specific content, and related activities.

Most of these choices are based on the resources available at the school and the department's institutionalized instructional inertia. It is crucial that teachers research and explore the various national frameworks, guidelines, and mandates provided by national contnetn or curriculum organizations and filtered through state and other bureaucratic agencies. Each state and district modifies and adapts these as sources of guidance.

A quick search using various Internet search engines picked up too many hits to print. These sites feature a variety of content standards and guidelines in all content areas. Three valid and useful examples of national curriculum guidelines come from the National Academy of Sciences, the National Science Teachers Association, and the American Association for the Advancement of Science (Project 2061). It's clear that the overall usefulness of content standards in science has improved over the years. It is fair to assume that other content areas are updating and becoming more valid and useful to teachers also. In the past rarely would any of these documents filter down to the school site and classroom teacher. Today, because of access to the Internet, they are available to everyone. So now, rather than turning to the textbook or colleagues first, teachers may treat themselves to a more global perspective on how teaching and learning should be experienced by teachers and students alike.

In the recent past, the information in these documents was limited to what the authors of the guidelines thought should be taught. They have evolved their thinking and expanded their philosophy to present not only what should be taught but also how content should be taught, learned, and experienced by students. Most of them now include suggested content, delivery, and assessment strategies and standards. However, most don't give the teacher direct, concrete examples or activities ready for the classroom. They only suggest guidelines on how to create and construct a teacher's own experiences that are embedded in educational philosophy. If teachers are designing their own instructional strategies and activities, these types of documents are the best and most current sources of information available on a specific discipline. These articles can be interesting and motivating and should be visited and revisited in support of professional growth and inspiration.

Precautions and Possible Pitfalls

 Not all teachers keep current on the latest ideas in teaching and learning. Department or school politics can be a problem. Curricular leadership can come into play and conflict. The standards, mandates, guidelines, and frameworks can be interpreted in different ways, and philosophical differences could also be problematic. There is no way to predict how change will affect the relationships within a given school or department.

Sources

Bell, M., & Rakow, S. (1998). Science and young children: The message from the National Science Education Standards. *Childhood Education, 74*(3), 164–167.

DeCarlo, C. (1998). Standards that serve you. *Instructor, 108*(4), 71.

Strategy 28: Use out-of-school learning environments.

What the Research Says

Learning outside of school (informal education) plays a vital role in the development of competence in language, reading, mathematics, and a variety of other school-related domains. Assume that such learning also contributes to classroom learning, motivation, and attitudes. Informal learning experiences help preschool children acquire a wide range of early literacy before the children enter school. They learn a language, usually before entering any formal classroom.

In this study (Ramsey-Gassert, 1997), structured interviews of parents with elementary school children revealed the nature and scope of children's science-related activities outside of school. Research exposed a remarkable level of participation in extracurricular, science-related activities. Categories of participation included nonfiction and science fiction television shows as well as reading activities, computer use, community activities such as zoos, home observations and simple science experiments, questioning and discussion, and household interest and familiarity with science. Often, time and interaction with science-related activities outside the formal science classroom exceed time in the classroom.

While the Ramsey-Gassert (1997) study of informal learning looked primarily at science activities, it would come as no surprise to find the same sort of informal connections to other disciplines.

Classroom Applications

The studies make it clear that learning outside of school should not be ignored and can be a new source of motivating instructional strategies. If science students are required to spend only a few hours a week in science instruction, the overall role schooling plays in developing science literacy is questionable. The influence of home and community environments needs to become a factor in planning more formalized content instruction.

Simple structured interviews or questionnaires can yield insights and characterize the development of content thinking from outside the school boundaries. This knowledge can yield a perspective on common experiences (e.g., exhibits at a museum) that can facilitate discussions, interpret phenomena, and frame classroom lessons and activities. Information could also serve to highlight a range of motivations and competencies among students and help teachers identify areas in which student "experts" could make a contribution to classroom learning, content projects, or other activities. It also can help identify influential allies at home who can reinforce efforts with individual students or act as a broader class resource.

There is a full range of informal content-related activities students bring to class. While this informal activity or exploration may diminish or change as students get older, much of their background and attitudes are based on this informal education. It may also become more specialized as a student finds some disciplines more interesting than others.

By remaining cognitive of the influence home and community environments have on overall content literacy, teachers can begin to incorporate the information into their instructional practices. Creative teachers can explore, enhance, and develop a range of curricular connections to the students' informal background.

Precautions and Possible Pitfalls

School learning is often seen in a less enjoyable and sometimes more threatening light than the informal learning students encounter outside of the classroom. Much of the students' experience outside the classroom can be classified as "edutainment." Integrating the two realms is a challenging but very doable task. Research into the connections is just beginning to illuminate instructional relationships and doesn't yet offer a wide range of tested curricula to use the knowledge. Don't let the lack of formal connections become discouraging! Create strategies to integrate the two paradigms within instructional objectives and your comfort zone.

Using resources outside the classroom can be a source of inequity due to access problems. Not all students have supportive parents or parents who can provide resources. If teachers are going to offer credit or ask students to visit or use resources outside of the classroom, they should offer a classroom or school-based option to those who can't participate off-campus.

Sources

Korpan, C. A., Bisanz, G. L., Bisanz, J., Boehme, C., & Lynch, M. A. (1997). What did you learn outside of school today? Using structured interviews to document home and community activities related to science and technology. *Science Education, 81*(6), 651–662.

Ramsey-Gassert, L. (1997). Learning science beyond the classroom. *Elementary School Journal, 97*(4), 433–450.

Strategy 29: Use student peers to scaffold students' learning.

What the Research Says

Peer tutoring can promote learning at virtually all grade and school levels. Research shows that peers can scaffold each other's development of higher-level thinking and learning.

One study of seventh graders learning science assigned students to three different tutoring conditions: explanation only, inquiry with explanation, and sequenced inquiry with explanation. Students were assigned to tutoring pairs and trained to tutor. Tutoring occurred over five weeks on content the teacher had already covered. Researchers measured cognitive, metacognitive, and affective variables. The results showed that students do not have to be with other students who are more competent to develop their own thinking and knowledge. Students who are the same age and ability levels helped each other learn in all three conditions (King, Staffieri, & Adelgais, 1998).

A whole classroom of students helping other students has been found to be an efficient and effective method of enhancing achievement. Twenty teachers participated in a study of classwide peer tutoring with 40 classrooms in elementary and middle schools. Half of the schools implemented classwide peer tutoring programs, and half did not. Both urban and suburban schools participated in the study, and students came from diverse backgrounds, both culturally and linguistically. There were three different categories of students: average achievers, low achievers without learning disabilities, and low achievers with learning disabilities.

The peer tutoring programs were conducted three days a week, 35 minutes a day, for 15 weeks. Stronger students were paired with weaker students. Teachers reviewed each pair to ensure they were socially compatible. In all pairs students took turns serving in the roles of tutor and tutee. Student pairs worked together for four weeks; then teachers arranged new pairings. Teachers received training on how to train their students to be tutors. Tutor training included teaching students how to correct each other's errors.

Achievement tests were administered before and after the peer tutoring program. This was regardless of whether students were average achievers or low achievers, with or without learning disabilities. Students in the peer tutoring classrooms achieved at higher levels than those in the classrooms without classwide peer tutoring.

Classroom Applications

 There are many areas in all disciplines that lend themselves to a peer tutoring program. When there is a skill or skills to be learned, and all one needs is experience with success or in understanding of something covered by the teacher or text, then peer tutoring can provide an efficient way to monitor and support a student trying to master the skill or knowledge.

Disciplines other than math may have a full range of student math competencies within the same class. Say a student has difficulty with a math problem in an activity in a discipline other than math. If the student hasn't had geometry, others in the class might have and can act as tutors. Part of the student's problem is to recognize which calculation is called for and when more than one type of calculation may be used. It can get doubly confusing. Here a peer tutor (under the guidance of a teacher) can be quite beneficial. A student who has difficulty doing dilution factors or converting moles could find a peer tutor a genuine asset in a chemistry class. Additionally, the tutors, in explaining these calculations to their peers, are also provided with an opportunity to strengthen their own understanding of both the concept of the application (a higher-order thinking skill) and the role of math in science. Thus, there is often a mutual benefit to a peer tutoring program.

Precautions and Possible Pitfalls

A tutor-training program offered by the teacher must precede peer tutoring. Tutors must be given some instruction on how to conduct the sessions, what sorts of difficulties to look for on the part of the tutee, and what points to stress in the sessions (based on the teacher's assessment of the class). Any individual difficulties on the part of the tutees should be mentioned to the tutor prior to the sessions. Tutors should be taught to guide student learning and not merely solve problems for students. Students with severe learning disabilities may pose a challenge to classwide peer tutoring, unless the tutors first receive individualized instruction from learning disabilities specialists.

Sources

Fuchs, D., Fuchs, L., Mathes, P. G., & Simmons, D. (1997). Peer-assisted learning strategies: Making classrooms more responsive to diversity. *American Educational Research Journal, 34*(1), 174–206.

King, A., Staffieri, A., & Adelgais, A. (1998). Mutual peer tutoring: Effects of structuring tutorial interaction to scaffold peer learning. *Journal of Educational Psychology, 90*(1), 134–152.

Strategy 30: Increase understanding of personal learning styles.

What the Research Says

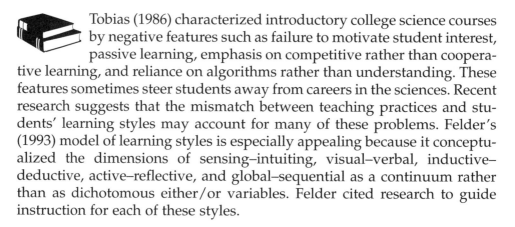

Tobias (1986) characterized introductory college science courses by negative features such as failure to motivate student interest, passive learning, emphasis on competitive rather than cooperative learning, and reliance on algorithms rather than understanding. These features sometimes steer students away from careers in the sciences. Recent research suggests that the mismatch between teaching practices and students' learning styles may account for many of these problems. Felder's (1993) model of learning styles is especially appealing because it conceptualized the dimensions of sensing–intuiting, visual–verbal, inductive–deductive, active–reflective, and global–sequential as a continuum rather than as dichotomous either/or variables. Felder cited research to guide instruction for each of these styles.

Classroom Applications

Felder (1993) recommended the systematic use of a few additional teaching methods that overlap learning styles and contribute to the needs of all students. These include giving students experience with problems before giving them the tools to solve them; balancing concrete with conceptual information; liberally using graphic representations, physical analogies, and demonstrations; and showing students how concepts are connected within and between subjects and to everyday life experiences.

Precautions and Possible Pitfalls

Students and parents often have an entrenched view of how a specific class is presented and will be experienced. If the teacher ventures too far from the norm, the students' comfort level can drop, and their anxiety rises. If the teachers feel they are presenting teaching or learning experiences (restructuring or reforming) that might be new or unfamiliar, they should consider clearly communicating these new strategies early. Teachers do not want to threaten students' potential success in their class or produce unneeded frustration.

Beware of the dangerous tendency to fall into the trap of labeling students, or allowing them to label themselves, as particular types of learners and restricting teaching and learning to the dominant styles. Ignoring nondominant styles can limit students' intellectual growth and development. The goal of thinking about students' learning styles is to facilitate learning—not constrain it.

Teachers shouldn't expect miracles of themselves. There can be an overwhelming number and variety of learning styles within a particular class, and it's unrealistic for teachers to regularly accommodate instruction to all of them. The key is to vary instructional methods and present information in multiple modalities.

Sources

Felder, R. (1993, March–April). Reaching the second tier: Learning and teaching styles in college science education. *Journal of College Science Teaching, 23,* 286–290.

Tobias, S. (1986, March–April). Perspectives on the teaching of science. *Change,* 36–41.

Strategy 31: Expand the range of opportunities rubrics offer.

What the Research Says

Research has found that teachers at various academic levels are exploring the use of rubrics in their classes. In this general survey (National Research Council, 1996), teachers at all levels used rubrics for assessment and for many other purposes within their instructional practices. Each application transforms the rubric to another purpose, and the rubric can become a specialized instrument. Researchers investigating the use of rubrics in their own secondary methods courses found certain benefits and detriments in their use.

The benefits include reflective practice among students and instructors within the methods class and among the students using rubrics in their own classes. The detriments are related to issues of time and the clarity of the rubric's content. Luft (1999) found that incorporating rubrics into instruction can benefit a course in two general areas. First, rubrics are tools that can be used to encourage reflective practice in both a temporal and a spatial sense. They model effective organizational strategies for students. Second, they are important in the development of professional knowledge through reflection and revisiting the rubric that is constructed. They force teachers to clarify the goals of the class and the goals of the specific lesson. Rubrics begin a discourse between students and teachers and instruction, content, and assessment.

More specific detriments include a class "addiction" to rubrics in that they learn to depend on them. In addition, students and teachers find that once implemented, sometimes the rubric doesn't fit and needs modification; therefore, its validity suffers.

Researchers found that 75% of teachers who experienced rubrics in secondary science methods classes now used rubrics in their own classes. Overall, like concept maps and portfolios, rubrics, once mastered and practiced, prove to be a positive addition to the teacher's instructional toolbox.

Classroom Applications

Before a discussion about rubrics can begin, it is important to clarify the term. The National Science Education Standards (National Research Council, 1996) states that a *rubric* is "a standard of performance for a defined population." Others have described rubrics as guidelines laid out for judging student work on performance-based tasks. Still others describe a rubric as an established set of criteria used for scoring or rating students' tests, portfolios, or performances.

Generally, rubrics must be able to answer the following questions:

- What do we want students to know and be able to do with the instruction?
- How well do we want students to know instructional information and related processes; what do we want them to do with the instructional information and processes?
- How will the teachers and others know when the student masters the instruction and related processes or how well they master it?

There are no prescribed procedures for developing rubrics in science education. Constructs are very dependent upon the context of their use. A transfer of one rubric to another teacher and class simply would not work most of the time. Yet examining rubrics from other classes is an important developmental activity and leads to professional growth.

One good suggestion for the construction of a rubric starts with writing performance standards. These can be found in many curriculum guides and frameworks. These standards should then be analyzed and divided into different components and complexity levels. The complexity and rigor of the rubric is then based on the experience and ability level of the students' and teacher's goals. Development of rubrics can come from three perspectives: holistic, analytical, or a combination of both. Holistic rubrics are instruments that contain different levels of performance that describe both the quantity and the quality of the task. The instructor determines the best fit for aspects of the lesson for the students. Analytical rubrics are constructs that consist of criteria that are further subdivided into different levels of performance. Start with criteria to be assessed and move on to different levels of performance for the criteria. Analytical rubrics tend to be more precise and concise while holistic rubrics contain broader descriptions about levels of performance.

Typing the word "rubric" into an Internet search engine can yield many good Web sites that can get a teacher started or can further refine and develop each personal rubric philosophy. Whichever style a teacher decides to synthesize, he or she should try to use the rubric to involve students in patterns of observation, reflection, thinking, and problem solving that follow the standards of the scientific community as mirrored in various standards for content and scientific processes.

Precautions and Possible Pitfalls

Teachers should keep in mind that a major long-term goal of instruction is to allow students to decide, on their own, what they need to know, how they need to know it, and when they need to know it. Rubrics can create dependence and do not foster "learning how to learn" strategies unless teachers deliberately build this goal into their strategies to reduce the students' dependence on them.

At some point the teacher should collaborate with the students in the development of mutually agreed-upon rubrics. The exercise becomes guided practice in transferring some responsibility to the students for their own learning.

Sources

Luft, J. A. (1999). Rubrics: Design and use in science teacher education. *Journal of Science Teacher Education, 10*(2), 107–121.

National Research Council. (1996). *National education standards.* Washington, DC: National Academy Press. Retrieved September 18, 2008, from http://www.nap.edu/openbook.php?record_id=4962

Strategy 32: Establish scaffolds for complex skills and procedures.

What the Research Says

Walberg (1991) suggested that in science it is especially useful for students to struggle with interesting, meaningful problems that can stimulate discussion about competing approaches. This idea can be stretched to include all disciplines. He recommended using what he calls *comprehension teaching*, more commonly called *scaffolding*, which involves providing students with temporary support until they can perform tasks on their own. Based on Vygotsky's (1978) concept of the "zone of proximal development," scaffolding is recommended for teachers to build from what students can do only with temporary guidance from a more competent person, gradually reducing and eventually removing this support as students become independent thinkers and learners who can perform the task or use the skill on their own. The *zone of proximal development* refers to the area within which the student can receive support from another to successfully perform a task until he or she is able to perform it independently. Scaffolding has been found to be an excellent method of developing students' higher-level thinking skills (Rosenshine & Meiester, 1992). Scaffolding is a strategy for gradually and systematically shifting responsibility and control over learning and performance from the teacher to the student.

Classroom Applications

Through a variety of methods (e.g., observation, listening, tests), assess students' abilities to perform and not perform important skills or tasks independently. Test their ability to perform or not perform these skills or tasks with assistance from another, in order to conceptualize their zone of proximal development. Teachers can use a scaffolding approach for skills and tasks that are within the students' zone. Scaffolds can range from a simple hint, clue, example, or question to a complex sequence of activities that begin with teacher-centered approaches (e.g., explaining, demonstrating) but end as student-centered (e.g., self-questioning, self-monitoring).

The example that follows is a scaffolding approach to teaching students to construct graphic organizers of text they have read. It is a complex sequence of steps that uses scaffolding to shift from teacher direction and control of creating graphic organizers to student self-direction and self-control over making them.

- Show and explain a variety of traditional examples of graphic organizers, such as flowcharts, concept maps, and matrices, made by both professionals and students.

- Inform students about what graphic organizers are and when, why, and how to use various types of them. One source (Jones, Pierce, & Hunter, 1988/1989) provided information on why and how to create graphic organizers to comprehend text. It provided illustrations of a spider map, a continuum or scale, a series of events chain, a compare–contrast matrix, a problem–solution outline, a network tree, a fishbone map, a human interaction outline, and a cycle. Another source focused on concept maps and Vee diagrams (Novak, 1998).
- As classwork or a homework assignment, give students a partially completed graphic organizer to finish on their own. Give students feedback on their completions.
- Assign classwork or homework that requires students to complete an empty graphic organizer structure entirely on their own. Give students feedback.
- Assign classwork or homework requiring groups of students to create their own graphic organizers. Give students specific criteria or rubrics for constructing and evaluating graphic organizers. Sample criteria include (a) neat and easy to read; (b) ideas are expressed clearly; (c) ideas are expressed completely but succinctly; (d) content is organized clearly and logically; (e) labels or other strategies (colors or lines) are used to guide the reader's comprehension; (f) main ideas, not minor details, are emphasized; (g) it is visually appealing; and (h) the reader doesn't have to turn the page to read the words.
- Once their graphic organizers are completed, the individual groups show their graphic organizers to the other groups, which critique the graphic organizers and give feedback based on the criteria identified above. Teachers should supplement the feedback as needed.
- For homework, students develop graphic organizers completely on their own, using the identified criteria. Group members give each other homework feedback on the extent to which they met the established criteria.
- Finally, students are expected to be able to create and critique their own graphic organizers, and support from others (students and teacher) isn't needed.

Precautions and Possible Pitfalls

To use scaffolding effectively, it is vital for teachers to consider issues such as what types of support to provide and when and in what order to sequence them, and to figure out the criteria for deciding when it is time to reduce or withdraw support from students. It is also very important to make sure scaffolding attempts are truly within the students' zone of proximal development. If they are below this area, activities will be too easy because the student can really do them independently. If they are above this area, no amount of scaffolding will enable students to perform independently because the skill or task is too difficult given the students' prior knowledge or skills.

Sources

Jones, B. F., Pierce, J., & Hunter, B. (1988/1989). Teaching students to construct graphic representations. *Educational Leadership, 46*(4), 20–25.

Novak, J. (1998). *Learning, creating and using knowledge: Concept maps as facilitative tools in schools and corporations.* Mahwah, NJ: Lawrence Erlbaum Associates.

Rosenshine, B., & Meiester, C. (1992). The use of scaffolds for teaching higher-level cognitive strategies. *Educational Leadership, 49*(7), 26–33.

Vygotsky, L. S. (1978). *Mind in society: The development of higher psychological processes.* Cambridge, MA: Harvard University Press.

Walberg, H. (1991). Improving school science in advanced and developing countries. *Review of Educational Research, 61*(1), 25–69.

Strategy 33: Create more stimulating and successful questioning techniques.

What the Research Says

There is evidence that much of teaching amounts to "telling," which students find boring. Research suggests that when teachers do ask questions, most of them are at a relatively low level. When teachers ask a majority of low-level questions (e.g., identify, define, describe), student achievement does not reach levels as high as when students are asked mostly higher-level questions (e.g., predict, justify, evaluate; Redfield & Rousseau, 1981).

Research was conducted to investigate what questions teachers asked and why they asked them (Redfield & Rousseau, 1981). Thirty-six high school teachers from five schools, representing all subject areas, participated in the study. They were asked to give examples of the questions they asked, to explain how they used them, and to tell to whom the questions were addressed. These results, along with findings from previous research by Bloom, Engelhart, Furst, Hill, and Krathwohl (1956), Tisher (1971), and Smith and Meux (1970), led to a system of classifying types of questions teachers ask in the classroom.

Brookfield (2008) looked at Nelson Mandela's autobiography, *The Long Walk to Freedom,* which describes how an iconic political activist and freedom fighter reflected on, and sometimes modified, four core assumptions at the heart of his struggle to overturn the White supremacist, minority hegemony and create a free South Africa. Critical reflection's focus is on understanding the dynamics of power (and how to manipulate these) and on uncovering and combating ruling-class hegemony. It is assumed that Mandela was unaware of education's utilization of the idea of critical reflection. Mandela's thinking on tactics and strategy, his awareness of the need to reappraise assumptions that previously were viewed as truth, and his use of multiple perspectives through which to view his actions as a freedom fighter exemplify the educational practice of critical reflection. Brookfield's work focused on a thematic content analysis of Mandela's own personal account of events, which others have challenged.

Classroom Applications

There are many types of questions to use, as well as many to avoid. Learning science requires understanding. When a topic that requires thought and deduction is being considered, it is usually helpful to ask lots of questions. Questions should be formulated with respect to long-term learning goals and should be succinctly structured to guide students' development so they can think like scientists. Questions can range from those that require low-level responses (e.g., recalling facts for definitions and descriptions) to those requiring intermediate-level responses (e.g., classifying and comparing or contrasting) to those requiring high-level responses (e.g., predicting, evaluating), which may have no definite answer but require a judgment to be made. The following is the classified system, mentioned above, of types of questions teachers ask in the classroom.

Cognitive Questions

- Recalling data, task procedures, values, or knowledge. This category includes naming, classifying, reading out loud, providing known definitions, and observing. These are low-level questions. For example, "How many stages are there in meiosis?"
- Making simple deductions usually based on data that have been provided. This category includes comparing, giving simple descriptions and interpretations, and giving examples of principles. These are intermediate-level questions. For example, "How does the Vietnam conflict compare with World War II?"
- Giving reasons, hypotheses, causes, or motives that were not taught in the lesson. These are high-level questions. For example, "What are possible explanations of the latest stock market decline that are not in our book?"
- Solving problems, using sequences of reasoning. These are high-level questions. For example, "What steps would you take to solve that problem? What order do they go in?"

- Evaluating one's own work, a topic, or a set of values. These are high-level questions. For example, "Did I make any careless mistakes? How can I verify my answer?"

Speculative, Affective, and Management Questions

- Making speculations, intuitive guesses, creative ideas or approaches, and open-ended questions (which have more than one right answer and permit a wide range of responses). For example, "Approximately how long will it take before the chemical reaction we're expecting takes place? How do you think we'll know if it worked? How else could we produce that reaction?"
- Encouraging expressions of empathy and feelings. For example, "How do you think she felt when her ceramic art project was dropped?"
- Managing individuals, groups, or the entire class. This category includes checking that students understand a task, seeking compliance, controlling a situation, and directing students' attention. For example, "Which groups solved the problem? Which groups need help?"

There are many different questioning taxonomies teachers can consult to help them vary the types and levels of questions they ask. Sigel, McGuillicudy-DeLisi, and Johnson's taxonomy (1980) has three levels: low (e.g., identify, describe), intermediate, and high. Teachers should spend most of their time questioning at intermediate and high levels.

Intermediate-Order Questions

Intermediate-order questions require the answerer to

- Describe or infer similarities
- Sequence
- Describe or infer differences
- Analyze
- Apply
- Classify
- Estimate
- Synthesize

Higher-Order Questions

Higher-order questions require the answerer to

- Evaluate
- Verify
- Infer causal relations

- Conclude
- Propose alternatives
- Predict outcomes
- Resolve conflicts
- Generalize
- Transform
- Plan

Finally, Brookfield (2008) examined the "real world" thinking of Nelson Mandela and the critical questioning, thinking, and reflection he did about culturally shared assumptions. The types of thinking and self-questioning lead to radical changes to philosophies deeply entrenched in the collective conscious. There are models of questioning out there in the real world that can model the types of behaviors we want our students to assimilate. It's a good idea in an instructional strategy to connect the desired outcome to concrete examples outside the classroom.

Precautions and Possible Pitfalls

 Even good questions can lose their value if they are overused. Avoid asking ambiguous questions and questions requiring only one-word answers, such as yes–no questions. Focusing on a questioning style as indicated above, but without proper concern to the subject matter, would be a misuse of this strategy.

Sources

Bloom, B. S., Engelhart, M. D., Furst, E. J., Hill, W. H., & Krathwohl, D. R. (1956). *Taxonomy of educational objectives: The classification of educational goals.* New York: David McKay.

Brookfield, S. (2008). Radical questioning on the long walk to freedom: Nelson Mandela and the practice of critical reflection. *Adult Education Quarterly, 58*(2), 95–109.

Brown, G. A., & Edmondson, R. (1984). Asking questions. In E. C. Wragg (Ed.), *Classroom teaching skills* (pp. 97–120). New York: Nichols.

Redfield, D., & Rousseau, E. (1981). A meta-analysis of experimental research on teacher questioning behavior. *Review of Educational Research, 51*(2), 237–245.

Sigel, I. E., McGuillicudy-DeLisi, A. V., & Johnson, J. E. (1980). *Parental distancing beliefs and children's representational competence within the family context.* Princeton, NJ: Educational Testing Service.

Smith, B., & Meux, M. (1970). *A study of the logic of teachings.* Chicago: University of Illinois Press.

Tisher, R. P. (1971). Verbal interaction in science classes. *Journal of Research in Science Teaching, 8,* 1–8.

Strategy 34: Make the most of one-on-one student contacts.

What the Research Says

Frequent contact between teachers and students helps students develop academically and intellectually. Rich teacher–student interaction creates a stimulating environment, encourages students to explore ideas and approaches, and allows teachers to guide or mentor individual students according to their specific needs.

Classroom Applications

Working with individual students in a traditional classroom setting is not practical for long periods of time. While students are working independently on an exercise, the teacher should visit with individual students and offer them some meaningful suggestions. Such suggestions might include hints on moving a student who appears frustrated or bogged down on a point toward a solution.

These private comments to students might also be in the form of advice regarding the form of the student's work. That is, some students are their own worst enemy when they are doing a geometry problem and working with a diagram that is either so small that they cannot do anything worthwhile with it or so inaccurately drawn that it, too, proves to be relatively useless. Such small support offerings will move students along and give them that very important feeling of teacher interest.

In some cases, when a student experiences more severe problems, the teacher might be wise to work with individual students after classroom hours. In this situation, it would be advisable to have the student describe the work as it is being done, trying to justify the procedures and explain concepts. During such one-on-one tutoring sessions, the teacher can get a good insight into the student's problems. Are they conceptual? Has the student missed understanding an algorithm? Does the student have perceptual difficulties or spatial difficulties?

Precautions and Possible Pitfalls

To work with individual students and merely make perfunctory comments, when more might be expected, could be useless when considering that the severity of a possible problem might warrant more attention. Teachers should make every effort to give proper attention to students when attempting to react to this teaching strategy. Teachers should keep the student's level in mind so that, where appropriate, they can add some spice to the individual sessions by providing a carefully selected range and choice of challenges to the student so that there may be further individualization in the learning process. Teachers should make sure students don't get bored. Challenge them by giving them more difficult problems to solve, having them tutor other students, or having them evaluate alternative approaches to solving a problem.

Be aware that some students can become very needy. They often lack confidence or the ability to work comfortably in an independent manner. This can compel them to begin to dominate teacher time. When this occurs, give them the same general attention given to others. When their demands begin to dominate the class, invite them to come after school or at a time when they can be given undivided attention. To conserve time, consider combining a few students with the same problems and address their needs together. Or have students who understand the material serve as tutors, mentors, or group leaders.

Source

Pressley, M., & McCormick, C. (1995). *Advanced educational psychology.* New York: HarperCollins.

4

Using Student Assessment and Feedback to Maximize Instructional Effectiveness

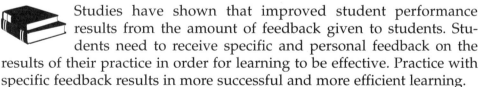

Strategy 35: Improve student performance with specific teacher feedback.

What the Research Says

Studies have shown that improved student performance results from the amount of feedback given to students. Students need to receive specific and personal feedback on the results of their practice in order for learning to be effective. Practice with specific feedback results in more successful and more efficient learning.

Pitts (2005) conducted a small-scale study regarding feedback on music students' written work. Staff and students were asked to evaluate existing practice and suggest possible changes. The researcher asked those in her study to rate the usefulness of existing feedback comments and also generate their own. The overall study illuminated the challenges in developing practice even when the changes were far from radical. Suggestions were drawn that provide ways to improve practice.

Classroom Applications

Within instructional practices in most disciplines there are usually many opportunities to practice the skills presented. By pairing students and having them read each other's work, or by having students compare their work to model solutions, a form of feedback can be obtained regularly without a great expense of time. Teachers might also systematically review a small and different sampling of student papers each day and, from this small number of collected papers, provide some meaningful feedback to the students. For example, suppose that a classroom is situated in rows of students. The teacher may randomly call for papers from everyone sitting in the first seat of each row, from the students sitting on the diagonal, or from everyone in the third row.

If a teacher wants to check on a particular student's paper a second day, as there may be some serious questions about the student's work, then the teacher can ask for the student's paper by including him or her in the second day's set of collected papers. This can be achieved by calling on a second group that also corresponds to the particular student's seat, such as the third row one day and then, since the target student is sitting in the last seat of the row, a call for the papers from all students sitting in the last seat of a row the second day. This would inconspicuously include the target student a second time.

Since it is unreasonable to expect the teacher to do a thorough reading of everyone's paper every day, there are alternative ways to provide feedback to students on their homework. One could search for parent volunteers or retired teachers who might like to take on some part-time work in reading and reacting (in writing) to student work. One might also try to engage some older and more advanced students to undertake a similar activity, using a cross-age tutoring approach. This would also serve them well as they can benefit by looking back over previously learned material from a more advanced standpoint. By doing this not only are the target students being helped but the older students are deepening their knowledge of the discipline, theme, or process.

Regarding written feedback, the Pitts (2005) study found that scribbled comments or hasty judgments were often seen by students as an indicator of lack of caring or active engagement in the students' work. This lessens the students' trust in the teacher's professional judgment and can sabotage the development of the students' self-esteem and confidence. Sample feedback from the Pitts study includes the following comments:

> Irritating if it's difficult to read. Feel a little bit more effort could have been put in after all student's effort.

If the tutor writes messily and criticizes at the same time, it makes it twice as bad!

If it seems that a tutor has taken time and effort to write feedback, then I am more inclined to take the comments on board (e.g., word processed, a decent length).

Other students were more pragmatic in their views on presentation and style.

I would rather have lots of messy feedback than two lines of beautiful print. We understand that time is precious.

Don't think it really matters—notes and bullet points make just as much sense as full sentences.

The results of the study were mixed on the types of feedback students wanted, and teachers would likely receive similar comments from classes. Students' wishes for clear and individual feedback might be met through short, precise comments, or they might demand a more lengthy response. Opinions seemed to be divided on the values of brevity and depth.

It is suggested that teachers and students have a discussion on the types of feedback they prefer and reach some type of compromise that best serves the needs of both teachers and students.

Precautions and Possible Pitfalls

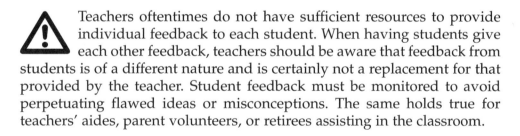 Teachers oftentimes do not have sufficient resources to provide individual feedback to each student. When having students give each other feedback, teachers should be aware that feedback from students is of a different nature and is certainly not a replacement for that provided by the teacher. Student feedback must be monitored to avoid perpetuating flawed ideas or misconceptions. The same holds true for teachers' aides, parent volunteers, or retirees assisting in the classroom.

Sources

Benjamin, L. T., & Lowman, K. D. (Eds.). (1981). *Activities handbook for the teaching of psychology.* Washington, DC: American Psychological Association.

Pitts, S. E. (2005). Testing, testing . . . : How do students use written feedback? *Active Learning in Higher Education, 6,* 218–229.

> **Strategy 36: When grading student writing, consider what is done well before noting what needs improvement.**

What the Research Says

In a review of current research, Gregg and Mather (2002) noted that many factors influence the perception that a student is not a proficient writer. They propose that, by considering writing skills (spelling, syntax, vocabulary, etc.) as well as the task format (dictating, copying, timed writing, etc.), teachers will discover a student's writing strengths and also notice areas that require support. They noted that it is vital to remember that writing is integrally related to social interactions and dialogue. In other words, writing is not simply the attempt to represent linguistic structures such as sentences, words, or phonemes; written expression requires a social process achieved through dialogue and interaction.

Classroom Applications

Students with disabilities often view writing as a hated task, and as standards move toward embedding writing in more curricular areas, poor writing skills can lead to a broader dislike of school and classwork in general. Writing itself is a very personal enterprise, and for a student who struggles with it, writing can be a very personal failure.

When teaching writing, teachers should pay close attention to how students view themselves as writers and encourage them to focus on finding and writing in their own unique voice. By modeling the writing process for them—showing how ideas come first, then a rough draft to give the ideas shape, followed by an editing process that addresses the mechanical aspects of the writing—teachers can begin to facilitate student success.

When assessing written assignments, teachers should consider grading the first draft for content only, engaging the student in a written dialogue about what the student is saying in his or her writing. Teachers must quell their urges to point out paragraphing, capitalization, and spelling errors as they read. They should demonstrate the difference between content and mechanics by isolating them in the teaching and assessment and evaluation process.

Experienced teachers recognize that writing skill develops on a continuum, and they help their students to see individual growth along that continuum. Students who understand that what they have to say is unique and valuable are much more likely to risk committing their thoughts and ideas to paper. They know that the mechanical components of writing can be addressed concretely farther along in their writing process.

Precautions and Possible Pitfalls

 In recent years many teachers and parents have lamented the lack of spelling and grammar instruction in schools. Students need to learn the principles behind spelling patterns as well as the basic grammatical components of standard written English. Most students learn these basic rules more effectively in context, so teachers should consider embedding a lesson on a specific rule of grammar by asking the students to correct it or apply it in their own writing.

Source

Gregg, N., & Mather, N. (2002). School is fun at recess. *Journal of Learning Disabilities, 35*(1), 7–23.

 Strategy 37: Use assessment as a teaching and learning opportunity.

What the Research Says

 Research shows that tests and other assessment devices can be used to improve learning, rather than just evaluating students' mastery of content. One study (Foos & Fisher, 1988) compared the test performance of students who took an initial or pretest with those who did not take an initial test. The results showed that students who took the initial test did better than those who did not, indicating that they actually learned from the test experience.

Assessment is most effective when it also includes students' self-monitoring and self-evaluating so that they can regulate or manage their own learning. One way of promoting students' ability to self-assess their performance is through error analysis (Hartman, 2001). Research on teaching students to use such strategies demonstrates that students need to be able to answer the following self-questions about such a strategy before it is used effectively in a variety of situations and tasks (Schunk, 2000).

- What is error analysis? It's a systematic approach for using feedback metacognitively to improve one's future performance. It involves obtaining strategic metacognitive knowledge about one's mistakes and recycling that knowledge for self-improvement.

- When and why is it used? Error analysis has several potential benefits. First, it gives students a second opportunity to master important material. Second, it develops students' metacognition, both strategic knowledge and executive management, as students evaluate their test performance, identify errors and possible error patterns, and plan for the future. For example, it can help students anticipate their specific likely errors and self-correct them before turning in a test. Third, it helps internalize students' attributions so that they recognize that their educational outcomes (grades) are a result of their own efforts, actions, and strategies—factors within their control. This is in contrast to attributing their performance to external factors outside their control, such as the teacher or bad luck. This could improve students' feelings of self-efficacy and their academic self-concept in the specific subject area and perhaps transfer to their general academic self-concept. Thus, error analysis improves critical thinking abilities of self-monitoring and self-evaluating one's performance and can improve students' feelings about their ability to succeed in this discipline.

- How is an error analysis performed? Error analysis requires identifying the correct information, answer, and approach and identifying what errors, omissions, and so on were made; determining why they occurred; and planning how to prevent them in the future. When performing error analyses, students should (1) identify what their wrong answer was and what the correct answer is (declarative knowledge), (2) determine specifically why they got the answer wrong (contextual knowledge), and (3) formulate an action plan on how they have now learned and understand the material and how they will remember this information (procedural knowledge).

Error Analysis Model

- What answer did I have? **AND** What really was the answer? **OR** What did I do wrong? **AND** What should I have done?
- Why did I choose the wrong answer? **OR** Why did I do it wrong?
- How will I remember what I now know is the correct answer? **OR** How will I make sure I don't make the same mistake again?

In all three steps, the student must focus on the specific content involved in the error rather than focus on general causes of errors.

Pelley and Dalley's (1997) question analysis was intended to help students make a broader analysis of test questions than a literal interpretation because a narrower, more literal interpretation can constrain their studying and limit learning. Their procedure has four steps: identifying topics, understanding the correct answer, understanding wrong answers, and rephrasing the question. Pelley and Dalley encouraged students to ask questions such as, "How would I have had to study to know that the correct answer was right?" and "How would I have had to study to know that each wrong answer was wrong?" Focusing on the topic rather than the question helps students understand material more deeply, so they understand how ideas are interrelated, and therefore students are able to correctly answer more and different questions.

Classroom Applications

 Following are examples of error analysis on a biology multiple-choice test item and on a research report (Hartman, 2001).

Multiple-Choice Item

Question: Which of the following is the correct characterization for the resting membrane potential of a typical neuron?

(a) It is negative outside compared to inside.
(b) It depends on high permeability of the membrane to sodium and potassium ions.
(c) It carries impulses from one region to another.
(d) It results from the unequal distribution of ions across the membrane.

Error Analysis of Item

1. What did I get wrong, and what is the right answer? I thought the answer was "b," but now I know the answer is "d."
2. Why did I get it wrong? I knew there was high permeability to potassium, but I forgot it was impermeable to sodium.
3. How will I remember this and prevent future similar mistakes? I'll remember that the resting potential of a neuron depends on the imbalance. The unequal distribution of ions results from the difference in permeability between sodium and potassium. The membrane is highly permeable to potassium, but it is impermeable to sodium. This causes it to be negative inside compared to the outside. I'll also try to use the process of elimination more so I can rule out some of the answer choices.

Alternative Error Analysis

1. What did I get wrong, and what should I have done? I lost credit because I did not properly cite all of the sources of my information in the text and on the reference list at the end. I should have put the authors' last names and publication years in the body of the report where I discussed them in addition to their names in the list at the end of the report. All names have to be in both places; I had some in one place but not the other.
2. Why did I do this wrong? We didn't have to do this before or in other classes, so I didn't know it was the correct procedure. I didn't understand "plagiarism." I also didn't read the assignment sheet carefully enough to see this was required. I just read it to get a general idea of what was expected and missed some of the details.
3. How will I prevent similar mistakes in the future? I'll remember to cite my sources in the text because I'll think about how I would feel if someone took my ideas and didn't give me credit for them. I'll also read my assignment sheets more carefully, looking for specific details instead of general ideas. Finally, I'll use a checklist to make sure I really do everything I plan to do. The checklist will have two sections for each thing I have to do. One section will be to track my progress; the other will be to rate the quality of the work I've done.

Precautions and Possible Pitfalls

Students historically have differing degrees of difficulty with different parts of an error analysis. The first question, about what students got wrong and what the right answer is, tends to be relatively easy for students. The second question, requiring students to explain why they erred, is moderately difficult, especially when it comes to specifics. Students try to get away with general excuses such as, "I didn't study enough," instead of making specific analyses of why their lack of sufficient studying caused them to make the particular error they made. The third question, about how students will use what they learned to improve their future performance, is the most difficult for students. Developing retention strategies and learning improvement plans requires hard and sustained thinking.

Sources

Foos, P. W., & Fisher, R. P. (1988). Using tests as learning opportunities. *Journal of Educational Psychology, 80*(2), 179–183.

Hartman, H. (2001). Developing students' metacognitive knowledge and strategies. In H. Hartman (Ed.), *Metacognition in learning and instruction: Theory, research, and practice* (pp. 69–83). Dordrecht, The Netherlands: Kluwer.

Pelley, J. W., & Dalley, B. K. (1997). *Successful types for medical students.* Lubbock: Texas Tech University Extended Learning.

Schunk, D. (2000). *Learning theories: An educational perspective* (3rd ed.). Upper Saddle River, NJ: Merrill.

Strategy 38: Learn when to de-emphasize grades.

What the Research Says

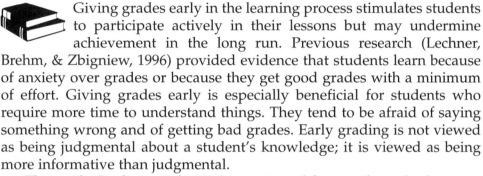

Giving grades early in the learning process stimulates students to participate actively in their lessons but may undermine achievement in the long run. Previous research (Lechner, Brehm, & Zbigniew, 1996) provided evidence that students learn because of anxiety over grades or because they get good grades with a minimum of effort. Giving grades early is especially beneficial for students who require more time to understand things. They tend to be afraid of saying something wrong and of getting bad grades. Early grading is not viewed as being judgmental about a student's knowledge; it is viewed as being more informative than judgmental.

This study (Lechner et al., 1996) investigated four ninth-grade classes on the effects of giving grades at an early stage of knowledge acquisition. To show the effects of early marking, the four classes were separated into two groups. Both groups received computer-aided instruction and got a grade after every step. The first group did not get to know about their grades, while the second group was informed about their grades. The achievements of the groups were compared on the basis of the grade after every step and on a final test. Students who knew their marks did slightly better on the interim tests. Their learning was enhanced by the grades. In contrast, on the final test, students who did not know their interim grades did noticeably better. They were not pushed by the pressure of marks. They used additional work to develop self-control. In this way, they dealt with the issue of their learning needs, they understood it profoundly, and they achieved at higher levels.

Classroom Applications

Teachers should avoid giving grades at an early stage of learning. Early marks can easily frustrate students who are not interested in a particular topic or even the whole subject, and their motivation can sink even further. Although early grades can promote rapid success, in some cases this leads to students resting on their laurels. During the period students are acquiring new knowledge, the teacher should use grades sparingly.

Teachers need to remember that not all feedback needs to be evaluated with a grade. The process of learning and putting together a product increasingly is seen as more important than the finished product itself. Simply checking off a step or stamping work as completed before moving on to the next could be enough incentive (with feedback) to keep instruction and learning moving.

Precautions and Possible Pitfalls

 The teacher should not stop all assessment during the early stage of learning. First, students need assessment to evaluate or at least estimate their own achievement. In addition, the teacher will always find some students who are entirely motivated by grades. Therefore, during the early learning phase, a teacher should use oral or nonverbal assessment techniques.

Source

Lechner, H. J., Brehm, R. I., & Zbigniew, M. (1996). Zensierung und ihr Einfluß auf die Leistung der Schüler [Influence of marks on student achievement]. *Pädagogik und Schulalltag, 51*(3), 371–379.

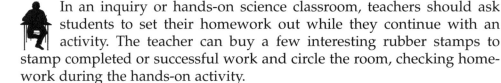

Strategy 39: Be prompt in giving students feedback about their performance.

What the Research Says

 Students need to know what they know and what they can do well. They also need to know what they do not know and what they cannot do well. Students often cannot make these evaluations on their own, so they need this kind of information from their teacher.

Information about their knowledge and performance, which is known as feedback, can help students focus their learning efforts and activities. This helps students learn. Feedback is more meaningful and more useful when delivered in a timely fashion.

Classroom Applications

In an inquiry or hands-on science classroom, teachers should ask students to set their homework out while they continue with an activity. The teacher can buy a few interesting rubber stamps to stamp completed or successful work and circle the room, checking homework during the hands-on activity.

The teacher can look over the homework while guiding and supporting the ongoing hands-on activity. The teacher doesn't have to correct it and has the chance to give each student instant verbal feedback! The work can then become part of the students' notebooks. This way the teacher's prep period or at-home time can be saved for grading work that requires more attention.

Teachers need to keep in mind that it is very tempting to spot-check homework by inspecting to see if the right answers are offered without looking at the method to reach the answer. Whenever possible, teachers should thoroughly examine students' homework answers and methods; they should give students information about the quality of their performance. With practice, teachers will learn to recognize problems with the assignment faster and more easily. Within a class, it is common to find that the same problems pop up as problematic for a number of students.

Where a class is too large to do a thorough check of the homework, the teacher can select different subgroups from within the class daily, picking their homework from the collected class set.

Precautions and Possible Pitfalls

 The teacher may either randomly select subgroups or select them by design. In any case, this selection should not be predictable by the students. Otherwise, those who anticipate homework inspection will do a better job. If feedback is not provided in a timely fashion, it will be of limited use to students.

Focusing on an assignment with the teacher's undivided attention can be difficult for some within a noisy and active class. It takes practice to become effective. The assessment and feedback must be authentic and not just rubber-stamped as completed, or teachers run the risk of devaluing the students' effort and work.

Source

Chickering, A. W., & Gamson, Z. F. (1987). Seven principles for good practice in undergraduate education. *Wingspread Journal, 9*(2), special insert.

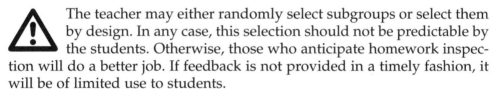

Strategy 40: Move beyond paper to a digital portfolio as an assessment alternative.

What the Research Says

 The Annenberg Institute for School Reform and the Coalition for Essential Schools, with the support of IBM, investigated the use of the digital portfolio at six schools. Digital portfolio software was used to create a multimedia collection of students' work and connect the work to performance standards. The sites represented rural, suburban, and urban schools that were both technology rich and poor. Digital portfolio software was customized for each school, and part of the effort included putting portfolio content online. In addition to the usual goals and objectives of the portfolio strategy, the aim of the digital portfolio was to expand the viewing audience to include college admissions and placement offices.

Word processing, scanning, and digitizing audio and video provided the means of entry into the multimedia portfolio. Researchers found the need for the targeted schools to support a schoolwide vision on how technology—and digital portfolios in particular—corresponds with the school's other systems. The main benefit of the digital portfolio, in contrast to its paper counterpart, seems to be its ability to become available to a wider audience. In addition, technology can add a few extra process steps that provide the students greater opportunity to reflect on and polish their presentations.

Classroom Applications

 While a schoolwide digital portfolio requirement might not be realistic or feasible, a digital portfolio option may be just the right thing for specific classes or students. Consider the following ideas.

- Allow motivated and interested students the option of a digital portfolio. Student artists or photographers could benefit by digitizing all their work, along with appropriate reflection and written content.
- Students interested in technology as a career could benefit by recording their mastery in the field as well as fulfilling a specific class portfolio requirement.
- A student could produce a digital job resume in portfolio form.
- Form a class portfolio and turn it into a class Web page that is available to a much wider audience.
- Include parents as collaborators and viewers in digital technology. Digital media provide another vehicle for sharing student work. Because it is a relatively new idea, the limits of technology have not been reached. Creative students and teachers can experiment with new and innovative uses of the digital portfolio as it finds its niche within other instructional strategies.

Precautions and Possible Pitfalls

 The research points to time as the major instructional concern. The technological learning curve has a huge time component, and the time needs to come from somewhere. Teachers can add new requirements on top of curricular goals and objectives. Try to realistically estimate the appropriate amount of time required to learn any new technology, and be prepared to let go of some other parts of curriculum or instructional activities.

Source

Niguidula, D. (1997). Picturing performance with digital portfolios. *Educational Leadership, 55*(3), 26–29.

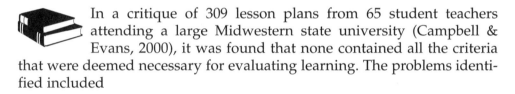

Strategy 41: Interface assessment strategies to instructional goals for powerful learning.

What the Research Says

In a critique of 309 lesson plans from 65 student teachers attending a large Midwestern state university (Campbell & Evans, 2000), it was found that none contained all the criteria that were deemed necessary for evaluating learning. The problems identified included

- An absence of a direct link between instructional goals and assessment
- Twenty-three percent featured nonobservable objectives, although the majority recognized the need
- Samples of 103 assessments, where only eight assessment strategies were deemed complete
- The absence of reliability and validity concepts
- A huge discrepancy between measurement instruction from their university classes and its practical application among student teachers

Classroom Applications

During the history of public education, there has never been a better time in which to find help on assessment and instructional practices. Today's course content has never been more analyzed by state framework writers, educational agencies, special interest groups, and parent organizations. The best of them feature not only content outlines but pedagogical and assessment suggestions and guidelines. In addition, most textbook publishers (who design their books based on the same documents) provide instruction and assessment strategies connected to their books' content.

Most subjects' content frameworks are now accessible via the Internet, and a master or supervising teacher can access the content textbook's support material. In addition, many veteran teachers use assessment strategies that connect to skills required on standardized tests. Teachers should analyze and use them all within their personal instructional contexts. It's clear the resources are there. The dilemma for new teachers is deciding which to use. Some of these resources offer more valid and reliable information, and the trick is finding a secure bridge between instructional goals, classroom instruction, and assessment. Also, all new teachers come with their own ideas about assessment, or they adopt their master teachers' goals. Some framework and supplemental textbook information seems to be written by people who have never been in a classroom. Some others stand out and seem to have been written just for new teachers with their goals in mind. As a beginning teacher, survey as much information as possible before synthesizing personal strategies.

The trick for new teachers is to construct the unit or lesson in a complete package with equal attention to goals and objectives; instructional delivery systems; and fair, reliable, and valid assessment strategies. If assessment is considered and addressed before beginning instruction, teachers will find peace of mind and security as they move the students toward final assessment. The teacher will know what the students need to be successful as the lesson progresses and will always have that in mind. In this way, the teacher can always make adjustments to instruction and shorten or lengthen the pace, simplify or rework instructional trouble spots, or tweak the assessment a bit if necessary. There is a saying that if you don't know where you are going, you will probably never get there. With assessment, teachers should take that to heart; their students will thank them, and they will feel much more confident as a teacher.

Precautions and Possible Pitfalls

For a new teacher, politics plays a heavy role in assessment. New teachers often find themselves split between using their master teachers' assessment instruments and strategies and developing their own. A solution to this dilemma is to codevelop the lesson or unit, including assessment, with the supervising teacher. Teachers should develop a resource bank of frameworks and other guidelines of their own and bring them to the table to support their ideas and practices.

Also, students are often quick to blame the teacher for their lack of success on the assessment. The teacher needs to be prepared for these arguments. This is where veteran teachers can offer suggestions and help the beginning teachers as they prepare strategies for such situations, as they are better able to provide strategies due to their experience. This is an area where clearly defined scoring guides can be extremely helpful.

Source

Campbell, C., & Evans, J. A. (2000). Investigation of pre-service teachers' classroom assessment practices during student teaching. *Journal of Educational Research, 93*(6), 350–355.

 Strategy 42: Consider alternate assessment instruments.

What the Research Says

 Ramsey-Gassert (1997) began by looking at Frank Oppenheimer, the originator of the Exploratorium in San Francisco, who argued against formal assessment in science centers and moved on from there. He saw the inherent value of informal learning in promoting science education and science and opposed the dominant, narrow view of science education taken in traditional, in-school science. Because informal learning is not graded, no one flunks an informal encounter with science. This view can be shared within other disciplines.

Some believe that many informal experiences are so individual and multifaceted that they cannot be assessed with letter grades or scores. Some see the lack of evaluation as an obvious strength in engaging individuals in a more social, open-ended, learner-directed experience, with a less planned and nonevaluative contact with science. Trying to evaluate so many potential unintended outcomes is just not fair to students.

Out of four research papers that examined out-of-school informal educational activities, all used students' written reflections (some used a rubric to guide students' responses) to survey the students' perception of how much they learned and its quality.

Classroom Applications

The assessment instruments identified in this research (Korpan, Bisanz, Bisanz, Boehme, & Lynch, 1997; Ramsey-Gassert, 1997) were not designed to yield a score or grade. They were designed to measure the overall effectiveness of the encounter. This information could then be used to modify the encounter itself and not rate the students' success or failure. Movies, plays, art galleries, and a host of other out-of-classroom activities can be used as authentic curricula that can provide interesting and motivating learning pathways.

One study (Korpan et al., 1997) featured assessment that was produced by parents interacting with their child. Students were stimulated by their parents' involvement, and the students felt comfortable with their parents. Researchers found this type of assessment to suffer from low reliability and validity, but it had its advantages. The collaborative, nonthreatening nature of the informal project fostered active and meaningful learning and an integrated school, home, and community.

It's clear that traditional content assessment may miss the point of the out-of-school experience or informal in-school learning. There is a wider range of attributes and facets that need to be measured, and a content test would send the wrong message to students about what is important. Extending the experience by expanding it with a related performance-based project, writing activity, or other application would be a better gauge of mastery than a traditional test. Korpan et al. (1997) felt that projects with appropriate scoring rubrics, where students combine discipline content from the classroom and the informal experience, are the best way for students to demonstrate this type of learning. Ultimately, the teacher wants to facilitate growth of enthusiasm and motivation.

Precautions and Possible Pitfalls

Consider a student who usually performs poorly in the traditional classroom yet exhibits enthusiasm and interest in more hands-on activities and participation in out-of-school learning experiences. This situation presents teachers with a dilemma as to how to encourage students like this and not penalize them with narrow-range, traditional classroom assessment devices. The teacher should not turn the students' enthusiasm off. Balancing opportunities for successful assessment and evaluation gives students in this group more than one pathway to find and demonstrate success. Oral presentations, project display boards, student videos, computer-generated presentations (e.g., PowerPoint), and other instructional outcomes can help these students find success.

Another challenge is providing equal access and opportunity for all students in class. Sometimes parental support is not available to all students. The teacher needs to make learning outside the classroom an option with an in-school component for those that can't participate in off-campus activities. For example, in a marine biology class in a high school located near the coast, an intertidal visit and beach walk had an alternative in-class option for those who couldn't get to the beach during low tides.

Sources

Korpan, C. A., Bisanz, G. L., Bisanz, J., Boehme, C., & Lynch, M. A. (1997). What did you learn outside of school today? Using structured interviews to document home and community activities related to science and technology. *Science Education, 81*(6), 651–662.

Kurth, L. A., & Richmond, G. (1999). Moving from outside to inside: High school students' use of apprenticeship as a vehicle for entering the culture and practice of science. *Journal of Research in Science Teaching*, 36(6), 677–697.

Ramsey-Gassert, L. (1997). Learning science beyond the classroom. *Elementary School Journal*, 97(4), 433–450.

Strategy 43: Keep feedback positive to bolster student confidence.

What the Research Says

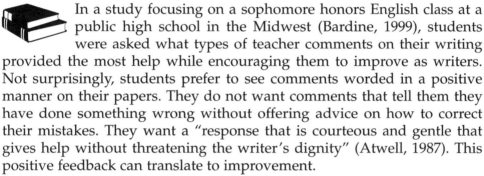

In a study focusing on a sophomore honors English class at a public high school in the Midwest (Bardine, 1999), students were asked what types of teacher comments on their writing provided the most help while encouraging them to improve as writers. Not surprisingly, students prefer to see comments worded in a positive manner on their papers. They do not want comments that tell them they have done something wrong without offering advice on how to correct their mistakes. They want a "response that is courteous and gentle that gives help without threatening the writer's dignity" (Atwell, 1987). This positive feedback can translate to improvement.

At least three studies (Daiker, 1983; Dragga, 1986; Harris, 1977) showed that teachers usually do not praise students' writing often enough. Daiker, Kerek, and Morenberg (1986) found that the vast majority of comments (89.4%) "cited error or found fault; . . . 10.6% of them were comments of praise" (p. 104).

Classroom Applications

The goal of student writing is improvement. Therefore, the more specific a teacher can be about students' work, providing comments that include thorough explanations and just, deserved praise of what they have done right (as opposed to taking the dreaded red pen and marking only what is wrong), the more likely students will feel supported and will work to improve. Teachers must also look at their own commenting style. Do teachers comment only on form, or do they include content? Do they consider the ideas the student is proposing? If the objective is to improve over several drafts, then certainly grammatical errors such as spelling and punctuation should not formulate the majority of a teacher's comments. These parts of writing are important, but can be revised in a later draft, after the student has the content-oriented problems ironed out. Do teachers tell students what is right with their work as well as give them a thorough explanation of what needs to be done to correct mistakes?

Telling a student to be more specific has little or no meaning if a teacher does not tell them which part of their text needs to be more specific and possibly give examples.

Precautions and Possible Pitfalls

Whether they are writing papers for English, science, or history, most students want their writing to reflect improvement. The teacher needs to be careful not to use praise that is too general or patronizing. At the beginning of a course, the teacher should go over the specific commenting style with students and discuss whether symbols will be used as well as written comments. The teacher should make sure students understand what these symbols mean. In addition to written comments, the teacher should talk to students on a regular basis about their papers and encourage students to ask questions if the comments they are given aren't clear.

Sources

Atwell, N. (1987). *"In the middle": Writing, reading, and learning with adolescents.* Portsmouth, NH: Boynton/Cook.

Bardine, B. A. (1999). Students' perceptions of written teacher comments: What do they say about how we respond to them? *High School Journal, 82*(4), 239–247.

Daiker, D. (1983, March). *The teacher's options in responding to student writing.* Paper presented at the annual conference on College Composition and Communication, Washington, DC.

Daiker, D. A., Kerek, A., & Morenberg, M. (1986). *The writer's options: Combining composing* (3rd ed.). New York: Harper.

Dragga, S. (1986, March). *Praiseworthy grading: A teacher's alternative to editing error.* Paper presented at the Conference on College Composition and Communication, New Orleans, LA.

Harris, W. H. (1977). Teacher response to student writing: A study of the response pattern of high school teachers to determine the basis for teacher judgment of student writing. *Research in the Teaching of English, 11*, 175–185.

Strategy 44: Help students embrace their errors for more meaningful instruction.

What the Research Says

Teachers often give students less-than-useful information about their academic performance. Studies have shown that students benefit more from learning about when they are wrong than when they are right. In addition, for students to improve their future performance, they need to know why something is wrong. Research shows that teachers often fail to provide students with this kind of information about their performance. When students understand why something is wrong, they are more likely to learn appropriate strategies to eliminate their errors.

Classroom Applications

Even with the emphasis on high-level thinking skills and teaching processes, in general, there are lots of opportunities for students to give a simple right answer or a wrong response to their answers. For a teacher to merely indicate the right answer, or to indicate that a student's response is wrong, does little to aim the student in the right direction. Teachers should analyze incorrect responses to see if the errors are in reasoning, incorrect interpretations of major concepts, faulty work with the concept details, or problems with reading the question correctly. Oftentimes, such an analysis can be time-consuming but extremely worthwhile, for it is the discovery of the error (resulting from their error analysis) that can be the key to helping students sort out their comprehension or learning difficulties. Remember, more meaningful instruction usually contributes to retention of more than just one-shot coverage.

There are several types of errors that occur in the normal curriculum–student interaction in classrooms. First, there are the errors that are common to a large portion of the class. These can be attributable to a misunderstanding in class or to some prior learning common to most of the class that causes students to similarly react incorrectly to a specific situation. When the teacher notices this sort of thing, a general remark and clarification to the entire class would be appropriate. The misconception may be one of not understanding the details or background behind a concept. Understanding the grammar or math leads to mastery of the concept. Analysis of errors in thinking and quick and instant feedback can turn potential drudgery into pride of understanding.

Wrong answers and misconceptions provide teachable moments and quick feedback opportunities. In this case, rapid feedback is important in helping students avoid the frustration that turns them off. Most of them have had the math but not within an authentic context.

Precautions and Possible Pitfalls

It is possible that, through an analysis of a student's work, several errors may turn up. To point out too many faults at one time could confound the student and consequently have a counterproductive effect. The teacher should arrange the discovered errors in order of importance and successively discuss them with the student one by one, going on to the next one only after successful completion of the earlier one. Teachers should follow up to see if the students successfully followed their error-correction plans and rectified previous errors, especially recurring errors.

Source

Bangert-Drowns, R. L., Kulik, C. C., Kulik, J. A., & Morgan, M. (1991). The instructional effect of feedback in test-like events. *Review of Educational Research, 61,* 213–238.

 Strategy 45: Look beyond test scores by keeping a range of student work.

What the Research Says

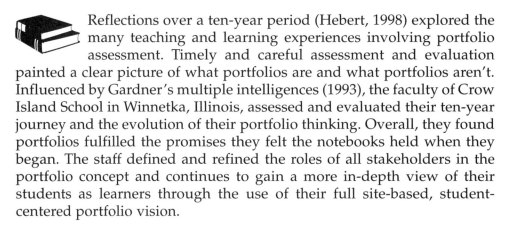 Reflections over a ten-year period (Hebert, 1998) explored the many teaching and learning experiences involving portfolio assessment. Timely and careful assessment and evaluation painted a clear picture of what portfolios are and what portfolios aren't. Influenced by Gardner's multiple intelligences (1993), the faculty of Crow Island School in Winnetka, Illinois, assessed and evaluated their ten-year journey and the evolution of their portfolio thinking. Overall, they found portfolios fulfilled the promises they felt the notebooks held when they began. The staff defined and refined the roles of all stakeholders in the portfolio concept and continues to gain a more in-depth view of their students as learners through the use of their full site-based, student-centered portfolio vision.

Classroom Applications

 Points to consider when thinking about portfolios include the following:

- Portfolios in education, by most definitions, are created to tell a story. Teachers shouldn't be too rigid when deciding what goes into one. They should consider allowing and helping the students to decide what goes into the "story" of their learning and growth. Are the portfolios going to be teacher-centered or student-centered? Who decides what goes into one?

- Decide what work will go home and what should stay in the portfolio. Are teachers presenting parents a "chapter" at a time, or are they presenting a more temporal view within the portfolio paradigm?
- Whose portfolio is it? Should teachers assume the role of a portfolio manager and let students decide what will counterbalance test scores and enter the portfolio? If teachers decide to do it this way, they should help the students with decisions. They are developing competent and thoughtful storytellers. When students are first discovering what a portfolio is, they require a scaffolding strategy.
- Grading or attaching a letter grade to a portfolio seems to run contrary to the nature of the concept.
- Select a time frame for the history of the learning that a portfolio might represent. Is a portfolio a year's worth of work?
- For some students, "telling" a long-term story is too abstract. Defining an audience for the work contributes to a more concrete picture.
- Attach meaning to each piece in a portfolio by asking students to write a short reason for its inclusion in the story. *Reflection tag* was the term used in Hebert (1998). This contributes to the student's metacognitive growth and attaches further value and meaning to the individual content.
- Deliberately teach parents about the value of student portfolios and what they mean to the curriculum and students.

Precautions and Possible Pitfalls

 On the surface, portfolios sound like a simple concept. Do not underestimate the learning curve for teachers, students, and parents if the concept is to really function at its best. Expect some frustration during the implementation and transition to portfolio adoption.

Sources

Gardner, H. (1993). *Multiple intelligences: The theory in practice.* New York: Basic.
Hebert, E. (1998). Lessons learned about student portfolios. *Phi Delta Kappan, 79*(8), 583–585.

Strategy 46: Consider the use of open-book tests.

What the Research Says

This study (Phillips, 2006) involved 1,080 community-college students enrolled in general biology classes over a ten-year period. Phillips was interested in finding out whether three open-book tests over the length of the course could be used to improve study skills and whether the students with weaker study skills benefited more than students with moderate or stronger study skills. The mean improvement for the entire sample was 4.47 points; the students with weak study skills improved an average of 23.79 points, the students with moderate study skills improved 4.88 points, and the students designated as strong decreased 4.88 points. The most obvious reason for the improvement with the weak and moderate group stemmed from their being provided with study strategies and an opportunity to turn those strategies into skills. The most dramatic improvement was seen between the first and second open-book tests of the year. Phillips assumed that students with strong study skills were not assimilating any new strategies or they were not incorporating any new skills. However, after a drop in scores in the second test, they rebounded for the third test. Although they did not show an improvement in their overall study skills, their drop was minimal.

Classroom Applications

Phillips (2006) used his open-book tests as a vehicle for teaching study skills within only the three tests that made up a portion of overall class evaluation. These open-book tests targeted information that was related to lectures but not directly covered during class. He prepared students by going over examples of open-book questions and discussing strategies for effectively and efficiently using the class text. Finally, Phillips made the importance of completing the assigned readings clear early in the class.

He also taught instruction strategies for comprehending the layout of the targeted chapters and highlighting, tabbing, and using the index as well as the significance of bolded pages and bolded keywords within the text. The open-book test questions also contained contextual clues that directed the students to the correct chapters and subheadings. Students who used the study skills and read the material prior to the test could more quickly narrow their search.

Phillips's efforts were not typical of college and university classrooms. In this class instruction, goals included not only teaching the subject matter but also providing students with the study skills necessary to help them learn. To do this, teachers need to see testing, assessment, and evaluation as an opportunity to embed teaching and learning devices within the targeted learning processes. This may take a change in perspective regarding using tests for evaluation purposes only. The rewards students take with them can be seen as greater than just subject-matter knowledge.

A variation of this technique is to give students test essay questions a few days before the test. Use those questions as an opportunity to teach study strategies. In this example, consider giving them ten essay questions out of which only two or three will be used on the actual test. They won't know which ones they will see until test day.

There are many other ways to incorporate the literacy-specific study skill agenda in testing. Again, teachers just need to see testing in a new way beyond mere assessment.

Precautions and Possible Pitfalls

Sometimes more successful students, especially in secondary schools, feel that their study skills work just fine and are not open to new or different ideas. If teachers try to push the agenda too hard, they will lose those students and they will lose respect for the rigor of the class. Teachers have to decide on the needs of the class, do their best to help those in need, and move on. Better test scores should reinforce and reward those who assimilate more effective study skills.

Source

Phillips, G. (2006). Using open-book tests to strengthen the study skills of community college biology students. *Journal of Adolescent & Adult Literacy, 49*(7), 574–582.

5

Celebrating Diversity in the Classroom

Strategy 47: Welcome the diversity of today's classrooms.

What the Research Says

That today's schools are more diverse than ever is undeniable. According to the Federal Interagency Forum on Child and Family Statistics (1998), one in every three students attending primary or secondary schools today is of a racial or ethnic minority. Predictions are also that students of color will make up almost 50% of the U. S. school-age population by 2020 (Banks & Banks, 2001). With the large influx of immigrants in the past several decades, children of these immigrants make up approximately 20% of the children in the United States, providing a kaleidoscope of cultural and language differences in many classrooms (Dugger, 1998).

Cultural and language differences are only a part of the diversity in our schools. One in five children under the age of 18 currently lives below the poverty line. The traditional two-parent family is becoming the minority. Less than half of America's children currently live with both biological parents, with almost 60% of all students living in a single-parent household by the time they reach the age of 18 (Salend, 2001). All this is occurring at a time when schools are working toward mainstreaming and the inclusion of nearly 11% of school-age children who are classified as disabled (U.S. Department of Education, 1995). Certainly the challenges that face today's classrooms have never been greater. Teacher preparation programs are including classes to help prepare future teachers for cross-cultural, inclusive instruction. Zeichner (1993) proposed that the key characteristics of these programs provide for the dynamics of prejudice and racism.

Classroom Applications

Even in today's society, some classrooms seem to be focusing on the differences and difficulties involved in multicultural education rather than embracing these differences as being enriching, desirable, inevitable, natural, and welcomed. Teachers must not only acknowledge the obvious diversity issues such as color and physical disability, but also be aware of the cultural diversity of students and families.

In selecting curriculum it is important to see if examples of diversity are represented. Are the visual examples only of Whites? Are the holidays represented in literature only those celebrated by Christians? Are the needs and emotions of the handicapped presented? When having a discussion of families, it is important to stress that not all family units are alike. When sending a note home to parents, it is better to have it addressed to the "parent or guardian of" instead of "mother" or "father."

A teacher once asked her students to describe their bedrooms and draw pictures of them. What this teacher didn't realize was that several students did not have their own bedrooms but shared a room with four or five siblings. Disclosing this information to the class by reading their stories and showing their drawings might have been embarrassing for these students.

By the same token, new teachers must be especially aware of district and state education codes with regard to celebrating religious holidays in the classroom. What about the student who doesn't celebrate Christian or Jewish holidays? Rather than asking students to write a story about their favorite Christmas memory, the teacher might require students to write about a favorite family tradition.

One question a teacher should consider is, "Could this question, example, or assignment make a student feel uncomfortable with regard to their race, religion, or ethnic or cultural background?" Designing a richly diverse curriculum does not have to be difficult; it simply takes thought and consideration. The use of cooperative learning groups lends itself particularly well to teaching students with differing abilities in the same classroom. Students should be grouped with consideration to differences in gender, race, ethnicity, and ability. Using assignments and activities that incorporate the recognition of multiple intelligences is particularly necessary and effective in responding to student diversity.

Precautions and Possible Pitfalls

 Frequently it is beginning teachers who find themselves with the most diverse classroom. It is of the utmost importance that these teachers are prepared for cross-cultural, inclusive instruction. Classes in teacher education programs must include information about the characteristics of prejudice and racism, provide successful examples of teaching ethnic- and language-minority students, and ingrain instruction that provides both social support for students and an intellectual challenge.

Teachers must also be sensitive to issues involving money. Perhaps every child in class wouldn't be able to afford the cost of a field trip. For one high school that considered putting ATMs on campus, the realization of the ways this could further divide students into "haves" and "have-nots" caused administrators to rethink their decision.

Teachers should consult with experienced, exemplary, veteran teachers or school administrators before meeting with parents of immigrant students to determine if a translator might be needed or if there is any specific information about that student's family culture that might assist the teacher in having a successful meeting. The same is true for a student with disabilities. The special education teacher and the IEP (individual education plan) can provide beneficial information to the novice teacher. The more a teacher is sensitive to the richness of the diversity in the classroom, the more successful and equitable today's classrooms will become.

Sources

Banks, J. A., & Banks, C. A. M. (2001). *Multicultural education: Issues and perspectives* (4th ed.). New York: John Wiley & Sons.

Dugger, C. W. (1998, March 21). Among young of immigrants, outlook rises. *New York Times*, A1, A11.

Federal Interagency Forum on Child and Family Statistics. (1998). *America's children: Key national indicators of well-being.* Washington, DC: U.S. Government Printing Office.

Salend, S. J. (2001). *Creating inclusive classrooms: Effective and reflective practices* (4th ed.). Upper Saddle River, NJ: Merrill.

U.S. Department of Education. (1995). *17th annual report to Congress on the implementation of IDEA.* Washington, DC: Author.

Zeichner, K. M. (1993). *Educating teachers for diversity.* East Lansing, MI: National Center for Research on Teacher Learning.

Strategy 48: *Confront personal ethnic and cultural stereotypes.*

What the Research Says

The introduction to Howard's (2001) research paper described a range of published research projects that consistently document the consequences of multicultural insensitivity by teachers from the student perspective. The consequences range from passive and active educational resistance as a form of disapproval to nonengagement, cheating, and disruption of class or withdrawing quietly as a way of coping.

Howard's (2001) analysis examined the historical range of research that attempted to gauge the loudness of a multicultural student's voice in the educational equation that all stakeholders share. Howard found that culturally relevant pedagogy recognized the cogent role that cultural socialization plays in how students receive, analyze, and interpret information. Culturally sensitive teaching and learning must go well beyond content modification. Modifying content does little to change how students perceive and respond to a noncaring environment.

Howard's (2001) study also examined student perceptions and interpretations of instructional practices used by four elementary school teachers in four urban settings who were identified as culturally responsive teachers for African American students. A total of 17 students were used in the study. Data were collected through observations and interviews with students. The purposes of student interviews focused on two areas. The first was to gain insight into viewpoints of ethnically diverse students that are rarely revealed in research about teaching and learning. The second was to balance the perceptions and interpretations of teaching practices between the student's viewpoint, the observer's viewpoint, and the teacher's intended goals and objectives.

Results indicated that culturally relevant teaching and learning should focus equally or more on how students are taught rather than what students are taught.

Classroom Applications

The students' perceptions and interpretations of their teachers' pedagogy revealed important insights into the dynamics of young African American learners. Howard (2001) suggested three specific strategies or areas that teachers could focus on:

1. *Caring.* Explicit and implicit showing of sincere concern and care that teachers have for their students is vital. Positive

reinforcement, expression of high expectations, and taking the time to find out about students' lives outside the classroom are vital to ethnic and cultural sensitivity. The commitment to both the academic and social development of students is the most important expression of concern and care.

2. *Establishing community.* The students in this study repeatedly mentioned their fondness for family or community-like environments in their classrooms encouraged by kindred relationships in academic settings, the elimination of homogeneous ability groupings (both formal and informal), establishing appropriate democratic principles, and the promotion of interdependence.

3. *Engaging classroom environments.* Creating exciting and stimulating classroom environments is not a new idea, but this goes beyond the physical environment and focuses on the style of discourse. Connecting course content to the students' lives and modifying the style of discourse in ways that are more interactive, engaging, and entertaining for students are suggested.

Surprisingly, the study (Howard, 2001) found that no students mentioned teacher race or ethnicity. The job for teachers is to acquire an understanding of the various cultural and learning characteristics their students bring to the classroom. Teachers who want to acquire an authentic understanding of the cultural aura students possess need, among other things, to abandon deficit-based stereotypes about the cognitive capacity, socio-cultural backgrounds, and overall learning potential different ethnic groups bring to the classroom. There must be a willingness to make changes to pedagogy to align more with the students' way of knowing, communicating, and being. Far too often, ethnic groups are asked or expected to leave their cultural identities at the door and conform to the teachers' way of thinking.

To make all this happen, teachers need to realize that this type of knowledge comes not only from books, but more important from parents, students, and community members. This may mean that teachers should immerse themselves in the day-to-day environment that the students experience. For new teachers, a strong will and courage may be their most needed assets.

Precautions and Possible Pitfalls

When developing effective teacher–student relationships, it is often difficult for new teachers to create clear, workable boundaries between the roles that all teachers have to play in dealing with students. Enabling questionable behavior in the quest for acceptance can create huge discipline and management problems. In the long run, setting reasonable and high standards for behavior, discourse, and pedagogy will establish a teacher's reputation as being fair and culturally sensitive.

By the time the second and third years of teaching roll around, teachers' reputations will help alleviate misunderstandings about their role, their teaching style, and any expectations they might have for the class before students enter the room. Finding a comfort zone in how a teacher deals with students takes time and is always considered work in progress. A teacher should look at establishing a three-year plan and should try not to ignore the challenges students present or find quick-fix solutions, which usually means trying to adopt another teacher's system. Rather, the teacher should be reflective, examine personal core philosophies, and adjust them for more long-term solutions. A teacher should see good teaching more as a journey than a destination.

Source

Howard, T. C. (2001). Telling their side of the story: African-American students' perceptions of culturally relevant teaching. *Urban Review, 33*(2), 131–149.

 Strategy 49: Become culturally literate when entering diverse school districts.

What the Research Says

The purpose of this specific study (Birrell, 1995) was to examine how ethically encapsulated first-year teachers coped with and responded to Black youths' ethnic behavior in a desert southwest school. It is not surprising that the research found that beginning teachers who are not prepared for oppositional ethnic behavior can act in ways that diminish Black children's (and, we assume, children from other ethnic groups') school learning and cultural identity. It was found that when underprepared White teachers confronted oppositional behavior from ethnically mixed environments, their educational techniques increased racial tension, hindered their own development, reduced student achievement, and reduced ethnic sensitivity in the school.

In Birrell (1995), a case study of a first-year, White male teacher provided multiple sources of data from reflective journaling, interview transcripts, and field observations. Reduced enrollment in his monocultural home community forced the new teacher to seek a teaching position elsewhere. His first school featured demographics with Whites being the minority culture. Because of a surplus of teachers, after the fifth week he was transferred to another urban school position within the same district. Four months later, finding he could not cope with the behavior of the mostly Black student body, he arranged to be transferred to a high school like the one he attended, where he was again part of the majority culture. Management strategies with which he was most familiar failed and only increased negative ethnic attitudes. He was not able to develop productive relationships with Black students. Ethnic origins, cultural experiences, and beliefs about schooling were issues limiting influences on how this teacher and his Black students viewed themselves and each other. The need to establish one's cultural identity (symbolic or otherwise) through behavior brought social consequences that hindered the development of an educational relationship.

Classroom Applications

The findings in this study (Birrell, 1995) suggested that principals in multicultural or multiethnic schools should know something about the racial attitudes of the teachers they hire. Most new teachers just want to find work, and their child-centered perspectives provide them with a false sense of security in dealing with multicultural settings. Their positive attitudes can become very short-lived. Beginning teacher demographics tell us that the majority of these teachers have had few opportunities to explore racial attitudes during preservice programs. They typically have limited experience in minority cultures before entering their first classroom.

If teachers find themselves in this position, they should not underestimate the rigors and potential consequences of the situation. They might consider seeking out skilled mentors to help them cope with the acclimation to unfamiliar territory. A culturally sensitive mentor could help new teachers explore their own feelings and help them reflect on the assignment. Beginning teachers should do what they have to do to find the help needed. There are no rules on where to find this help. Principals may be able to suggest someone onsite or within a local university education department, or teachers might expand their search to other departments where culture and ethnic sensitivity is important and there are knowledgeable people willing and able to help.

Precautions and Possible Pitfalls

For many good reasons, teachers may find they are indeed better suited for classrooms like those that the new teacher in the study (Birrell, 1995) experienced. A teacher may also be better or best prepared to teach in that setting. See this as an option. However, if a person is a good teacher, teaching in an upper-middle-class suburban school will do little to help reverse the social, political, economic, and educational factors that perpetuate the multicultural divide.

Sources

Birrell, J. R. (1995). "Learning how the game is played": An ethnically encapsulated beginning teacher's struggle to prepare Black youth for a White world. *Teaching and Teacher Education, 11*(2), 137–147.

Burant, T. J. (1999). Finding, using, and losing voice: A pre-service teacher's experiences in an urban educational practicum. *Journal of Teacher Education, 50*(3), 209.

Terrill, M. M., & Mark, D. (2000). Pre-service teachers' expectations for schools with children of color and second-language learners. *Journal of Teacher Education, 51*(2), 147–153.

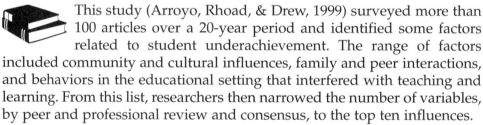

Strategy 50: Be aware of the wide range of specific factors associated with underachievement.

What the Research Says

This study (Arroyo, Rhoad, & Drew, 1999) surveyed more than 100 articles over a 20-year period and identified some factors related to student underachievement. The range of factors included community and cultural influences, family and peer interactions, and behaviors in the educational setting that interfered with teaching and learning. From this list, researchers then narrowed the number of variables, by peer and professional review and consensus, to the top ten influences.

The study focused its efforts on meeting the needs of diverse student populations in urban schools and then made research-based recommendations for school personnel. These recommendations or interventions included instructional strategies, methods of image building, and changes in the behaviors of academic professionals. Their goal was to be able to focus on the key variables related to underachievement and to make specific recommendations for school personnel in assisting underachieving urban students.

Classroom Applications

Many new teachers come from a background of success as students in the way they have experienced the institution of education. In fact, they liked it so much they wanted to be part of it and worked very hard to return to the classroom as teachers! From this perspective, teachers—especially new teachers—have a difficult time understanding why certain students don't feel the same way they do about the classroom, learning, and school. Underachievement can be outside a new teacher's personal paradigm. Not understanding where an underachieving student is coming from frequently leads to teacher confusion, frustration, and avoidance of the student and the problem.

It is also common for many teachers, as they become more experienced and acquire a little political power within their school, to try to isolate themselves from underachieving students rather than try to work with them. However, with insight, reflection, empathy, and effort, teachers can gain some confidence in their ability to be successful with traditionally underachieving student groups. Information about the possible causes along with a willingness to try to understand and create educational strategies can go a long way toward professional and personal fulfillment. The ten top influences, reviewed by experts in student underachievement and students at risk for failure, are listed here. All school personnel need to consider and act on these ten top influences.

1. Teacher behavior refers to the teacher's actions that demonstrate care, respect, and interest in the personal, as well as academic, growth of their students.
2. Teacher expectations for students' achievement of realistic academic standards are directly or indirectly communicated to students and usually result in the students' attainment of those standards.
3. Curriculum relevance refers to the students' perceptions of how meaningful and usable the content material and the instructional methods are in their personal lives.
4. Class size is the number of students enrolled in a classroom.
5. Disengagement from school-related activities pertains to the lack of student involvement in and identification with the school community.
6. Confidence in the students' ability to achieve refers to the students' belief and expectation that they can learn academic material and be successful in school.
7. High mobility in school attendance or transferring from one school to another can cause both students and parents to feel alone and disconnected from the new school or school environment.
8. Parental expectations and involvement refer to the parents' realistic academic performance standards and goals for their children as well as their active engagement in meeting those goals.
9. Level of parents' education is the number of years parents have been involved in formal education as well as their level of

academic accomplishments (e.g., high school graduation, bachelor's degree).
10. Poverty or low income (e.g., annual family income falling below poverty standards) often creates conditions in the family that, if uncorrected, could result in student underachievement.

While the study (Arroyo et al., 1999) went on to identify specific strategies to mitigate these influences, it concluded with three particularly noteworthy findings that emerged from threads connecting all ten influences, which are summarized here.

- First, engagement level and expectations for success are critical not only for students but for school personnel and parents as well. The more confident all parties are in their ability to overcome barriers, the greater the chance for success. Past successes should be invoked as evidence that challenges can be overcome.
- Second, high mobility and attendance problems created learning and teaching environments characterized by disconnection and feelings of being alone. The effects of this relate to not only the students, but also the parents and the school community as a whole. Schools can take positive steps to decrease the negative influence of mobility by inviting parents and students to become more involved and take a more active part in the school community.
- Third, school personnel have more influence over some conditions associated with chronic underachievement (e.g., teacher behaviors and expectations, curriculum relevance) than over others (e.g., low income of parents). The researchers found that school personnel could proactively address problems caused by some of the influences that they may not be able to control directly. Creating an environment where parents are included as vital members of the team was cited in numerous studies. Most of the recommendations offered by the study involved a change in the strategies used by counselors, tutoring services, parent organizations, and caring teachers—systems already in place. Personnel need to use these traditional resources to address the common influences related to underachievement. Their study indicated that there was little need to develop new systems.

Precautions and Possible Pitfalls

No system or program will replace a single caring and involved teacher. This starts with one teacher dealing professionally and emotionally with one student at a time. This is done with the help, input, and insight of support services and other caring and insightful school personnel and the student's family. Be aware that not every family or family member will be useful in mitigating the student's problems. Some are the source of the problems.

It can't be emphasized enough that this is a team effort. Gather all the information possible from others who know the student or students before acting. Make sure other experienced school personnel are informed.

Source

Arroyo, A., Rhoad, R., & Drew, P. (1999). Meeting diverse student needs in urban schools: Research-based recommendations for school improvement. *Preventing School Failure, 43*(4), 145–153.

Strategy 51: Support the needs of challenged students with a team effort.

What the Research Says

 Veteran teachers realize the benefits of collaborating with colleagues to problem solve and troubleshoot. In today's classrooms the challenges new teachers face in trying to meet the educational, social, and emotional needs of diverse learners can be overwhelming. Teacher educators are increasingly realizing the benefits of teamwork. With school reform, restructuring, and the "least restrictive environment" practice taking the spotlight, co-planning and co-teaching may provide powerful ways to address the demands of students with special needs (Hafernick, Messerschmitt, & Vandrick, 1997). Many schools are now using the model of co-teaching for their special needs population. In this model, the general education and special education teachers co-teach in the same classrooms.

In a 1999 study by Duchardt, Marlow, Inman, Christensen, and Reeves, the special education faculty of a university in Louisiana initiated collaborative opportunities with the general education faculty for co-planning and co-teaching. Teachers met once a week, over lunch, to discuss course content and lesson delivery. As an outgrowth of these meetings, participants developed a co-planning and co-teaching model to assist other educators who wished to collaborate. A step-by-step design of this model follows.

> *Stage 1.* Choose a trusted teacher with whom to collaborate. Obstacles can result when misunderstandings or miscommunications occur. The goal of collaboration is clear: success for special

education students. The more this goal is discussed and used as a motivating factor, the more trust can be established and the greater the rapport that is generated.

Stage 2. Find pockets of time to plan. Carve out small blocks of time in the beginning to meet with other team members to discuss course content. Down the road, planning can occur on an as-needed basis, or even by phone or e-mail.

Stage 3. Brainstorm! After discussing course content, team members can brainstorm options for co-teaching the lesson. Brainstorming helps establish the expertise of each team member and permits planning to advance easily and without delay.

Stage 4. Prepare the actual lesson. The team members discuss, prepare, and develop a written guide for co-teaching the lesson. Consider having the lesson videotaped to assess and amend the lesson plan for future use.

Stage 5. Co-teach the lesson. The first time a lesson is co-taught, the two teachers must test the new instructional strategies. At this point the preparation time will be obvious in its value. Until the lesson is taught, the teachers will have no idea if the first four strategies are working or if additional strategies for co-teaching will be needed. Once the lesson is done, the teachers can evaluate its success.

Stage 6. Support team members. A necessary skill for the effective teacher to possess is the capability to be flexible and add to or emphasize key points throughout the lesson. Each team member needs to establish a comfortable and secure working relationship as well as trust in the intentions of the other team members.

Stage 7. Assess the lesson. After the lesson is presented, each team member can provide the presenting teacher with feedback. If the lesson was videotaped, team members can view the ways in which the lesson can be improved or polished. Having other trusted colleagues view the lesson might also provide valuable insights.

According to the study by Duchardt et al. (1999), co-planning and co-teaching arrangements can result in nine positive outcomes.

1. Collaboration and development of trust
2. Learning to be flexible and collegial
3. Finding pockets of time to co-plan
4. Learning through trial and error
5. Forming teaching and learning partnerships

6. Challenging ourselves and developing professionally
7. Solving problems as a team
8. Meeting the needs of diverse learners
9. Meeting the needs of teachers as problem solvers

Classroom Applications

The African proverb "It takes a village to raise a child" can be adapted in education today to read, "It takes the whole school to educate a child." With the needs of special education students and other diverse learners, co-planning and co-teaching offer students (and teachers) opportunities for success. The collaboration between general education teachers, special education teachers, school counselors, speech therapists, and other school professionals can make a critical difference in helping students with special needs achieve.

In one West Coast high school, this model has been used extremely effectively. Taking a team approach has resulted in greater collaboration among all the staff members. The co-teaching model is so successful that other districts have come to observe and talk to participating teachers. General education teachers feel supported when dealing with their students with special needs, and special education teachers can assist their students in succeeding in mainstream classes.

Precautions and Possible Pitfalls

While more and more schools are using a team approach when dealing with students with special needs, caution should be taken. Team members must be committed to making this model work. Each member of the team provides expertise and insights critical to the success of students involved. Also, general education teachers sometimes aren't used to team teaching and may feel uncomfortable having another teacher in their classrooms. Co-teaching should be just that. The special education teacher should not become an aide for the general education teacher but an integral part of the lesson. This is where planning is of critical importance.

Sources

Duchardt, B., Marlow, L., Inman, D., Christensen, P., & Reeves, M. (1999). Collaboration and co-teaching: General and special education faculty [Special section: Culture and the schools]. *Clearing House, 72*(3), 186–191.

Hafernick, J. J., Messerschmitt, D. S., & Vandrick, S. (1997). Collaborative research: Why and how? *Educational Researcher, 26*(9), 31–35.

> ## Strategy 52: Tap the strengths of students with Attention Deficit Hyperactivity Disorder (ADHD).

What the Research Says

Zentall, Hall, and Grskovic (2001) reported that the most effective instructional strategies for students with attention deficit hyperactivity disorder (ADHD) were those that included personal attention, opportunities to be in leadership or helper roles, and the use of preferred activities as incentives. The least effective instructional strategies were those that took away or withheld activity.

Classroom Applications

The frustrations of beginning teachers dealing with lesson planning, state testing schedules, classroom management, managing the paper load, and just trying to find enough hours in the day to accomplish it all can be overwhelming. Add to these responsibilities students with special needs (such as ADHD) and new teachers may feel like they are navigating in choppy seas.

For a beginning teacher working with a student with special needs, the first person to seek out for support can be a veteran special education teacher who has a thorough understanding of the student's IEP (individual education plan). Using special education teachers to help plan activities and lessons can be a tremendous resource for the new teacher. They can also provide helpful hints in dealing with discipline issues, preferential seating, and the importance of presenting clear, specific, and simple directions.

Stimulation through social interactions and activity-based lessons has been found to be effective for students with special needs. Teachers should avoid lengthy doses of seat time and sedentary work. The use of hands-on and manipulative activities is also more effective with students with special needs and may enable them to be successful. Providing the student with opportunities to move around the classroom can also be helpful. Allowing the student to run an errand, hand out papers, clean the board, or help out in the classroom can help reinforce appropriate behavior.

Because students with ADHD may experience greater difficulty in starting and organizing tasks, the teacher should consider breaking assignments into smaller pieces while remembering to check for understanding at regular intervals.

Precautions and Possible Pitfalls

 Having a student with special needs in class can be challenging for any teacher. If the teacher is organized and has straightforward and concise classroom rules and procedures, with consequences clearly stated, the chances for student success increase. Teachers need to be sensitive to students with special needs and not announce to the class that "John" is allowed extra time on an assignment because of his disability. Most students with special needs don't want attention drawn to them. Any modifications that are discussed with a student should be done in a one-on-one setting away from other students.

Source

Zentall, S. S., Hall, A. M., & Grskovic, J. A. (2001). Learning and motivational characteristics of boys with AD/HD and/or giftedness. *Exceptional Children, 67*(4), 499–519.

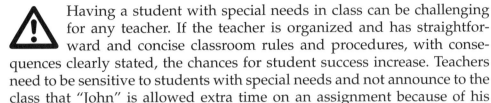

Strategy 53: Be patient with learners who require more reading practice than other students.

What the Research Says

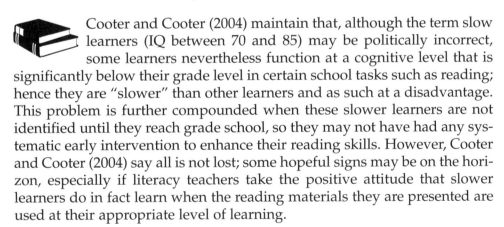 Cooter and Cooter (2004) maintain that, although the term slow learners (IQ between 70 and 85) may be politically incorrect, some learners nevertheless function at a cognitive level that is significantly below their grade level in certain school tasks such as reading; hence they are "slower" than other learners and as such at a disadvantage. This problem is further compounded when these slower learners are not identified until they reach grade school, so they may not have had any systematic early intervention to enhance their reading skills. However, Cooter and Cooter (2004) say all is not lost; some hopeful signs may be on the horizon, especially if literacy teachers take the positive attitude that slower learners do in fact learn when the reading materials they are presented are used at their appropriate level of learning.

Classroom Applications

 First, Cooter and Cooter (2004) suggested that teachers set up an atmosphere in which reading is possible by attempting to reduce distraction. One way of doing this is to provide students with a quiet, private place to read. Then, during the instructional process, teachers should also emphasize students' strengths and use legitimate praise and reinforcement frequently because slow learners crave positive feedback. More specifically, Cooter and Cooter (2004, p. 683) suggested that teachers utilize the following framework when teaching slow learners:

1. Make the reading lessons short, using several short periods rather than one long one.
2. Add variety to the academic routine, such as games and puzzles.
3. Work on material that is somewhat challenging but also allows success. For this to be achieved, a process of ongoing assessment may be necessary to help teachers keep students within their learning range. Encourage parents to talk to their child to build language and vocabulary. Parents will need to be coached on how to ask, for example, about their child's day at school in order to develop the child's language skills.
4. Include an amount of repetition in instruction. This is because slow learners need to over-learn various reading strategies and skills.
5. Provide meaningful, concrete activities rather than abstract ones. Have students continuously make cognitive connections to what they already know by engaging in concrete activities.
6. Give short, specific directions and have students repeat them.
7. The teacher should read in front of the students in order to set a good example.
8. Use a buddy reading system whenever possible because struggling readers can often help each other.

Precautions and Possible Pitfalls

It is always difficult to define who "slow learners" are, and if or when teachers do, these students may be stigmatized by other teachers and/or their peers. Reading teachers must be careful not to tell these students that they are "slow" and instead treat them as usual learners who have a different reading curriculum. In addition, Cooter and Cooter (2004, p. 683) cautioned teachers to be mindful that slower learners can "master reading skills only after massed and distributed practice over time." Thus, teachers must be patient with their students' progress.

Source

Cooter, K. S., & Cooter, R. B. (2004). One size doesn't fit all: Slow learners in the reading classroom. *Reading Teacher, 57*(7), 680–684.

> *Strategy 54: Think beyond content, as English-language learners come with a variety of challenges and needs.*

What the Research Says

This research and reflection (Valdez, 2001) centered on the fact that one in four California students is an English-language learner. It also reflected on the fact that 90% of teachers in California are monolingual English speakers. This article examined how legislation and institutionalized practices affect teacher preparation in forcing teachers to accept roles emphasizing a standards-driven, technical, one-size-fits-all approach in addressing the very complex and diverse needs of English-language learners.

Focusing on California, the researcher (Balderrama, 2001) showed little faith in the ability of California's teacher certification programs to prepare teachers for meeting the needs of English-language learners or immigrant students. Critical review of credentialing practices in California range from the Cross-cultural Language and Academic Development Credential (CLAD) and California Basic Educational Skills Test (CBEST) to Reading in California (RICA) and the California Commission on Teacher Credentialing performance standards. Balderrama stated that standards or examinations don't provide any opportunity for scrutiny of the role of the teacher in the socialization and schooling of youth. They tend to dance around the importance of culturally responsive teaching while de-emphasizing the more qualitative and effective aspects of teaching.

In apparent conflict are the standards-based assessment of good teaching and the more humanized standards most adults use to reflect on how they remember good teachers. In the end, it is the humanity that is emphasized in reflection, not teaching methods, techniques, or implementing standards.

Balderrama (2001) presented a context of teacher preparation with an emphasis on techniques and standards that tends to mis-prepare teachers in addressing the needs of an increasingly immigrant student population. The fear is that this mis-preparation will in turn mis-prepare the students academically.

Classroom Applications

Teacher education programs are ideologically based, and teachers need to understand the ideological underpinnings that tend to perpetuate social and economic subordination. Find a balance in the role as a teacher from a technical perspective and sometimes, more important, from a humanistic perspective.

When dealing with limited English proficiency students or English-language learners, teachers will find that content and standards can be some of the least important things they teach and learn in their lives. Balderrama (2001, p. 262) stated

> In attempts to raise their pedagogical consciousness, teachers examined two elements of their teaching: (1) their students, within a historical context, and (2) the context of schooling and teaching. Students, particularly English-language learners, must be seen up close, not abstractly, so that understanding of their individual, academic and learning needs are humanized and thus fully understood.

This type of teaching doesn't call for teachers to abandon all mandated guidelines, content standards, or expectations; it only asks that they find a larger and more relevant context.

Precautions and Possible Pitfalls

Beginning teachers need to be careful to take the pulse of their workplace. Colleagues may be under great pressure to raise test scores and student academic achievement. It would be a mistake for teachers to ignore or neglect their responsibility to support school or department goals. However, a teacher can create a more humanistic educational environment in which the teacher and students function. A teacher will be expected to be accountable, but that doesn't mean a teacher can't begin to explore a more humanistic approach to teaching and learning.

Sources

Balderrama, M. V. (2001). The (mis)preparation of teachers in the Proposition 227 era: Humanizing teacher roles and their practice. *Urban Review, 33*(3), 255–267.

Valdez, E. O. (2001). Winning the battle, losing the war: Bilingual teachers and post–Proposition 227. *Urban Review, 33*(3), 237–253.

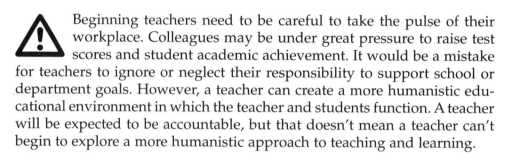

Strategy 55: Be sensitive to issues affecting gay and lesbian youth.

What the Research Says

 Several research studies suggested that approximately one in ten students served by public schools will develop gay and lesbian identities before graduation (Cook, 1991; Gonsiorek, 1988). Sexual orientation, however, appears to be established prior to adolescence, perhaps from conception, and is not subject to change (Gonsiorek, 1988; Savin-Williams, 1990).

The social stigma surrounding homosexuality discourages many gay and lesbian teens from discussing the confusion and turmoil they may feel about their emerging identities (Friend, 1993). Add to this the sense of confusion and isolation they may feel, and it should not come as a surprise that gay and lesbian youth are "two to six times more likely" than heterosexual teens to attempt suicide (Cook, 1991). While gay and lesbian teens account for 30% of all completed suicides among adolescents, they comprise only 10% of the teen population (Cook, 1991).

Classroom Applications

 Gay and lesbian youth face many of the same changes with regard to social, biological, and cognitive development as their heterosexual counterparts. However, the misconceptions and stigmas, combined with the homophobic cultural climate of our society, often add to the stress and turmoil that many of our gay and lesbian youth struggle with on a daily basis.

Adolescence is a difficult time at best, and these years can be hell on earth for students struggling with issues relating to their sexual orientation. Students can be very cruel to each other, and this seems to be heightened more so during adolescence.

The physical and emotional safety of every student in class should be paramount. Teachers of middle and high school students can do a lot to provide a safe and harassment-free environment. Not allowing derogatory words or comments in class is a start. If a teacher does not address these negative comments, the gay or lesbian student can further feel alienated and alone. Many times, silence from the teacher is interpreted as agreement with what is being said.

Because homosexuality sometimes appears to be one of the last bastions of "acceptable" discrimination, gay and lesbian youth may feel more isolated and withdrawn than heterosexual students. These perceptions of inferiority can lead to poor self-esteem, substance abuse, sexual promiscuity with the opposite sex (to conceal their true feelings), and possibly suicide. Teachers would not tolerate students calling each other by racial, ethnic, or religious slurs; they must not tolerate comments of a negative nature to gay and lesbian students either. It is up to each and every teacher to provide a safe, nurturing, and respectful environment for every student.

Precautions and Possible Pitfalls

 Just because a teacher doesn't have a student (or students) coming out to him or her doesn't mean that teacher doesn't have any gay or lesbian students in the classroom. Given many research studies, which estimate that one in ten persons is homosexual, it stands to reason that in a class of 30 students, a teacher might have three who are struggling with sexual orientation issues. Teachers shouldn't assume that if no one is coming forward to complain about harassment or name calling that the "problem" doesn't exist.

Students may pose questions to the teacher about homosexuality (is it okay, why are some people heterosexual and some people homosexual, etc.). It is not advisable to get into a discussion of right and wrong, okay or not okay. However, telling students that every person is entitled to respect, acknowledgement, and acceptance is not only okay, it is the right thing to do.

Sources

Cook, A. T. (1991). *Who is killing whom?* Issue Paper 1. (Available from Respect All Youth Project, Federation of Parents and Friends of Lesbians and Gays, P.O. Box 27605, Washington, DC 20038.)

Friend, R. A. (1993). Choices, not closets: Heterosexism and homophobia in schools. In L. Weis & M. Fine (Eds.), *Beyond silenced voices: Class, race, and gender in United States schools* (pp. 209–235). Albany: State University of New York.

Gonsiorek, J. C. (1988). Mental health issues of gay and lesbian adolescents. *Journal of Adolescent Health Care, 9,* 114–122.

Savin-Williams, R. C. (1990). Gay and lesbian adolescents. *Marriage and Family Review, 14,* 197–216.

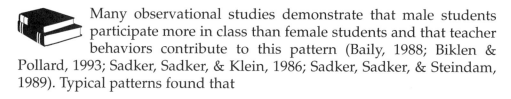

Strategy 56: Eliminate signs of subtle gender bias in classroom discourse.

What the Research Says

Many observational studies demonstrate that male students participate more in class than female students and that teacher behaviors contribute to this pattern (Baily, 1988; Biklen & Pollard, 1993; Sadker, Sadker, & Klein, 1986; Sadker, Sadker, & Steindam, 1989). Typical patterns found that

- Male students receive more attention and more specific feedback from teachers.
- Males are more likely to receive praise for the intellectual content of their answers.
- Teachers rarely wait more than five seconds for a response to a question and rarely call on nonvolunteers. This type of discourse favors aggressive male students.

- Many teachers are unaware of their own discriminatory behaviors until someone calls it to their attention.
- Gender equity is rarely a component of teacher education programs.
- Teachers have a misconception that they are not responsible for bias in the classroom and the students are. If teachers believe that students, not teachers, are to blame for gender bias, it will continue.
- Prospective teachers' beliefs may interfere with current concepts and ideas in gender-bias components of teacher education.

In this study (Lundeberg, 1997), 48 preservice teachers (21 male, 27 female) were involved in trying to answer the following questions:

1. How do preservice teachers' perceptions of gender interactions compare with actual gender interaction data?
2. Do prospective teachers become aware of the limits of their own perceptions in detecting inequities in classroom interaction?
3. What strategies do preservice teachers propose to ensure equity?
4. Do preservice teachers report changing any beliefs about subtle gender bias? (The answer to this question seemed to be beyond the scope of the study.)

These preservice teachers were all enrolled in sections of an educational psychology class. Gender interaction patterns were recorded and researched using a variety of techniques both in their classes and during outside field experience. Some of the highlights of Lundeberg's (1997) results included the following:

- 73% said they would promote equity and make a conscious effort to ensure equity in seating, lab work, cooperative groups, and athletic activities and ensure equity in curriculum content and language use.
- 24% said they would collect data to become aware of or to monitor gender bias (videotape, outside observers).
- 21% said they would become more aware of seating arrangements and pairing of males and females.
- 18% said they would balance guest speakers and gender bias in curriculum.
- Several planned to use inclusive language to switch gender roles for demonstrations, cleanup, and so on.
- 35% of the students reported changes of conformations of their beliefs about gender equity.

In discussions it was felt that interventions of this sort in teacher education programs increased awareness of gender bias. The majority of students discussed the need to collect data and monitor classroom interaction in order to ensure equity in their future classrooms.

Classroom Applications

There are two categories of action that teachers can take from this research: (1) Believe that gender bias exists and, just like preparing other components of pedagogy, keep gender bias as a highly considered element. View existing research on the subject and adjust teaching style where it is needed. (2) Informal action research can alert teachers to subtle biases they may not be aware of. Videotape a teacher's interactions or have someone observe a teacher. It doesn't need to be publishable, only personally reflective of the teacher's classroom discourse. Make appropriate changes to instructional strategies and classroom discourse.

Most of the students in Lundeberg's (1997) study believed that if they had not experienced gender bias, it was because they were not really aware of it. Once becoming aware of the fine details of gender bias in the classroom, the project showed them that their perception might not fit reality.

Precautions and Possible Pitfalls

Boys and girls have acquired their behaviors and roles over time. They need to be taught how to recognize gender bias in their own lives. There are many students who are so comfortable in their roles that they would resist changing. Teachers should consider keeping their equity goals as part of a hidden or subtle curriculum. Students acquired their roles over a long time and from many places, and teachers should keep their expectations reasonable. They may not see the desired changes in the short time they work with the students.

Sources

Baily, G. D. (1988). Identifying sex equitable interaction patterns in classroom supervision. *NASSP Bulletin, 72*, 95–98.

Biklen, S. K., & Pollard, D. (1993). *Gender and education. Ninety-second yearbook of the national society for the study of education (part 1)*. Chicago: University of Chicago Press.

Lundeberg, M. A. (1997). You guys are overreacting: Teaching prospective teachers about subtle gender bias. *Journal of Teacher Education, 48*(1), 55–61.

Sadker, M., & Sadker, D. (1994). *Failing at fairness: How America's schools cheat girls.* New York: Charles Scribner's Sons.

Sadker, M., Sadker, D. and Klein, S. S. (1986). Abolishing misperceptions about sex equity in education. *Theory into Practice, 25*(4), Sex Equity and Education, pp. 210-226.

Sadker, M., Sadker, D., & Steindam, S. (1989). Gender equity and educational reform. *Educational Leadership, 46*(6), 44–47.

Strategy 57: Understand that immersion experience can be the best teacher.

What the Research Says

Personal background is recognized as an important element in the development and formation of multicultural perspectives in preservice teachers. These previous experiences and backgrounds influence what is taught, the teacher's interpretations of classroom situations, student behaviors, and many instructional decisions.

The main background elements of this perspective are outlined as follows (Smith, 2000):

- Race, gender, and social membership
- Prior experience with diversity
- Support of ideologies of individualism

Two related studies (Smith, 2000; Wiest, 1998) looked at issues related to the following:

- How do the background experiences of preservice teachers influence inclusion of a multicultural perspective in teaching?
- How do preservice teachers' background experiences influence the effectiveness of a teacher education program in achieving multicultural education?
- How could a multicultural immersion program alter their perspectives?

Wiest (1998) examined two preservice teachers: one with limited multicultural experiences and background and another with multicultural experiences. Both were White, with one mainly isolated in her socioeconomic and cultural upbringing and the other immersed in and forced to fit into and adapt to other cultures in other countries. Both taught history in schools of roughly the same size. One teacher's school was slightly more diverse. Overall, the data, from observation, teacher reflection, and student responses, suggested noticeable differences in the two teachers' effectiveness as multicultural teachers. Background experiences and three specific factors—preservice teacher's race, gender, and social class; prior experiences with diversity; and support for ideologies of individualism—would appear to offer a partial explanation for these differences. While the two subjects seemed to be at opposite and extreme ends of the multicultural spectrum, the researchers felt there were valid concerns their work could bring to education programs regarding how background experiences influence sensitivity and cultural congruence; knowledge of students' backgrounds; awareness of learning styles; recognition of racism, classism, and sexism; and a high school student's perception of the teacher's teaching.

This case study (Wiest, 1998), while it included only two teachers, did provide tentative support for the explanatory power of background in a teacher's ability to respond to multicultural pedagogy. Important questions that the study did not answer were: "What experiences or strategies appear to be successful in expanding a preservice teacher's multicultural literacy?" and "Is it possible to broaden the experiences and beliefs of all preservice teachers, and should multicultural experiences be a prerequisite for admission to a teacher education program?"

Smith (2000) clearly found a connection between multicultural background and a teacher's ability to deal with multicultural settings. However, the researchers recommended further studies using larger sample sizes and a wider range of research questions.

Wiest (1998) examined how a very short-term immersion in a multicultural setting affected a group of student teachers or teachers within a teacher preparation program. Three classes of 86 students in their fifth year of a five-year education program were asked to immerse themselves in an unfamiliar multicultural experience of their choice and respond with project write-ups. Settings ranged from African Americans in church to gay bars and Quaker meetings. Students had to take the initiative in their self-growth by arranging their cultural immersion experience themselves. Most students were reported as being displeased with the project and expressed discomfort and anxiety. Afterward, they overwhelmingly endorsed the project as valuable and memorable and stated it was the most important course assignment. However, the experience did have a neutral effect on a few, and some made little effort to fully engage and immerse themselves. Some expressed feelings of guilt about infiltrating a group without explaining why they were there. Others were resistant to the situation they entered, and this compromised the effectiveness of the experience.

Judging from the feedback, Wiest (1998) felt that the project had a meaningful effect on the students but made no claims about the lasting or cumulative effect of other multicultural activities.

Classroom Applications

The research speaks to experience as the best teacher in preparation for a multicultural placement. Classroom discussions and activities can only go so far in their contribution to a new teacher's range of multicultural insight and tactics. Smith (2000), while narrow in scope, pointed to previous experience in multiethnic and multicultural settings as important in developing positive teaching attributes. Wiest (1998) placed education majors in multicultural noneducational settings with documented positive short-term results. Most of this should come as no surprise. If one is new to the teaching pool, there is a good chance a teacher's first job may be in an unfamiliar social, cultural, or ethnic environment. These studies point out a need for new teachers to fill in the multicultural gaps in their training.

Beginning teachers may not want to trust their teacher education program to do the job. Remember that getting a teaching job is only the beginning. The new teacher will be working toward keeping the job. More important, the teachers may want to personally feel effective and in control of any situation they are asked to tackle. The more a teacher experiences the conditions and the more understanding and knowledge one brings to the job, the more comfortable the teacher will feel. Suggestions include some of the following activities:

- Volunteer for placement in unfamiliar settings.
- Scout out the communities ahead of time.
- Reflect on fears and limits. What conditions can you overcome with preparation and which should be avoided?
- Find support in community groups and colleagues in preparation.
- Research and read the professional literature.
- Look for colleges and universities that offer proven and effective preparation. Go back to school if necessary or seek professional inservices and workshops.

Research indicates that experience beats outs classwork most of the time when preparing for multicultural settings.

Precautions and Possible Pitfalls

 Preparation for a multicultural setting is very individualized, and each new or potential teacher needs to be honest and very proactive. One program can't meet the requirements of all participants. Individuals, based on their unique needs and goals, may have to go well beyond the program to fill in holes in their preparation. One large pitfall would be to underestimate the challenges that a multicultural classroom of kids, their parents, and the community can present.

Sources

Smith, R. W. (2000). The influence of teacher background on the inclusion of multicultural education: A case study of two contrasts. *Urban Review, 32*(2), 155–176.

Wiest, L. R. (1998). Using immersion experiences to shake up pre-service teacher views about cultural differences. *Journal of Teacher Education, 49*(5), 358–365.

Strategy 58: Avoid creating expectations based on students' racial and ethnic backgrounds.

What the Research Says

 Tenenbaum and Ruck (2007) examined whether teachers' expectations, referral records, positive and neutral speech, and negative speech differed toward ethnic minority students (i.e., African American, Asian American, and Latino/a) as compared to European American students. The Tenenbaum and Ruck study is very compelling in its complexity and thoroughness. The researchers looked at a compilation of recent studies and also reviewed previous compilation studies. The earlier studies were more than 20 years old but did serve as a basis to see if patterns have changed.

It was found that teachers hold the highest expectations for Asian American students, followed by European Americans. Teachers also held more positive expectations for European Americans than Latino/a or African American students. Teachers made more positive referrals and fewer negative referrals for European American students than for Latino/a and African American students. Teachers directed more positive and neutral speech (questioning and encouragement) toward European Americans than toward Latino/a or African American students. However, they also directed an equal amount of negative speech to all students. Generally, teachers' favoring of European American students compared to African American and Latino/a students was associated with small yet significant effects. Again, generally, the study suggests that teachers' expectations and speech vary with a students' ethnic background.

Classroom Applications

As subtle as these Tenenbaum and Ruck (2007) findings are, it's clear teachers can predispose students to a less-than-fair classroom climate and reduce the educational opportunities for ethnic minority students. Every student in a class has different levels of need. There is no one-size-fits-all model of classroom discourse to suggest here. While the Tenenbaum and Ruck study posed some interesting and important results, it is hard to make concrete recommendations for practice. Each teacher will therefore need to examine his or her own situation and personal and professional discourse style and decide how to use the information from the study.

The topic could become an interesting discussion with students. Teachers need to be comfortable with the notion, however. It could be stimulating to hear how they perceive their treatment in the school system.

Teachers need to lay down some ground rules to control the discussion, protect the identity of other teachers, and generally keep the conversation civil. They could also consider videotaping a few classes and view how they interact with students. However, it may take a colleague and repeated videotaping to help point out potential issues to discuss.

Precautions and Possible Pitfalls

 The effects of differentiated expectations and discourse style are difficult to identify, subtle, and likely different for all students. Expectations also come from family, teachers, peers, and internally. It's common for teachers to praise students who are perceived as needing praise for motivation (positive speech) but to withhold it from others who don't appear to need it (neutral or negative). Teachers also tend to interact with students who initiate conversation more. Interpreting student–teacher discourse (expectations, etc.) is not easy to do.

Source

Tenenbaum, H. R., & Ruck, M. D. (2007). Are teachers' expectations different for racial minority than for European American students? A meta-analysis. *Journal of Educational Psychology, 99*(2), 253–273.

Strategy 59: Include multicultural works when developing a quality English curriculum.

What the Research Says

Even with the widespread calls for more multicultural texts and literature in secondary English curricula, teachers have encountered roadblocks to integrating new literature into their courses. Selections do not always hold up well against competition from the great works of more traditional canons. In this context, selected multicultural additions often are marginalized. Nontraditional authors do not fit comfortably into the curriculum.

Another concern is that students often distill a curricular march through the more classic selections as a search for "right" answers, with little connection to why the works were chosen or how they might connect to a larger purpose. The content has little or no context or connection to students or to other parts of the curriculum. Research seeks to discover a more "knowledge in action" discourse and current conversation about living traditions. The main concern is that lists of classics, or the selected tradition, predispose curriculum to a more teacher-centered and less student-centered pedagogy. A student-centered approach would strive to include multicultural texts as "curriculum in conversation" and use it as a framework for discussing multicultural literature.

In Burroughs's (1999) research, three teachers' experiences were used as part of a larger study of teacher decision making regarding curriculum involving eight English teachers in 19 classrooms in two high schools. The three teachers featured in the article came from the same high school, which had a diverse student body with more than 50% African American students. Observations were taken over a two-year period as teachers worked, with varying degrees of success and motivation, to integrate multicultural literature into the curriculum.

Of the three experiences, one included very little multicultural curriculum because the structure of the teacher's course and her teaching style crowded it out. A second included many multicultural works and changing conversations that put multicultural curriculum at the center of instruction. Another teacher actually established a multicultural curriculum course and changed what were defined as literary works while creating new conversations to analyze them. This teacher expanded what has been traditionally considered literature.

Classroom Applications

The task of creating a more multiculturally inclusive literary curriculum yielded three very different responses from the teachers in the study (Burroughs, 1999). Their responses also helped redefine and develop new ways of thinking about what curriculum is and how it should be selected. The research showed that changing to a more inclusive curriculum requires more than just selecting multicultural texts and a range of minority authors. While this is an essential and positive starting point, simply selecting is not enough. For example, teachers in this study expanded the term *literature* to include speeches, myths, plays, and journals, as well as novels and poems.

Beyond making selections, teaching and learning also require thinking about how teachers and students should experience and appreciate the content and its context. Scope and sequence were also seen as important, and the construction of "curriculum" needs to incorporate some intellectual continuity of discourse as a theme. Teachers in these studies found that the types of student conversations desired began to drive decision making. They found students responded well to some selections and not to others. Adjustments were made. In the Burroughs (1999) study, the least successful teacher added only one multicultural text to her existing curriculum, and students found little context and relevance in the scope and sequence of the course.

The major problem the teachers in the study encountered was the challenge of providing a scope and sequence without the class time and space. Teachers found that, unlike in a college course where literature can be more effectively grouped as a coherent curriculum, high school students lack the background and teachers have a difficult time making connections between time periods and source cultures. The literature range required for high school is too broad and time is too short.

One way two of these teachers solved the problem was to make textual selection criteria a more explicit part of the classroom conversation. One created a theme called "What Is American Literature," which allowed him to move away from a more traditional approach. In the new multicultural literature course, "World Cultures," the teacher created conversations to reflect cultural and individual differences within the classroom as well as within the literature. As teachers work to broaden the traditional literature canon, it is more realistic and useful to think about restructuring the entire curriculum rather than just adding a new text. Multicultural restructuring requires a look ahead as to how students will experience and use the new information they are given. Context and relevancy need to be considered, and strategies of discourse are very important. Although it was not mentioned in the research, the nature and makeup of each class can interact with curriculum in different ways. Diverse classes mean a variety and range of educational consumers, each with different expectations and mind-sets.

Given an opportunity, the three teachers in this study (Burroughs, 1999) responded to the challenge of inclusion with various degrees of motivation and success. What is clear is that inclusive curricular design is not easy. Giving a voice to traditionally marginalized groups is an art, not a science.

Precautions and Possible Pitfalls

 Restructuring is always a process loaded with workplace politics over funding, department policy, priorities, and so forth. It would be a mistake not to begin to make the effort now, because it will likely be mandated in the future. The only question individual teachers have to ask themselves is how are they going to respond to an inquiry about inclusion in their classrooms. They need to begin to develop a multicultural vocabulary when it comes to curricular discussions.

It is always a challenge for a teacher to replace curriculum. There are always worries that something taken out will be needed for a standardized test. Keep in mind that politics do play a part, and well-intentioned teachers can encounter resistance from all sides.

Sources

Agee, J. (2004). Negotiating a teaching identity: An African American teacher's struggle to teach in a test-driven context. *Teachers College Record, 106*(4), 747–763.

Burroughs, R. (1999). From the margins to the center: Integrating multicultural literature into the secondary English curriculum. *Journal of Curriculum and Supervision, 14*(2), 136–155.

 Strategy 60: Help boys make positive connections between masculinity and success as readers.

What the Research Says

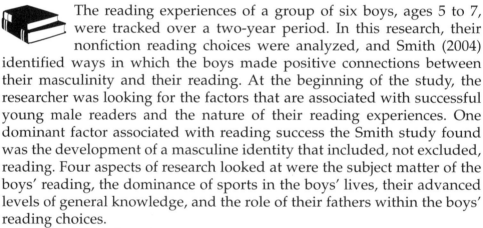 The reading experiences of a group of six boys, ages 5 to 7, were tracked over a two-year period. In this research, their nonfiction reading choices were analyzed, and Smith (2004) identified ways in which the boys made positive connections between their masculinity and their reading. At the beginning of the study, the researcher was looking for the factors that are associated with successful young male readers and the nature of their reading experiences. One dominant factor associated with reading success the Smith study found was the development of a masculine identity that included, not excluded, reading. Four aspects of research looked at were the subject matter of the boys' reading, the dominance of sports in the boys' lives, their advanced levels of general knowledge, and the role of their fathers within the boys' reading choices.

Smith (2004) found that their nonfiction reading centered on typical boy interest areas and hobbies (soccer, space, dinosaurs). It was found that the boys became "experts" in some of these areas. According to the research, this earned them the respect of their peers, especially other boys, and a positive masculine identity in the classroom. Thus, being a successful reader and having a positive male identity became compatible. This study found that reading was a desirable activity for boys in the sample group.

Classroom Applications

In schools there are many ways of being a "boy." There are also many ways boys experience literacy. In some settings, when boys connect to reading or school achievement, they risk being seen as different by their peers. Some young people see reading as being more of a female activity. In a subtle way, boys can see themselves as subordinating their masculine status if they read successfully.

Teachers need to look for ways to better connect some student versions of masculinity with classroom instructional literacy goals and endorse them. Once these connections are made or available, engaging in instructional literacy activities can be acceptable and even desirable for boys.

In the Smith (2004) study, the gender--reading compromise the boys made was to focus heavily on the stereotypical masculine interest areas of reading. Teachers made it a point to have these books available. The boys also exhibited stereotypical views on texts more suitable for male interests and also for female readers. It's clear their choices were socially and culturally influenced. One way to help them broaden their range of interests is to challenge their ideas and perceptions regarding masculine and feminine reading choices and help open their minds to a wider range of reading choices. With knowledge, boys can be encouraged to open up their reading choices. However, even if they don't accept this knowledge, keeping a genre of reading material that is acceptable and not threatening to a male's masculine sensibilities and identity is key.

While this was only one small study, it did produce tips and hints that could be very useful in many settings. Reading material needs to be carefully selected within the cultural and social constraints of classroom, school, and community.

It is important to use the range of book lists out there to help in selecting books appropriate for the age groups and their sensibilities. An Internet search will bring up many lists that can be used to help the teacher and students select books for the classroom, library, or home. The goal is to help young people find books they will enjoy and not threaten their social and peer group standing.

Precautions and Possible Pitfalls

 Peppered throughout the educational research is the perception that it is not always "cool" for males to be good students or readers in some settings. It would be a huge mistake not to very carefully evaluate and consider students' demographics before stocking the library or classroom bookshelves. Many small student peer and cultural or racial groups need to be accommodated with appropriate reading material. Selections can motivate or turn off and exclude any of these groups.

Source

Smith, S. (2004). The nonfiction reading habits of young successful boy readers: Forming connections between masculinity and reading. *Literacy, 38*(1), 10–24.

6

Integrating Technology in the Classroom

Strategy 61: Use the Internet as a classroom.

What the Research Says

"Kids as Global Scientists" (KGS), characterized as a telecommunication program, is an interactive, integrated, inquiry-based science curriculum project that has been developed by meteorologists and teachers from the University of Michigan and is sponsored by the National Science Foundation. It resides on the Internet, which makes it accessible to large numbers of teachers and students. Its current Internet project engages more than 200 schools in interactive investigations. Professional weather experts interact with students, answering their questions. The total length of a unit runs six to eight weeks.

The investigation and interaction is facilitated by the use of specialized interactive software that is designed specifically for the project. The software provides all textbook content and, in addition, connects students to the Internet, simulations, and current imagery collections of weather data and allows them to download data. In one project the program suggests a final project of building a hurricane-safe house and simulating the force of the hurricane by using a leaf blower.

The program provides teacher's guides, software, and all other material needed to empower the project. The program develops thematic units within the earth science discipline of atmospheric science and meteorology.

Research centered on the assessment and evaluation of one class participating in one unit or program (Mistler-Jackson & Songer, 2000). Six sixth-grade students representing three motivational levels were selected for intensive study to help illustrate how different students view learning science and the use of technology both before and after a technology-rich program. Pre- and post-assessment scores were analyzed for the entire class, and the six students' comments from individual interviews provided one example of evidence from each motivational level.

Overall, results indicated significant gains in content knowledge and a high level of motivation with the project. Students find the use of the Internet and telecollaborative environments engaging and motivating.

Classroom Applications

This use of the Internet as a classroom is an emerging use of the technology. In addition to the KGS program, there are other opportunities to engage students in similar programs. Distance learning (type the term in a search engine and you will find a large number of sites) is available as an alternative to site-dependent learning. Many colleges and universities and a few high schools now offer participation in digital classrooms. Electronic Advance Placement classes are now offered as alternatives for schools without the ability to provide such programs.

As an inquiry-based science experience, KGS offers an authentic, guided, safe experience that is not only content but also process rich. The use of technological tools provides a motivating vehicle to learn. Not all science works this easily in real life. However, for a taste of real science, this serves the purpose. The Internet educational market is growing. The KGS project is a packaged, user-friendly project.

NoodleTools, at http://www.noodletools.com, is a free suite of interactive tools designed to aid students and professionals with their online research. From selecting a search engine to finding some relevant sources and then citing those sources in MLA style, NoodleTools makes online research easier.

There are a number of Internet sites that act as repositories of data. Climate and weather data are easily available, and GenBank provides almost unlimited genomic and molecular science data. Imaginative, creative, and motivated teachers can develop their own inquiry-based opportunities. Many of these sites offer free data that can be used to answer student questions. The opportunities are open-ended in nature and can be as complex or as simple as the instructor desires. There are even digital libraries that offer access to periodicals and other sources of information.

Some access is limited to subscribers, and some sites must be accessed at a college or university that subscribes to the service.

There are too many sites to identify here. At the time of writing this strategy, typing the term *interactive lessons* in a search engine produced more than 5,000 hits or sites. Not all these sites are useful, but obviously there are a lot out there. The interactive nature of some of these sites was found only in software a few years ago. Now it's free.

Precautions and Possible Pitfalls

Although the technology provides an attractive and often motivating alternative to conventional hands-on experiences, the evaluation and preparation time remains the same. It does take time to find and survey the potential that Internet sites offer. Technology has its quirks and breakdowns, and access may not be available on demand or on the class's schedule. Online access can be a problem in some communities.

Appropriate use policies are a necessity, and Web surfing can keep students off-track for extended periods of time. The idea that the Internet can provide serious instruction sometimes requires an adjustment in perception and a context change with both students and parents.

Source

Mistler-Jackson, M., & Songer, N. (2000). Student motivation and Internet technology: Are students empowered to learn science? *Journal of Research in Science Teaching, 37*(5), 459–479.

Strategy 62: *Balance the rigors of new technology with content goals.*

What the Research Says

It's beneficial to teach students to set learning goals for different reasons, and different kinds of goals have different effects. Goal setting can affect students' achievement and motivation, and it can affect how students regulate their thoughts, actions, and feelings. Students can use the goals they set as standards for assessing their own progress. Goals focusing on the learning process emphasize the strategies that students use in acquiring skills or information. In contrast, goals focusing on the product of learning emphasize outcomes or results, such as how much was accomplished and how long it took. Research conducted on goal setting when teaching students to use the computer indicates that students who set process goals felt that they learned more effectively than did students who set product goals. Students in the process condition believed that they were more competent in performing hypercard tasks (i.e., they had greater self-efficacy) than did students in the product condition, and achievement results showed that process condition students indeed were more successful than students in the product condition in performing hypercard tasks.

Classroom Applications

Have students regularly set process goals when acquiring new knowledge or skills. Use a think-aloud procedure and write on the board to model for students how they should set process goals. Have students brainstorm, individually or in groups, process goals they can set for a particular computer task. Require students to write their process goals in their notebooks, and periodically check their notebooks to assess their progress in achieving their goals, looking for new goals to replace those that have already been accomplished. Some process goals may require more time than the product goals. Teachers should not underestimate the rigorous and challenging learning that technology requires to make progress toward a more primary goal or product. The following are some situations that would require sometimes as much or more time learning than actually doing the primary task. Teachers should help students make realistic time estimates, including the technology learning curve.

- Student groups needed to learn a spreadsheet and graphing program to be able to manage and summarize the data from a statistics experience. They needed to complete a tutorial and manipulate a few small data sets before looking at their own data.
- Students using a laptop computer with a physiology-sensing capacity needed to learn the accompanying software to make their experiment and data collection fully functional.
- An earth science group accessing a weather and climate Web page was required to learn the Web page's specific programs to manipulate its temperature and rainfall data.
- Students from a high school located near a university needed to master the university library's digital library and e-journal access to acquire the background information for their research paper.
- Students needed to evaluate many curriculum-related Internet sites to assess which sites were the most accurate and useful.
- A graphics program needed to be learned in order to develop overheads and slides to be used in an English presentation.

These are all examples of process goals that may need to be mastered before finishing a project or activity. A teacher shouldn't underestimate the potential techno-process pitfalls and should be patient with students who may have a limited background in technology.

Precautions and Possible Pitfalls

 Teachers should not just let students copy their process goals for learning to use computers or other technology. Self-generated goals are more personally meaningful to students than teacher-imposed goals.

Source

Schunk, D., & Ertmer, P. (1999). Self-regulatory processes during computer skill acquisition: Goal and self-evaluative influences. *Journal of Educational Psychology, 91*(2), 251–260.

 Strategy 63: Don't let technology overwhelm subject matter.

What the Research Says

A traditional undergraduate physics course on math methods was redesigned to incorporate the use of a computerized algebra program throughout all aspects of the course. The goal of this redesign was to expose beginning students to professional tools currently used by mathematicians and physicists. At the same time, a new multimedia physics class sought to integrate math and physics content with other multimedia forms. These two classes served as research laboratories to begin a qualitative case study to first describe the course and then develop an understanding of the effect technology had on instruction and learning in the courses. It was found that the instructors of both courses made rather substantial changes in their courses the second time through based on their early experience.

The research (Runge et al., 1999) provided an overview of the issues as follows:

- Students resisted the additional process orientation of adding technology as another layer of course requirements. Computers add another layer of process skills to learn.

- Teachers needed to be better prepared and have their own technological act together.
- The advanced workload preparing for such courses is enormous and goes unnoticed by the students. To the students, book content represents the curriculum; a reduced use of books leads to a student perception of a reduction in content and course structure.
- There needed to be a means for demonstrating the technology and a backup plan in case of problems.
- Clear procedures needed to be developed for students to follow when they encountered problems.
- Whenever students seemed to have strong learning preferences and styles, their expectations about how they ought to be taught conflicted with the design of the courses. Expectations needed to be described explicitly and explained for possible conflicting expectations. Problematic conflicts in how and why instruction is implemented needed to be resolved.
- Instructors somewhat underestimated the basic instruction needed. Teachers were challenged to provide guidance and examples without providing "simple" templates that structure the students' homework with little imagination or editing. Technology used as a professional tool required in-class instruction that modeled real problem-solving modes.

Overall, the research suggested that the necessary transition from traditional instruction to tool-based instruction is dramatic and fraught with difficulty for teachers and students. The researchers found their data far less positive or encouraging than they would have liked. As experienced teachers, as technology users, and as scientists foreseeing drastic changes in the kinds of intellectual skills that students are likely to bring to the professional world, they saw a long developmental road ahead.

Classroom Applications

When movable type was invented and the first books were printed, all the formatting, running heads, tables of contents, page numbers, indexes, and so on were not included. The technology of the book is standardized today. Teachers are all familiar with these book standards, and so are the students. When you teach a course from a book, most of the time, everyone involved knows what to expect.

Calculators, seen as routine today, required a good deal of time to filter through instructional practices and find a niche. Most teachers today have no problem finding a context in their courses for calculators. There are no such standards yet on the World Wide Web.

As new technology continues to filter into the classroom, teachers first await better-trained students from below. Second, teachers need to address the concerns listed in the research and accept a rather steep learning curve for implementing technology for themselves and their students. The researchers found a remarkable similarity in problems and pitfalls between these two independent classes using very different technologies. Real-world professional tools impose a rather drastic transition for all stake-holders. Become as informed as you can about the technology, but also be aware of the potential transitional pitfalls a teacher will need to address as a professional educator.

Precautions and Possible Pitfalls

 Teachers should not underestimate the amount of work, for both themselves and their students, involved in making technological transitions. Frustrated students can sabotage teachers' best efforts by not authentically engaging in the new type of instruction. Students that would do well in traditional classes need nurturing and assurance when the rules change.

Source

Runge, A., Spiegel, A., Pytlik, L., Dunbar, S., Fuller, R., Sowell, G., et al. (1999). Hands-on computer use in science classrooms: The skeptics are still waiting. *Journal of Science Education and Technology, 8*(1), 33–44.

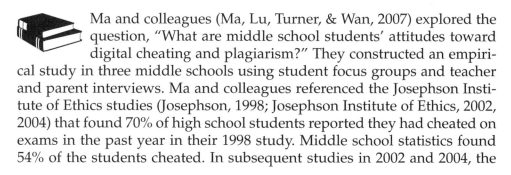

Strategy 64: Use multiple strategies to help combat digital plagiarism.

What the Research Says

Ma and colleagues (Ma, Lu, Turner, & Wan, 2007) explored the question, "What are middle school students' attitudes toward digital cheating and plagiarism?" They constructed an empirical study in three middle schools using student focus groups and teacher and parent interviews. Ma and colleagues referenced the Josephson Institute of Ethics studies (Josephson, 1998; Josephson Institute of Ethics, 2002, 2004) that found 70% of high school students reported they had cheated on exams in the past year in their 1998 study. Middle school statistics found 54% of the students cheated. In subsequent studies in 2002 and 2004, the rates of cheating increased. Sadly, it was also found that students had a more lax attitude toward cheating as well.

The big questions Ma et al. (2007) tried to answer were: How do young people decide to cheat? What are the students' attitudes toward plagiarism? How do students define plagiarism? What are teachers' attitudes toward plagiarism?

Ma and colleagues (2007) found that peer pressure or peer culture contributed to the deterioration of ethics within student groups. They also found that students only had vague ideas about intellectual property and related ethical decisions. The deterioration of ethics seems to be related to increased Internet use. The findings also pointed to the notion that activities that are engaging and more relevant to the students' own lives and interests can help reduce plagiarism. They also found that building a social community online and offline helps students comprehend the concept of plagiarism.

Classroom Applications

Teachers should not expect their students to be experts on the topics they are usually asked to write about, unless it is autobiographical and even then one never knows. However, do expect them to support their research and investigation with evidence and arguments by experts either from those who are the primary producers of the knowledge or by those who review, report, or critique the primary producers.

Students need to comprehend the value of a paper that acknowledges its sources and that citing those sources doesn't have to diminish the value of their conclusions and opinions. Conversely, a well-documented and referenced paper usually adds to the value of their work and their authority as consumers of information. The whole idea is to get students to respect intellectual property rights and document how they have done that within the assignment context. It's about changing the perception on how to use fairly the information generated by others. This should be the first line of defense against plagiarism. Often students, especially younger students, don't know they are doing anything wrong, and many don't think it is a serious issue. Teachers can do a lot to change attitudes here and let kids know what's appropriate and why.

Also, teachers constantly need to ask why they assign research projects and other writing assignments. How much of the assignment's purpose is to learn MLA or APA formatting; develop note taking skills or outline construction, footnoting, and referencing primary sources; or compile bibliographies? Does the topic have value, or is it mostly about form?

In the Ma et al. (2007) study of three middle schools, it was found that the strategies and policies adopted were generally too narrow in scope. The most common strategy used was to clarify the concept of plagiarism and the use of punishment.

Beyond that, one might consider looking at the high-tech defense approach against high-tech cheating. Blocking, filtering, and rating systems can be used. Software packages such as turnitin.com (http://turnitin.com/static/home.html) can help instructors detect digital cheatings. Turnitin is one of the best known. Schools can subscribe to the service, and students submit their digitized papers to the teacher's class at the Turnitin Web site. This site upgrades and fine-tunes the idea of putting a passage of a student's paper into a search engine in order to find a source. Turnitin makes a "digital fingerprint" of each paper and then converts the words into long numbers. These numbers are then compared with the digital fingerprints of other papers in multiple databases. One of the databases focuses on newspapers and professional journals, and another is a complete collection of every student paper ever submitted to Turnitin. Turnitin receives 50,000 to 60,000 papers a day in its student paper database. Finally, the last database is the Internet itself. Turnitin updates this database at the rate of 60 million pages a day. Turnitin generates reports in which any unoriginal text is underlined, and teachers can then decide what is plagiarized and what isn't. Internet "cheat sites" are rendered useless because any paper can't be turned in more than once. After the Turnitin report, teachers are left with the problem of what to do about the information they get. It is recommended that teachers use the information as a service that aids in helping students understand that original thought is important in academic work. This is in contrast to focusing on embarrassing, sanctioning, or punishing students.

Next, teachers can consider bringing parents into the equation and encourage them to be alert and help develop their child's sense of ethics and honesty. Like the students, many parents will need to be taught to appreciate the concept of intellectual property. They need to become part of the projects. Teachers can consider strategies in their assignments to engage the parents in monitoring the students' work and work strategies. Teachers shouldn't just make it a one-shot effort. They need to address intellectual property issues in every assignment.

Help schools teach plagiarism ethics and develop, with the students, strict policies to deter digital cheating and plagiarism. This includes working on developing a peer culture by clarifying the concept of plagiarism. Have teachers share strategies that work and make it a schoolwide effort.

Teachers and schools need to establish clear and specific rules and consequences for breaking them. Teachers should try to develop policies that avoid the "gotcha" mentality. Developing prevention strategies is more important than coming up with punishments or consequences.

Finally, teachers can find ways to compliment model behaviors, such as showcasing original student work or highlighting evidence of creative thinking. Construct learning environments to cultivate peer pressure as a strategy to combat cheating and plagiarism; the research found that plays an important role.

The cut-and-paste Internet mentality is nothing new and not much different than copying out of encyclopedias.

Precautions and Possible Pitfalls

⚠ Teachers shouldn't forget that creative, challenging assignments can go a long way toward avoiding other ways to mitigate cheating and plagiarism. Many students in the Ma and colleagues (2007) study felt that cheating and plagiarizing were acceptable if the assignments they were engaged in were meaningless and boring, yet they wanted a good score. If work tended to be interesting to them, they would take the time to really engage in reading the information they found. For example, in the study a teacher reported that one student had a family member who had developed leukemia. During a science assignment, students were asked to explore disease information Web sites. The student told the researcher how he took pains to read and reflect on the online journals of a little girl who developed leukemia. He didn't write his report simply through copying and pasting.

Creative, well-thought-out assignments can do much to motivate students to take an honest approach to doing assignments.

Sources

Dudley, B. (2006). Cut, paste, and get caught: Plagiarism and the Internet. *The Education Digest, 71*(9), 40–43.

Ma, H., Lu, E. Y., Turner, S., & Wan, G. (2007). An empirical investigation of digital cheating and plagiarism among middle school students. *American Secondary Education, 35*(2), 69–82.

Josephson, M. (1998). *1998 Report Card on the Ethics of American Youth.* Los Angeles, CA: Josephson Institute of Ethics. Retrieved September 24, 2008, from http://charactercounts.org/programs/reportcard/

Josephson Institute of Ethics. (2002). *The Ethics of American Youth.* Retrieved September 24, 2008, from http://charactercounts.org/programs/reportcard/

Josephson Institute of Ethics. (2004). *The Ethics of American Youth: 2004.* Retrieved September 24, 2008, from http://charactercounts.org/programs/reportcard/

Strategy 65: Become Web site literate.

What the Research Says

As part of a larger study that focused on the Web presence of elementary, middle, and high schools, Hartshorne, Friedman, Algozzine, and Isibor (2006) investigated 50 high school Web sites. These sites served as a rich source of data. They looked at basic Web design rules in their evaluation but really focused on the functionality of each site. Each site was accessed using a checklist that included sections on structure, design, content, and general use issues. The Web sites were rated as either having or not having a specific feature. If the characteristic was present, points were added to the overall score.

Researchers were encouraged to find that virtually every high school Web site examined appropriately addressed basic Web design principles and was represented in a logical, orderly fashion rather than just posting information. Schools were able to represent themselves to their viewers. The majority (94%) also included a school calendar.

Specific Web site elements that concern researchers included sites that did not illustrate student work (only 30% did). Reviewers felt the illustration of student work acted as an important motivating factor for students. In their research reviews, a number of studies pointed to this Web element as a factor in increasing achievement.

Also, none of the Web sites evaluated gave any indication that they had been "Bobby Approved." A Bobby approval is an indicator of the site's commitment to special education inclusion for those with disabilities and other access issues. Bobby is provided by CAST (Centre for Applied Special Technology) and is a free piece of software available online or to download. It assists Web page authors in identifying obstacles to accessibility for individuals with disabilities. Bobby's analysis of accessibility is based on the W3C Web Accessibility Initiative. To become "Bobby Approved" and display the Bobby Approved icon, a Web site must successfully address all of the Priority 1 WAI issues that Bobby identifies. (The WAI guidelines are located at http://www.w3.org/TR/WCAG10-TECHS/#Abstract.) The researchers found this disheartening because a stated goal of many high schools is to provide and foster knowledge from diverse populations.

It should come as no surprise that research found the high school sports community well served. School athletic teams generally serve as a point of pride for high schools. Finally, researchers found, again to no surprise, that accountability (testing results) played a large role in the Web site information (82%).

Classroom Applications

Researcher in the Hartshorne et al. (2006) study found the majority of high school Web sites handled Web design issues but needed to improve other features such as presenting student work, overall accessibility for diverse populations and languages, and parent–teacher communication. Only 48% had links to career or job sites, yet 78% featured links to SAT or test prep information and 82% offered college and university admission information.

In order to fully benefit from a Web presence, schools and teachers must move beyond merely providing general school information. Class syllabi, schedules, course homework, and general classroom information can also be a part of any school's site. Sixty-four percent of the sites visited had links to teachers' or course Web pages. Sadly, less than 50% of the teachers contacted in the study had Web pages linked to school sites.

Here are a few considerations for school Web site design.

- Ownership is important, and all voices need to be heard in planning and development of a school site.
- It sounds simple, but research and planning for the site needs to occur before development and implementation, building a sense of shared planning and buy-in.
- Teachers can study and identify the factors that encourage and discourage school Web site development and maintenance. Five or more other Web sites should be investigated by staff with information compiled from an online survey to provide a starting point. This information could be supplemented with discussions with Webmasters, administration, and teachers to provide more in-depth information about factors that facilitate or constrain the development of a successful Web site.
- Focus on what the audience will want to see, including students, prospective students and parents, local investors, school faculty and staff, and others who may visit the site.
- Teachers can focus on all the benefits of school Web sites mentioned in the research. The majority of the sites in the study posted general information as opposed to creating sites that promote the involvement of all stakeholders.
- Teacher buy-in and easy access is important. Teacher gateways need to be seen as user-friendly and not time-intensive. Most teachers don't need the added responsibility of learning more technology.
- Follow the general Web design rules that can be found in many books.
- Design the site being cognizant of future changes and editing.

Precautions and Possible Pitfalls

Hartshorne et al. (2006) published their Web page research checklist in an appendix. Most of the factors or elements dealt with the technical components of a Web page. However, the following content checklist, part of the larger checklist (which is available in Hartshorne et al.'s journal article), describes basic features that stakeholders routinely find important. These elements are important considerations for any school, and designers and administrators of school Web sites should be sure to include

- School administrative information
- Teacher contact information

- Teacher and course sites
- Conference, advising, and guidance information
- Testing and accountability (NCLB) information
- School district information (this could include a link to the main school district site)
- School information (map, address, etc.)
- Student- and child-centered links and resources
- College and university admission information (deadlines, sites, etc.)
- SAT and standardized test information
- Job search links
- Scholarship and financial aid information
- Graduation information and requirements
- Resources for applying to college
- Parent–Teacher–Student organization information

Source

Hartshorne, R., Friedman, B., Algozzine, T., & Isibor, T. (2006). Secondary schools online: Are high school Web sites effective? *American Secondary Education, 34*(2), 50–66.

Strategy 66: Develop Internet-based literacies.

What the Research Says

Bos (2000) conducted research to examine the Internet as a source of valid information for science students. The World Wide Web is an exciting and challenging information resource now available to many teachers and students. It is so convenient for students that it can become their primary source of information while conducting research for their assignments and projects. The Internet is challenging because of the diverse and often uneven nature of the information presented. This presents both students and teachers with the need to develop new skills of critical analysis and evaluation. Critical evaluation skills have always been an important part of media literacy for students in the context of a science class. Bos's study focused on two aspects of critical evaluation: summarization of science content and evaluation of credibility.

Participants in Bos's (2000) study were students in two 11th-grade science sections at an alternative high school in a medium-sized Midwestern college town. The class involved in these studies was in the third year of a

"Foundations of Science" sequence, an integrated science curriculum that follows the principles of a project-based approach. It also has a heavy technology component. Forty-four students (27 females and 17 males) took part in the project. The study centered on answering three questions.

1. Can students summarize scientific resources that they find on the Web?
2. Can students identify and evaluate evidence in the scientific resources that they find on the Web?
3. Can students identify the source and potential biases (points of view) of the scientific resources that they find on the Web?

The project produced 63 student Web reviews published by the students. Content analyses showed that student summaries were usually accurate. However, students had problems assessing how comprehensive and detailed sites were. When asked to evaluate credibility, students struggled to identify scientific evidence cited or present supporting Web site claims. This was a problem because many Web sites do not present evidence as it might be found in a scientific journal format. Students could determine the publishing source but were challenged in identifying potential biases with Web publishers.

The findings of Bos's (2000) study can provide teachers with a solid grounding for further development of media literacy activities. Technical and pedagogical scaffolding based on site-specific goals and demands facilitates students acquiring or reinforcing critical evaluation skills.

Classroom Applications

This research (Bos, 2000) has clear implications for science teachers. Many teachers in the sciences present students with opportunities to critically review the validity of science information, content, and resources as a normal part of scientific thinking. With easy access, the Internet is rapidly becoming students' primary source of information beyond the textbook for many curricular activities. Therefore, acquiring Internet-critical evaluation skills will become crucial in developing overall media literacy.

There are many ways to embed critical evaluation into projects or as a separate independent activity. Ideally, experienced students will be able to critique Web site information routinely. However, to get to that point, a teacher may need to begin by creating prompts or triggers to serve as review categories. This could be as detailed and complex as needed for beginning student researchers. A simple prompt worksheet might look like the box on page 151.

Again, the level of guidance, triggers, and prompts can be adjusted to the class and the experience of the students.

1. Content

What is the purpose of this resource? Who is the target audience? What scientific claims are made? What information and content are available here?

2. Source Credibility

Who is publishing this Web site? Are there any potential biases or conflicts of interest? How much support or evidence exists for the claims made within the resource? Is it referenced or academically cited to back up the claims or information beyond common knowledge?

3. Overall Organization

How well organized is the information? Is there a central Web page where everything is accessible? Are there links to other relevant Internet sites? How technical is the information?

4. Appearance

Is it a professionally designed resource? Do the graphics support the information and help communicate it? Does the resource "teach" the information beyond the textbook for many curricular activities?

Precautions and Possible Pitfalls

At its best, the Internet and its resources provide students with an easily accessible source of valid resources for a variety of curricular activities. However, it can also be a source of biased content and misinformation. Web site text can be copied and pasted into word processing programs. Some students will rely too much on the Internet and not use other, more traditional resources. Teachers should be careful to make these points clear to students. Students should be encouraged to plan ahead and use other sources of information.

Source

Bos, N. (2000). High school students' critical evaluation of scientific resources on the World Wide Web. *Journal of Science Education and Technology, 9*(2), 161–173.

Strategy 67: Maximize effectiveness of available technology.

What the Research Says

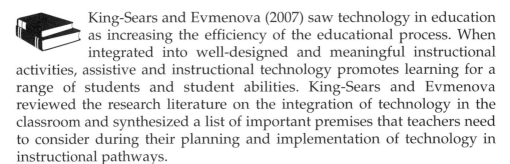

King-Sears and Evmenova (2007) saw technology in education as increasing the efficiency of the educational process. When integrated into well-designed and meaningful instructional activities, assistive and instructional technology promotes learning for a range of students and student abilities. King-Sears and Evmenova reviewed the research literature on the integration of technology in the classroom and synthesized a list of important premises that teachers need to consider during their planning and implementation of technology in instructional pathways.

Classroom Applications

In the world of business, advances in technology abound and continue at a rapid pace. The business world thrives on and successfully competes in the free economy by mastering useful technology, training people to operate it, and trying to do what they do more efficiently than the competition. Businesses capitalize on using technology quickly, as this is the way successful business is done. Teachers must capitalize on using technology as an integral way that teaching and learning occur in their classrooms. But teachers don't usually have information technologists helping them sort through the factors of being a good consumer of technology. King-Sears and Evmenova (2007) came up with three basic premises for integrating technology into instruction, along with a number of basic principles for integrating technology. They are well worth considering.

Premises

1. *Technology used well in schools can prepare students with disabilities for careers that require some level of aptitude with technological skills.* Technology must be a part of the instruction because the students' futures will require proficiency in technological skills. Successfully mastering technology provides students the opportunity to match their school skills with their career skills.
2. *Technology enhances the learning process: Technology is not learning.* The technology itself must not become the focal point of instruction. Technology should be used in the direct context of specific instructional subject-matter content goals and not as an isolated focus or distraction.

3. *Technology changes quickly.* Teachers need to be involved in knowing about new advances in technology and what products are on the market. While considering these new advances, teachers need to keep in mind instructional integration and the support, both technical and instructional, they might need to install or implement new technology. Schools aren't always the most supportive places when a teacher needs a maintenance worker to install a receptacle or when a cable is missing. Sometimes there are also hidden costs associated with new technology, such maintenance contracts, service agreements, or the cost of consumable parts (bulbs, cables, etc.).

Principles

1. *Choose technology that aligns with curriculum outcomes.* The very first principle is choosing instructional technology that clearly matches and aligns with the curricular outcomes. It needs to mesh with and complement the students' learning in a straightforward manner. It needs to promote student learning, not just entertain or keep the students busy.
2. *Match students' instructional needs with the technology.* Whatever technology teachers are using, they will need to match the way they use it with the students' instructional needs. It shouldn't make the content harder or too easy to teach or learn. It's important to carefully consider the students' learning stages before selecting a software program. Some drive and practice programs can actually impede rather than support learning.
3. *Choose technology that helps students blend in with peers.* Some researchers cited in the King-Sears and Evmenova (2007) study suggested seeking student input when selecting technology. They further suggested selecting technology the peers perceive as challenging and "cool."
4. *Choose a parsimonious alternative.* Teachers need to get what they want out of the technology by considering efficient and cost-effective choices that meet instructional needs. More money doesn't always mean better for instruction. Choose low-tech and low-cost options when they really work best and have high instructional value.
5. *Target the students' needs and the learning outcomes.* A learning outcome is synonymous with a curriculum standard, content goal, or similar terminology that educators use to describe the desired knowledge or skill acquisition teachers expect from instruction. Teachers need to consider not only the outcome but the degree of complexity of the outcome. Within every class there is a range of background knowledge that the students bring to

class. Also, there is a range of learning abilities in a typical class. Teachers need to ask themselves, "What is the learning outcomes complexity from the students' perspective? Will the technology contribute to this complexity or make their job easier?"

6. *Examine the technological choices, then decide what to use.* Know what the choices are and assess them by doing a cost–benefit analysis. What are the costs and time commitments beyond the purchase price for teachers and students?

7. *Handle the implementation, and monitor the impact on the students' learning.* Many times, teachers plan what they think are perfect lessons and watch them fall apart when implemented. As a general rule, a teacher needs to run through a new lesson three times to really get it down and make it work for a full range of students. Many times, teachers don't know the pitfalls until they run through a lesson.

Precautions and Possible Pitfalls

Deng and Zhang (2007) conducted two surveys to measure and compare the perception of learning achievements, instructors' teaching methods, and classroom instructional technology. This survey took place in a multimedia classroom (187 students) and a more traditional classroom (110 students) in a mid-south state university. The results of the survey showed no significant differences in the perception of learning achievements between the two classes. However, there were significant differences in the perception of the instructors' teaching methods by students in both classes. Students in the multimedia class had more positive perceptions of the instructor's teaching methods than those students in the traditional class.

The Smartboards, acoustics, video conferencing, touch-screen panel monitors, and technology as a whole were seen in a positive way. Students liked the learning and teaching environment being enhanced with emerging technology and left many positive comments.

The research presented a few questions. If the learning achievement is the same between high-tech and low-tech environments but students expressed greater satisfaction with the instructor's teaching methods, then how should schools respond? Does the novelty of the new technology wear off, and if achievement isn't enhanced, is it worth the money? Evaluating teaching tools is complicated. Most teachers don't have the time to quantify the effectiveness of any teaching method or tool. It is hard to predict what teaching tools will work best with any specific instructor. In the end, it's the teacher who makes any technology come alive. Before schools buy in to trendy technology, there needs to be a buy-in by the teachers along with the time and support needed to learn the technology. Schools and teachers should not underestimate the rigor of implementing technology or a change in teaching style.

Sources

Deng, H., & Zhang, S. (2007). What is the effect of a multimedia classroom? *International Journal of Instructional Media, 34*(3), 311–322.

King-Sears, M. E., & Evmenova, A. S. (2007). Premises, principles, and processes for integrating technology into instruction. *Teaching Exceptional Children, 40*(1), 6–14.

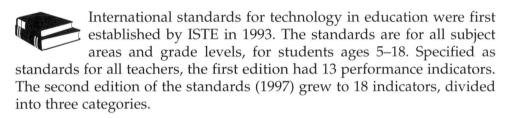

Strategy 68: Learn what the International Society for Technology in Education (ISTE) says about standards and student learning.

What the Research Says

International standards for technology in education were first established by ISTE in 1993. The standards are for all subject areas and grade levels, for students ages 5–18. Specified as standards for all teachers, the first edition had 13 performance indicators. The second edition of the standards (1997) grew to 18 indicators, divided into three categories.

1. Basic computer/technology operations and concepts
2. Personal and professional use of technology
3. Application of technology to instruction

The third edition of the standards, *ISTE National Educational Technology Standards for Teachers*, consists of 23 performance indicators that are grouped into six categories.

1. Technology operations and concepts
2. Planning and designing learning environments and experiences
3. Teaching, learning, and curriculum
4. Assessment and evaluation
5. Productivity and professional practices
6. Social, ethical, legal, and human issues

Technology is not only here to stay, its influence is exploding exponentially in education and all other aspects of life. Teachers need to integrate it into their instruction now, or their students will be left behind in the future.

The RAC model, which consists of three phases in technology integration—Research, Analysis, and Communication—is an instructional framework for integrating technology into the curriculum through lesson planning and assessment across subjects and grade levels. Research suggests that teachers identified the following benefits of RAC lessons:

1. It includes more student-centered learning.
2. Students engage in more critical thinking.
3. Material can be integrated across subject areas.
4. It is easily incorporated into performance-based classrooms.
5. Students are required to apply important skills in a meaningful context.
6. It provides opportunities to evaluate students' work.

Classroom Applications

To plan the use of technology to meet the national standards for both teachers and students, teachers can visit the ISTE Web site (http://www.iste.org) and download or view the standards. The Web site also has numerous instructional resources to help teachers integrate technology into their instruction in virtually all grades and subjects. Resources include a database of lessons in which a teacher can search for lesson plans that integrate technology into science teaching, specifying the particular topic and grade level needed. The site also contains resources that have been developed for multidisciplinary units and allows teachers to enter their own lesson plans.

According to the ISTE Web site, the "Multidisciplinary Unit Resources" section includes resource units designed to provide powerful themes around which multidisciplinary learning activities can be built. Each unit addresses the theme with a variety of activities, related technology, and thematically relevant information, tools, and resources. Each activity is designed to address content standards from two or more subject areas while also addressing the National Educational Technology Standards (NETS) for student performance indicators. Units for each grade range provide developmentally appropriate themes, tools, and resources from which teachers can choose when developing specific learning experiences.

Implementing the RAC model involves the following three phases:

1. *Research.* Students gather information from various resources, not just paper and pencil. For example, they go to various Internet sites to acquire information about specific concepts within the curriculum.

2. *Analysis.* Data analysis depends on the results of the research. Students must think critically and use the information they gathered. For example, students have to gauge the validity of the resource information, whether it is the most current, unbiased, or complete enough for their use.

3. *Communication.* Students prepare products to share their results. For example, students can communicate the new information to a wider audience for critical review and critique.

Precautions and Possible Pitfalls

 Teachers should not expect themselves or their students to meet all 23 performance indicator standards the first or second time around. Teachers and their students may need more time and experience to assimilate new information and develop new skills. Teachers can use the standards as longer-term goals and to establish performance criteria for assessment purposes.

Source

Bowens, E. M. (2000). Meeting standards with technology. *Learning and leading with technology: Serving teachers in the classroom, 27*(8), 6–9, 17. Retrieved September 24, 2008, from http://www.iste.org/Content/NavigationMenu/Publications/LL/LLIssues/Volume_27_1999_2000_/May17/Research,_Analysis,_Communication,_Meeting_Standards_with_Technology.htm

 Strategy 69: Look to out-of-school uses of the Internet for instructional literacy strategies.

What the Research Says

 Burnett and Wilkinson (2005) enthusiastically commented on all the possibilities for engaging with information that is associated with a wide variety of literacy practices. Their study explored the purposes for which young children, with routine availability, access the Internet; the attitudes and orientations they demonstrate in their approach to Web-based texts; and what has enabled them to develop as Internet users. The focus of the study was out-of-school uses. Their findings are used to make suggestions for supporting and framing the literacy uses of the Internet. They defined "reading" Internet and digital texts as functionally distinct from print-based text, as decoding text, moving images, still images, sounds, and words. Meaning is created in different ways.

Their study focused on six 6-year-olds, three boys and three girls from a small rural primary school. Individual and whole-group interviews were conducted over a six-week period focusing on key questions regarding Internet use to gather the following information:

- Reasons why children used the Internet
- Descriptions of the sites they liked and visited
- Advice for the students on how to access these sites
- General reflections on skills needed to be effective Internet users
- Experiences that had been significant in enabling them to become users

The researchers found the students' reasons for using the Internet were diverse. The most common reasons were as a source of free stuff such as games, for downloading music, images, and so on; to enter into special interest communities for shared interests and enthusiasts; and to communicate with the world around them. The researchers ended by offering suggestions on how to use this knowledge in the school setting.

Classroom Applications

Students rarely see the use of the Internet as "literacy" or learning activity. Their agendas are usually very un-school-oriented. As Burnett and Wilkinson (2005) found, the most common outcomes of Internet use for younger students were accessing free stuff such as games, music, and images, and sharing in special-interest communities. As students get older, e-mail and research for school activities become focuses. Veteran teachers of students in the upper grades know the educational pitfalls of easy access to questionable information. Because of such pitfalls, younger students can really use help accessing Web information appropriately. This is where the Internet can become the focus of literacy-based school activities in the younger grades.

The Internet is an ideal mechanism for encouraging students to assume responsibility for their own learning and build on and improve skills some have already developed. As students find different learning resources on the Internet, they become active participants in their quest for knowledge and information. Incorporating the Internet into the classroom provides students with more opportunities to structure their own explorations and, hopefully, learning. Once trained, students are able to define their learning needs, find information, assess its value, build their own knowledge base, and engage in discourse about their discoveries. Yet before teachers and students can begin to use the Internet in the classroom, students need the foundation of two main sets of skills to help them navigate the Internet and manage the large amounts of information they find.

People rarely read Web pages word by word; instead, they scan the page, picking out individual words and sentences. Morkes and Nielsen (1998) found that 79% of their test users always scanned any new page they came across; only 16% read word by word. So how do teachers train students to utilize Internet information well? What are "information literacy skills"?

Few teachers read Web pages word by word. That means they're already familiar with two very important strategies for reading on the Web: skimming and scanning. Skimming and scanning help find needed information, without reading everything on a Web page. Skimming is glancing quickly over a text to get a general idea of the topic. When skimming, quickly look over the entire page, focusing on any titles and headings. Look at the illustrations, diagrams, and captions. What do they describe?

Scanning is looking for key words and phrases that will give the specific needed information. When scanning, look for key words, headings, and terms in bold or italics that refer to needed information. Read the first and last sentences of the paragraphs on the page to see if they connect to needed information.

The amount of information available over the Internet, on the news, in newspapers, and in magazines and books is overwhelming for most adults, let alone children. Beyond just gaining Web page fluency, therefore, it is critical that students learn to find, analyze, use appropriately, and credit the information at their fingertips. These are information literacy skills, and the sooner teachers begin teaching them, the better students' chances are of succeeding in the Information Age.

Information literacy skills entail complex thinking and reasoning. These types of skills take time and practice to learn, and many students passing through classes do not have strong information literacy skills, so teachers need to be patient and encourage students to practice, practice, practice.

Many of the following information literacy skills and techniques can be taught by first discussing the concept, then following up with modeling and guided practice. As students watch the teacher and other students manage information, they will think aloud about what is being analyzed, reach conclusions, and begin to use similar strategies for themselves.

Many of these skills are defined as advanced thinking skills by Higher-Order Thinking Skills (HOTS) or Bloom's (1956) taxonomy criteria. The Bloom's taxonomy skill(s) used in each strategy are included in parentheses at the end of each numbered skill set.

1. Identify if there is a need for information within a task (Comprehension): Recognize when information is needed to solve a problem or develop an idea, concept, or theme.

   Brainstorm multiple pathways for approaching a problem or issue. Identify, organize, and sequence tasks and specific activities to complete an information-based project.

2. Locate, identify, categorize, and analyze information needed (Comprehension and Analysis):

Formulate questions based on information needs.
Use effective search techniques; use keywords to search for information.
Analyze various sources for validity and overall relevance.
Read competently to understand what is presented.

3. Assess the information found (Analysis and Evaluation):

Evaluate the quality of information by establishing authority.
Determine age, accuracy, and authenticity.
Distinguish among opinion, reasoned arguments, and fact.

4. Organize the information (Application):

Learn how knowledge is organized.
Organize and store data in searchable formats.
Organize information for practical application.

5. Use information effectively to address the problem or task (Synthesis):

Create new information by synthesizing data from primary and secondary sources.
Integrate new information with existing knowledge.
Summarize information found in sources.

6. Communicate information and evaluate results (Application and Evaluation):

Present information in a product form.
Revise and update the product in ongoing evaluation.

7. Respect intellectual property rights:

Develop knowledge for how information and knowledge is produced.
Document sources using appropriate formats.

As a teacher, work through the information literacy skills with students. It is important to remember that these are not the types of skills one can model and teach once and assume students will learn and utilize. Teachers are building on skills they have already developed on their own. They require very advanced thinking and organizing skills, and therefore need multiple visits with hands-on and minds-on practice. Teachers should keep in mind that every classroom has a range of information literacy, and it is important to assess prior knowledge before starting a unit on information literacy.

Once students have basic skills on searching and navigating the Internet and strategies to manage and make sense of the information they find, teachers can begin using the Internet in their lessons, learning centers, and individual assignments and projects.

Precautions and Possible Pitfalls

The Internet is a "time bandit" and without structure, and it is easy for kids to lose their direction and purpose. Here are a few hints.

- Give students a few selected Web sites related to their unit (in worksheet form) that relate directly to the lesson. Never start lessons by having students only use search engines.
- Require students to find very specific information, not just surf. A rubric might be appropriate here.
- Always require students to write down the URLs of the sites they use for reports in a bibliographic format. Teach them a cut-and-paste technique to help develop their bibliography or references.
- Don't send the entire class to the same site at the same time. Once you get them started, encourage the development of search engine techniques.
- When possible, try to preview sites or do easy keyword searches before students visit them.

Sources

Bloom, B. S. (1956). *Taxonomy of educational objectives, handbook I: The cognitive domain.* New York: David McKay.

Burnett, C., & Wilkinson, J. (2005). Holy lemons! Learning from children's uses of the Internet in out-of-school contexts. *Literacy, 39*(3), 158–177.

Morkes, J., & Nielsen, J. (1998). *Applying writing guidelines to Web pages.* Retrieved April 26, 2006, from http://www.useit.com/papers/webwriting/rewriting.html

Strategy 70: Balance the demands of traditional teaching with contemporary technological tools.

What the Research Says

Brit, Brasher, and Davenport (2007) looked back at education and schools during the previous ten years and examined the predictions that were made regarding educational technology by reformers during the 1990s and the reality of the use of technology in

the classroom today. They also reviewed past research on teaching and technology, most notably the work of Cuban (1996, 2001).

The Brit et al. (2007) study looked at Heritage Elementary School in Madison, Alabama, to see how teachers in a technology-rich environment use technology to support their teaching and student learning. Heritage is a school of about 1,000 students; it opened in 1999. The school is fully networked and filled with the most current classroom technologies. It was found that Heritage teachers use technology to enhance traditional teaching. Teachers use the Internet as a resource, present information through technology, and thread technology resources into lessons. However, the emphasis is on teaching and learning rather than on technology. Pedagogy reflects a balanced mix of traditional teaching with contemporary technological tools.

In contrast, Cuban's research (2001) and his opinion are summarized in this quote.

> The facts are clear. Two decades after the introduction of personal computers in the nation, with more and more schools being wired, and billions of dollars being spent, less than two of every ten teachers are serious users of computers in their classrooms (several times a week). Three to four are occasional users (about once a month). The rest—four to five teachers of every ten teachers—never use the machines for instruction. When the type of use is examined, these powerful technologies end up being used most often for word processing and low-end applications in classrooms that maintain rather than alter existing teaching practices. After all the machines, money, and promises the results are meager.

Cuban went on to explore why nine out of ten teachers routinely use technology at home but find it difficult to integrate it into instruction.

> Perhaps it is now time to recognize that getting teachers to integrate technology into daily teaching and learning is more than UPS delivering machines to the schoolhouse door; it is more than having workshops for teachers or pressing universities to change their teacher education programs. Important as such measures are, in the larger picture of why teachers are infrequent users of classroom technologies, these actions divert attention away from deeper causes for teacher behavior. Making changes in what teachers do in their classrooms requires paying attention to the daily workplace conditions and constant external demands, and the inherent unreliability of the innovations themselves. (Cuban, 2001)

Classroom Applications

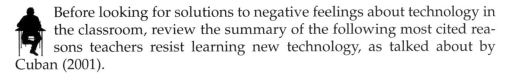 Before looking for solutions to negative feelings about technology in the classroom, review the summary of the following most cited reasons teachers resist learning new technology, as talked about by Cuban (2001).

- *No flexible workplace conditions.* Although information technologies have transformed most corporate workplaces and businesses, schedules and working conditions have changed very little in schools. Most teachers teach five classes a day, usually each 50 to 60 minutes long. Often teachers have two, sometimes three, classes to prepare for and sometimes need to do this in multiple rooms. Also, teachers see between 100 and 160 students a day. Teachers have usually one period a day set aside for planning lessons, seeing students, marking papers, making phone calls to parents or vendors, previewing videos, securing a DVD player or other equipment, and using the school's copy machines for producing student materials. Those professional demands haven't changed, yet other new time demands, such as learning new technology, are continually added. The demands on a teacher's time continue to accumulate while few demands ever disappear.
- *Content and professional demands.* In addition to managing workplace conditions, teachers are expected to be discipline experts, structure and manage classes, and create and set high standards. Teachers are also held accountable for test preparation and the results of high-stakes testing. Being a subject-matter expert and managing the learning of 150 students is exhausting. Adding quirky technology to this mix adds another layer of professional complexity to teaching. If something has to give, it's usually learning new technology.
- *Finicky technology.* Technology takes patience. Technology breakdowns and software glitches test even the most dedicated teachers. Many schools can't afford onsite tech people, and when schools have them, they are stretched thin. Getting parts in a timely fashion takes time, usually because the purchasing departments in schools don't operate like those in the business world. Servers crash and student files get lost or tampered with. New software doesn't always work on old computers, there's not enough memory, or the computer isn't fast enough to run it. Instructional aides need cables and bulbs. Technology wears out, and it costs more to fix it than replace it. Further, Internet blocking programs are not always precise and often can block access to desired Web sites, frustrating students and teachers.

So what is a teacher to do to overcome these obstacles? In addition to the cited research, there are many other papers, articles, and anecdotal opinion papers that find the same disconnect between technology, teachers, and the classroom.

When searching for strategies to become more involved in adopting technology, it was demonstrated over and over again that the teachers in these studies were shown to have a better attitude and adopted technology faster when they had conversations with peers about how they would integrate Web resources into their classroom practices. Modeling and sharing of successful uses of strategies in face-to-face peer collaborations led to increased frequencies of integrating new teaching strategies. Teachers who collaborated and shared successes and challenges in authentic context were more likely to develop successful approaches implementing new teaching strategies in their classrooms.

Knowing the state of a teacher's attitude is an important measure in predicting his or her predisposition to adopting new innovations such as the use of Web resources in his or her established teaching and learning practices.

The results of these investigations demonstrated that peer support for adoption of innovations could have accounted for higher levels of positive attitudes. Thus, an important component for training teachers in the use technological resources should include authentic skills and technical integration objectives in addition to providing opportunities for teachers to participate in focused collaboration after the training session ends. Teachers need to discuss successes and challenges to implementation and feel that they have others who can share similar experiences as they experiment with technology use in their classroom.

Establishing such discussion groups among teachers may be the most effective mechanism for promoting positive attitudes toward the use of technology in the classroom, thereby increasing the integration of such resources into teaching and learning environments.

Precautions and Possible Pitfalls

Examine the reasons for using technology. For the most part, teachers view technology as a more effective technique for transmitting content they want the students to learn or as a means for facilitating that transfer process by making learning easier, faster, or more interesting.

However, teachers should not lose sight of the fact that technology, especially computer technologies, can be used to promote constructivist approaches to learning and knowing, allowing students to be producers rather than just consumers of knowledge. In this sense, technology is used to foster increasing levels of cognitive complexity, reflective and higher-order thinking, and problem solving.

Some teachers seem clearly aware of the constructivist potential inherent in computer technology while others don't. However, it is not hard to understand the difficulties that many teachers face in addressing the demands of a more learner-centered perspective. There remains precious little time or institutional space for fostering the kind of innovation suggested by constructivist orientations to the use of technology.

Sources

Brit, J., Brasher, J. P., & Davenport, L. D. (2007). Balancing books and bytes. *Kappa Delta Pi Record, 43*(3), 122–127.

Cuban, L. (1996, October 9). Techno-reformers and classroom teachers. *Education Week*. Retrieved September 24, 2008, from http://www.edweek.org/ew/articles/1996/10/09/06cuban.h16.html?print=1

Cuban, L. (2001). *So much high-tech money invested, so little use: How come?* Retrieved September 24, 2008, from www.edtechnot.com/notarticle1201.html

Strategy 71: Accept that new technologies alter certain fundamentals of language and literacy.

What the Research Says

According to Hobbs and Frost (2003), the first large-scale empirical study measuring the acquisition of media literacy skills in the United States concluded that incorporating media message analysis into secondary-level English language arts curriculum can enhance the development of literacy skills. When 11th-grade students who received year-long media literacy instruction as part of their English course were compared to a control group enrolled in the same level course without the media literacy component, the media literate students outperformed the other students on the same assessment. Media literacy instruction improved students' multimedia analysis and reading skills; viewing and listening comprehension of print, audio, and video texts; message analysis and interpretation; and writing skills. The media literacy lessons were designed and integrated into existing curriculum by the classroom English teachers, an approach previous research suggested may be a more successful technique than using off-the-shelf curriculum.

Classroom Applications

Media literacy is the process of accessing, analyzing, evaluating, and creating messages in a wide variety of media modes, genres, and forms. It uses an inquiry-based instructional model that encourages people to ask questions about multimedia—what they watch, see, and read. It provides tools to help people critically analyze messages to detect propaganda, censorship, and bias in information, news, and public affairs programming and how they affect the information presented. Media literacy aims to enable people to be skillful creators and producers of media messages, both to facilitate an understanding as to the strengths and limitations of each medium and to create independent media. Media literacy is an expanded conceptualization of literacy. By transforming the process of media consumption into an active and critical process, people gain greater awareness of the potential for misrepresentation and manipulation (especially through commercials and public relations techniques) and understand the role of mass media and participatory media in constructing views of reality.

Teachers and students can begin to better judge the validity of a multimedia message or examine and analyze their own reasons or purposes for creating a multimedia message by asking the following questions. Creators of messages can more clearly tailor their messages for their intended audiences and avoid the pitfalls of unclear communication. Basic questions to consider are

- Media literacy is more than just a matter of learning how to consume media, but also the skills to produce media responsibly and effectively. What are the qualities of multimedia that make it communicate well?
- What group, person, or organization wrote, designed, and composed the multimedia message?
- What teasers or techniques did the creator of the presentation use to attract the viewers' attention?
- Different people, maybe from other countries or cultures, understand multimedia messages differently. Could the message be understood differently?
- What values, lifestyle choices, or perspectives are in the presentation, and which are being omitted?
- How are the multimedia messages constructed? Creative use of images and language can hide bias and the creator's agenda.
- Is the message informational, or is it to persuade or influence opinion? Why was the multimedia message created? (adapted from Jolls, 2008)

Using a search engine and a few keywords related to media literacy or multimedia literacy will produce many Internet sites with lots of information for curricular development. Here are a few sites that feature a variety of links featuring curriculum.

Media Education Foundation:
http://www.mediaed.org/resources/#mediaLiteracy

Media Literacy:
http://www.edselect.com/media.htm

Media Literacy Links:
http://www.emtech.net/media_literacy.html

Media Literacy Web sites:
http://www.studentactivities.com/links.htm

Precautions and Possible Pitfalls

Parents may go to great lengths to protect their child from exposure to violence, sex, and profanity in the media. Student minds are being bombarded by a constant stream of information from television, radio, newspapers, magazine, books, billboards and signs, packaging and marketing materials, video games, and Internet communications. There are motives behind each of these types of communication that may not be obvious to the casual observer. Media designers know that they must first catch viewer interest before they can sell their product. The techniques they use often include subtle messages about values, lifestyles, and points of view. The cumulative impact of these messages influences students and their decisions and shapes their worldview. Children are particularly vulnerable to media influence. Children learn social behavior through watching and imitating the behavior of others, including those they see in the media.

It would be a mistake not to include parents in media or multimedia literacy curriculum. Developing media- or multimedia-literate parents will allow families to help understand and filter out harmful messages that could twist children's worldview.

Shared homework assignments, questionnaires, and surveys including parents can help involve them in media literacy decision making. Shared analysis, reflection, and discussion can foster communication and understanding between parents and students.

Finally, teachers will need to carefully monitor multimedia work created by students. Many students are good at creating "edgy" messages that challenges their appropriateness for school settings. The same issues that come up with student newspapers and other student-produced communications come up in multimedia. First Amendment rights in schools can be a sticky issue, and it's always good to work with administration and parents to help define boundaries that work for everyone. Again, teachers should not work alone on these issues but keep an open dialogue with others to begin to define what is appropriate for a specific community and school.

Sources

Hobbs, R., & Frost, R. (1999). Instructional practices in media literacy and their impact on students' learning. *New Jersey Journal of Communication, 62,* 123–148.

Hobbs, R., & Frost, R. (2003). Measuring the acquisition of media literacy skills. *Reading Research Quarterly, 38*(3), 330–355.

Jolls, T. (2008). *Literacy for the 21st century: An overview & orientation guide to media literacy education* (2nd ed.). Malibu, CA: Center for Media Literacy. Retrieved September 24, 2008, from http://www.medialit.org/pdf/mlk/01a_mlkorientation_rev2.pdf

7

Enhancing Reading
and Literacy Skills

 Strategy 72: Keep in mind the three key elements of reading fluency.

What the Research Says

Hudson, Lane, and Pullen (2005) did a wonderful job of dissecting and defining the most important elements of reading fluency. They explained the concepts of accuracy in word decoding of connected text, automaticity in recognizing words (plain old word identification), and appropriate use of prosody (expressive reading characteristics), or the use of oral expression in reading aloud. As reading fluency is one of the defining characteristics of good readers, they also linked these skills as reliable indicators and predictors of comprehension problems. They went on to explore the links between reading accuracy and proficiency, reading rate and reading proficiency, and prosody and reading proficiency. Further, they explored various assessment techniques for accuracy, rate, prosody, and overall fluency. Finally, they went on to look at the various instructional methods.

Rasinski (2006) critiqued the work of Hudson et al. (2005) by validating much of what they had to say, but Rasinski did have some concerns regarding instructional priorities implied in their article. Hasbrouck and Tindal (2006) simply examined the use of oral frequency reading norms as an assessment tool for reading teachers. They felt that everyone associated with schools today needs to be aware of the increasing require-ments for number- or data-driven student performance accountability. They examined the use of assessments in oral reading fluency and its various components.

Classroom Applications

Accuracy in word decoding, automaticity in recognizing words, and appropriate use of prosody or meaningful oral expression is the pathway to comprehension. If these skills are mastered, the students' limited intellectual or cognitive resources can be used for greater compre-hension, which is the higher-order thinking goal of fluency. Rasinski (2006) took issue with teaching these three skills separately and felt that this type of instruction requires precious extra time out of the instructional day. Second, he felt that some of the activities focus only on gains in reading rates, or reading faster for the sake of just reading faster. He felt that classroom practice needs to unify accuracy, automaticity, and prosodic reading methods.

So where does that leave teachers? Teachers might be able to clinically engage younger students in separate instructional activities to strengthen these elements of fluency, but they pay a price for it. Students lose their motivation and incentive for reading when teachers take the comprehen-sion and meaning out of it. Repeated reading is a common strategy for increasing fluency. However, the older the students, the less likely they will be motivated to read using this method. It's like doing basketball or soccer drills in isolation and never engaging in a motivating, authentic game.

Rasinski (2006) made some good suggestions for fluency instruction. It is best described as authentic instruction. He suggested engaging stu-dents in performance of passages that combine all three instructional goals. Any type of performance requires repeated readings, practice, or rehearsal. He went on to say that if performance is the incentive to prac-tice, then what kind of texts lend themselves to expressive oral perfor-mance? Many types of texts are important yet offer limited opportunities for expressive interpretations. As he pointed out, there are a specific num-ber of texts meant to be performed that can be considered easy to per-form. Songs, poetry, lyrics, plays, scripts (theater, movie, TV), monologues, and other types of oral presentations work well for expressive oral read-ing and mastery of meaning. This strategy exposes students to a wider range of reading material and also motivates students to master the ele-ments of fluency and comprehension.

Rasinski (2006) stated that his purpose was to reinforce the recommen-dations by Hudson et al. (2005) that repeated reading was a key instruc-tional strategy. To this notion Rasinski added that it should also be meaningful and motivating and provide expressive oral potential. Teachers should be looking for text and activities that bring these ideas together to keep reading motivating and important in the students' lives.

Precautions and Possible Pitfalls

As with any type of performance, a teacher has to create a safe environment and a trusting relationship with his or her students. Many students with reading problems simply won't want to risk the social consequences of a public performance. While Rasinski (2006) touted the success of reading performance as an instructional tool, he failed to talk about the social factors involved in this type of activity. An empathetic teacher will need to use all of his or her skills to build an environment where students are willing to take very personal risks.

Sources

Hasbrouck, J., & Tindal, G. A. (2006). Oral reading fluency norms: A valuable assessment tool for reading teachers. *The Reading Teacher, 59*(7), 636–644.

Hudson, R. F., Lane, H. B., and Pullen, P. C. (2005). Reading fluency assessment and instruction: What, why, and how? *The Reading Teacher, 58*(8), 702–714.

Rasinski, T. (2006). Reading fluency instruction: Moving beyond accuracy, automaticity, and prosody. *The Reading Teacher 59*(7), 704–706.

Strategy 73: Make it routine practice to foster self-efficacy and motivation in readers.

What the Research Says

Walker (2003) summarized the major points of other authors and researchers since 1990 regarding the concepts of self-efficacy and the steps teachers can take to promote it in the teaching and learning environment. She then proposed and defined responses teachers can choose to increase self-efficacy, which in turn increases performance in reading and writing. Her premise was that understanding students' motivation, particularly those exhibiting self-efficacy, can help educators better engage students in literacy activities, because young people who are effective are more likely to work hard, to persist, and to seek help to complete challenging tasks they sometimes believe are beyond their ability.

Classroom Applications

Efficacious students do achieve and exhibit a group of attributes that make our teaching efforts rewarding. Self-efficacy refers to people's belief in their capabilities to carry out actions required to reach a high level of achievement. This success motivates the students to engage in more literacy activities, which in turn increases their reading and writing performance. Even when teachers know all this, they often fail to engage students in appropriate literacy activities that foster self-efficacy. It's no secret that the basic approach is to plan and provide interesting topics and clever activities to motivate students. However, motivation in self-efficacy is complex and difficult to nail down for curricular purposes. It is not easy for students to assess their own progress and achievement regarding self-efficacy in reading comprehension and writing.

Individuals develop their academic self-efficacy in a number of ways. Most commonly, successful learning experiences that are somewhat challenging yet doable create a sense of accomplishment that may significantly foster self-efficacy. Second, a strong source of self-efficacy is positive verbal response from parents, teachers, or peers that convey the student's capacity for performing literary activities. Related to this are accurate positive self-attributions developed by providing task-specific comments on student success and attributing that success to tasks that are learnable within the school environment. It is also helpful to reinforce the use of a variety of strategies to solve problems and work through activities. When faced with challenging activities, students with high self-efficacy apply metacognitive skills and strategies by asking themselves questions about concepts and content while checking their understanding.

Cultivating self-efficacy within a curricular framework is difficult. A number of authors have suggested that self-efficacy can be cultivated in low-performing students. Following are five suggestions mentioned most frequently.

- Give students choice within activities.
- Encourage strategic thinking about activities.
- Provide opportunities and tools for self-assessment.
- Change the assessment purpose and context.
- Incorporate choice that asks students to make decisions about their interests and what they may already know about a task.

When given a choice, students bring more effort to activities. Allowing choice in literacy activities increases motivation and authentic engagement. Teachers can provide a choice of activities within the day-to-day educational environment by offering personal reading and writing time, inquiry-oriented activities, and collaborative discussions based on student interests.

Many less-than-successful students look at failure and success differently than their more successful counterparts. In their eyes success and failure are products of factors beyond their control. Luck, the teacher's attitude toward them, and the difficulty of the material have more influence on outcome and products of learning than their own ability and effort. Often they do not recognize or acknowledge the effective strategies they use. Their mistakes are looked on as a continuous or repeated stream of blunders that have little value for learning. Learning from failure is rarely an option for them; failure just reinforces a negative self-image. They read and write without using or learning alternative strategies. What they are really saying is, "I don't have strategies and I don't know how to do it."

Because of these phenomena, teachers need to teach reading and writing strategies such as monitoring of meaning and understanding and elaboration. Teachers can help students deal with mistakes and use alternative strategies when students confront difficult or challenging curriculum. Selected strategies can be modeled by the instructor, and student strategies can be defined and recognized as legitimate coping strategies. Low-efficacious students need this type of help.

Related to how failure and success work in the lives of low-efficacious students is the notion of self-assessment. Many low-performing or low-efficacious students believe they are not up to doing many tasks; therefore, they assess their work and abilities negatively. Literary progress is very difficult for students to assess. Positive self-evaluation and assessment raise self-efficacy because students understand the complex relationships between performance and their strategy and the literary processes.

Teacher-produced rubrics and checklists emphasizing the strategic steps within tasks help support effective adoption of strategies. Specific checklists help students revisit and rethink their strategic actions and help students see clearly the connections between strategy and personal success. Defining and quantifying the steps in strategies and showing their connections to success cultivate self-efficacy and empower students. These assessment tools help students attribute their success to strategic actions. Checklists also allow students to evaluate how their literacy and strategies are progressing. The checklist and rubric strategy work well in both reading and writing activities.

Grades and learning are supposed to go hand in hand, yet grades today often create a sense of false security for teachers, students, and parents. Students often believe grades equate to learning. Rather than focusing on grades, low-efficacious students should be focusing on what they are learning and what they can do. Changing the assessment context supports a learning notion rather than a performance orientation. Both specifically designed portfolios with carefully crafted requirements and student-led conferences with parents and teachers can become learner-centered, rather than grade-centered, assessment strategies.

Within a portfolio students can evaluate their success with instructional activities and also help measure progress over time. Parents, students, and teachers can collaboratively review the students' work and what students can do. This all shifts the goals of assessment and evaluation from grade performance to specific learning goals that empower students and hopefully increase student efficacy. Past tasks are used to measure what students are learning, not to get better grades. The focus is on what they can do and how they are achieving their literacy goals.

By giving choices, learning literacy strategies provide self-assessment strategies, and by changing the focus of assessment, teachers can help guide students through more positive learning environments within more rigorous curriculum. All this contributes to increased ownership of learning, authentic engagement, and motivation and effort to continue to read and write, in turn enhancing self-efficacy.

Precautions and Possible Pitfalls

Another element to consider when designing curriculum, assessment, and instructional strategies does take time and adds another layer of complexity. However, self-efficacy is one of those educational intangibles that can't be measured, yet is one of the most important characteristics a teacher can enhance. Nothing is more satisfying than having a room full of empowered students. Consider it a necessity during curricular development and not just another required mandate. Self-efficacy is a gift teachers can help students open.

Source

Walker, B. J. (2003). The cultivation of student self-efficacy in reading and writing. *Reading and Writing Quarterly, 19,* 173–187.

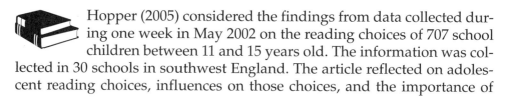

Strategy 74: Find the "out-of-classroom" forces that shape reading habits and reading choices.

What the Research Says

Hopper (2005) considered the findings from data collected during one week in May 2002 on the reading choices of 707 school children between 11 and 15 years old. The information was collected in 30 schools in southwest England. The article reflected on adolescent reading choices, influences on those choices, and the importance of profiling all reading experiences beyond books. This includes "new" literacies such as the Internet, magazines, newspapers, comic books, and other areas not typically considered traditional literacy activities.

Evidence from the study supported past research that there has been no significant decline in student literacy habits.

Classroom Applications

There is an intellectual gap between what teachers provide as reading material and what young people choose to read, both in class and for private reading. This can most likely be attributed to a generation gap. Teachers need to distinguish between promoting curricular reading and fostering the students' personal reading interests. The goal here should be to make the connections to the development of a reading habit that will empower young people as learners and future citizens beyond the classroom curriculum. Being aware of how teens choose their reading material will help begin this journey toward offering them a wide range of attractive choices for personal reading.

Giving students access to a range of appropriate reading books and other literacy activities requires an understanding of what triggers students' choices. Hopper (2005) rated clear categories of factors affecting choice that emerged from the study. Listed in descending order of importance, these categories can provide insight that you can use to foster students' personal reading choices.

- Prior knowledge of the book or author
- The appearance of the book
- Recommendation
- Television or film
- Genre

Students often exchange information with others in their lives, creating prior knowledge before deciding on a book to read. Prior knowledge connects with recommendations students might get from others. Young readers also read books as part of a series they might already be familiar with. This was a common response, as was reading multiple books from the same author. Genre choices, such as fantasy, were popular, and specific interest in nonfiction subject matter was also mentioned, especially by boys. Current trends and detailed knowledge of available books that students mention—and also books in the same or related genre or by the same authors—can be important.

The appearance of a book on the shelf also played a role in a student's decision to read. The color, pictures, or font could be a significant factor in choice. Publishers know this and create covers with images that affect the targeted demographic. The *Harry Potter* series is a great example of this. In addition, the same book might have different covers for different markets.

Television and film can also play a role, although a lesser one. The media hype certain books; again, the *Harry Potter* series as well as the *Lord of the Rings* received lots of media play. Oprah's Book Club influences choice, and sales jump for any book she recommends.

Genre is easy to connect to choice. Kids often become fans of a specific genre, such as science fiction or sports. These two genres are safe choices for boys.

Regarding other forms of reading materials or nonbook sources (93% in Hopper's study cited reading nonbook texts during the study week), girls spend more time reading magazines. You can see this in what students carry around with them at school. Girls show more interest in love, sex, celebrity, fashion, and health magazines, and boys show interest in technical, computer, and sports magazines. In the Hopper (2005) research, magazines proved to be an important reading choice for teens. Following magazines, newspapers were a significant nonbook reading source, and teens tended to read what was brought into their own households. Although not as popular as magazines or newspapers, the Internet was also cited as a source of nonbook reading.

Not surprisingly, teachers play a small role in influencing choice except for required class readers. This could be attributed to teachers' general lack of knowledge regarding what teenagers want to read.

What should teachers do with this information? They should use it to gain insight for stocking libraries or creating reading lists to share with students. They can also use it to integrate more popular reading choices into curriculum. They can use it to provide gender-specific choices to appeal to both boys and girls and to hard-to-reach groups of nonreaders.

Precautions and Possible Pitfalls

Developing an ongoing awareness of the reading preferences of teenagers takes time, and the job is never done. It's almost like predicting the type of music they are going to like. Many online book lists can help, and most are updated regularly. Do an Internet search for book lists and pick the ones that seem to be the most valid and useful, offer the greatest insight, and are the most current. There are also many agencies, clubs, and organizations that give book awards, and these are good sources of literary information. There is no one right way to develop this knowledge, but once teachers begin to tap into it, they will be better able to inspire teens and expand the range of what literacy can be for them in a school setting.

Source

Hopper, R. (2005). What are teenagers reading? Adolescent fiction reading habits and reading choices. *Literacy, 39*(3), 113–128.

> ### Strategy 75: Explore ways to encourage students' interaction with text.

What the Research Says

Reading is said to be an active rather than a passive process in which good readers actively monitor their reading process. Carrell (1998) observed that successful, strategic readers monitor their reading and state of learning, plan to use specific reading strategies, and are not afraid to adjust appropriately and evaluate their efforts (whether they have been successful or not) after reading. Zygouris-Coe, Wiggins, and Smith (2004) suggested that reading teachers can better engage their students with the text by following what they call a 3-2-1 strategy in which the students are first encouraged to summarize important points from text they are reading, then share whatever insights they got on topics or any aspects of passages they found interesting, followed by a questioning strategy that gives students opportunities to ask questions about the text they have been reading. The goal of this 3-2-1 strategy is to maximize students' interaction with text, and Zygouris-Coe et al. maintained that this strategy gets the students more involved with the text and encourages them to think independently by inviting them to become personally engaged in and with the text. This strategy can be used when students read a textbook, a novel, an article, or other instructional texts.

Classroom Applications

Zygouris-Coe et al. (2004) suggest that teachers model and provide opportunities for students to interact with text. The 3-2-1 strategy works as follows for any text or book: teachers first ask students to discuss three things they discovered after reading the text, then to discuss two interesting things they want to note as a result of reading the text, then to ask one question they still have after reading the text. When discussing three things the students discovered, the teacher must first teach them summary skills, which he or she can do by getting them to summarize small sections of the text to make sure all are participating. A summary, of course, is a short, to-the-point outline of the main ideas in the text. When the students discuss two interesting things about the text they noted, teachers can encourage them to think about what they enjoyed most or what was most relevant to their everyday lives. The final step of the 3-2-1 strategy is to get students to write one question they still have about the text. This question can link the text to their everyday lives.

Precautions and Possible Pitfalls

As noted previously, teachers must model this strategy to their students slowly and carefully before asking them to do it, because they must also teach their students how to summarize; thus, although this 3-2-1 strategy is useful, teachers should note that it may take some time before their students are comfortable using it, and they may have to model it several times. Obviously, teachers can use this strategy only after their students know how to summarize.

Sources

Carrell, P. L. (1998). Can reading strategies be successfully taught? *ARAL, 21*(1), 1–20.
Zygouris-Coe, V., Wiggins, M. B., & Smith, L. H. (2004). Engaging students with the text: The 3-2-1 strategy. *The Reading Teacher, 58*(4), 381–384.

> ### Strategy 76: Reexamine the nature of "content literacy."

What the Research Says

Behrman (2003) examined content-area literacy by observing a summer six-week high school biology class. The class featured a problem-based instructional approach by examining and working with biology-related realistic scenarios that included a community component.

The community component required students to spend a considerable amount of time outside of school interacting with community mentors and biology-related workplaces. Each scenario must be analyzed and acted on in a somewhat workplace-like procedure. Students were free to select any sources of information that would help them learn and respond successfully to the problems, as problem solving was stressed over information retrieval. This can best be described as "field-based learning."

Behrman (2003) found that students placed high reliance on human resources (mentors) and the Internet and limited their use of print media and sources. Behrman explained that the use of multiple literacies and varied print material calls for reexamining the definitions of content literacy and adolescent literacy in general. The limited instructional focus on traditional print-based literacy needs to be expanded to include multiple texts, including electronic, spoken, nonlinguistic, and other representations of meaning and knowledge.

Behrman's data sets included notes of classroom observation and events, instructional experiences with mentors at field sites, and interviews with students and the teacher. In addition, students provided end-of-the-course surveys and reviews of student project reports. Data were analyzed qualitatively.

Behrman (2003) found that, without a textbook, the class supported students in a rich assortment of literacy activities. Students sorted out digital and oral forms of content information to construct responses to project prompts and the authentic problems posed within the scenarios. The Internet was used far more than the class library of traditional print texts and other reference material. The author concluded by asking readers to rethink the primacy of print text in acquiring content knowledge.

Classroom Applications

It is common for teachers to help students learn to use and read traditional textbooks. However, more and more textbooks are taking a back seat to the oral transfer of information, the multimedia Internet, and other sources of information (television, radio, magazines). Most teachers are now aware of the problems and benefits the Internet provides. Textbooks in many classes have been reduced to use only for reference or a source of answers if a lecture is not totally understood. The biggest problem, when the textbook is no longer the primary source of information, is determining the validity and relevance of information from other sources. A second problem is outright plagiarism as students copy and paste Internet information into their papers.

The strategy here is to extend the potentially limited scope of how content literacy is defined beyond the textbook. Many times when students are asked for their sources, they just say, "I mostly used the Internet," indicating an absence of a human intellect in evaluating sources. They place a higher value on Web-based sources than text-based sources without carefully assessing the validity of the content.

Ongoing curriculum development is needed in all classes to reflect content-area learning in nonschool sources (nontextbook or other school material) and contexts. To further this idea, teachers need to consider how information is obtained in most workplace settings and use that information in curricular design, stressing how to move content learning beyond the traditional textbook.

How do teachers quickly find a site on the Internet containing useful information related to classroom units and at an appropriate grade level? One strategy is to simply use a search engine or a directory organized for teachers and children, one that also screens out sites inappropriate for children. Teachers might begin with one of these locations:

Yahooligans (http://kids.yahoo.com) is a directory and a Web guide designed for children. Sites are appropriate for ages 7 to 12.

Ask Jeeves for Kids (http://www.askkids.com) is a directory and a search engine based on natural language. Simply type in a question, and it finds the best site with the answer. Sites are appropriate for use by children.

Searchopolis (http://www.sunstorm.com/amazing/search.htm) is a directory and search engine organized for students in elementary, middle, and high school.

KidsClick! (http://www.kidsclick.org) is a directory and search engine developed for kids by the Ramapo Catskill Library System.

A second strategy is to select one of several central sites for each subject area and explore the resources for use during an Internet workshop. A central site is one that contains an extensive and well-organized set of links to resources in a content area. In a sense it is like a directory for a content area: reading, math, science, social studies, or another topic. Most are located at stable sites that will not quickly change. As teachers explore the Internet, they will discover these well-organized treasure troves of information. They will become homes to often return to, and teachers will develop favorites. The following are a few examples of central content sites.

Science

Eisenhower National Clearinghouse—http://www.goenc.com
Science Learning Network—http://www.sln.org

Math

Eisenhower National Clearinghouse—http://www.goenc.com
The Math Forum—http://mathforum.com/

Social Studies

History/Social Studies for K–12 Teachers, CoreComm—
    http://home.core.com

Reading/Literature

SCORE Cyberguides to Literature—http://www.sdcoe.k12.ca.us/
score/cyberguide.html

The Children's Literature Web Guide—http://www.ucalgary.ca/
~dKbrown/

The Literacy Web—http://www.literacy.uconn.edu

Designing a specific activity could be the third step related to the learning goals of a unit, using a bookmarked site. The activity may be designed to introduce students to a site used in an instructional unit, to develop important background knowledge for an upcoming unit, to develop navigation strategies, or to develop the critical literacies that are so important to effective Internet use.

It is important during this step to provide an open-ended activity for students, in which they have some choice about the information they will bring to the project. If everyone brings back identical information, there will be little to share and discuss during the activity session. You may wish to prepare an activity page for students to complete and bring to the Internet activity discussion, or you may simply write the assignment in a visible location in classroom.

The potential for innovative approaches to Internet literacy is endless. Be prepared to teach students to retrieve information in ways that will serve them well both inside and outside the classroom while respecting intellectual property rights.

Precautions and Possible Pitfalls

"I just don't have the time!" This is a common response for teachers who have not integrated the Internet into their literacy curriculum. There are usually two different explanations for this statement. Some teachers say they don't have time in their schedule; other teachers say they don't have time to learn new instructional strategies for using a complex tool like the Internet.

More sources of information are available to students than ever before. The textbook and the school library were once the extent of 95% of class research. Now information can come from anywhere. It would be a mistake to not help students sort and deal with the vast range and quality of content information out there. Avoid many problems with plagiarism and related issues by embedding respect for intellectual property rights into the assignment and curriculum in general. By doing this, teachers will also help students become better writers and turn in more interesting papers. Preparing children for their future is not an extra; it is central to a teacher's role as a literacy educator.

Source

Behrman, E. (2003). Reconciling content literacy with adolescent literacy: Expanding literacy opportunities in a community-focused biology class. *Reading Research and Instruction, 43*(1), 1–30.

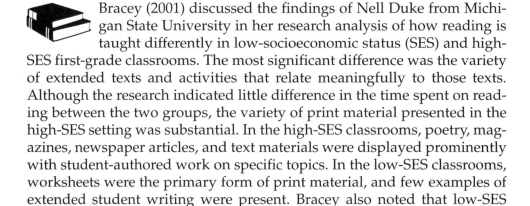

Strategy 77: Utilize a variety of print materials to inspire student reading and writing.

What the Research Says

Bracey (2001) discussed the findings of Nell Duke from Michigan State University in her research analysis of how reading is taught differently in low-socioeconomic status (SES) and high-SES first-grade classrooms. The most significant difference was the variety of extended texts and activities that relate meaningfully to those texts. Although the research indicated little difference in the time spent on reading between the two groups, the variety of print material presented in the high-SES setting was substantial. In the high-SES classrooms, poetry, magazines, newspaper articles, and text materials were displayed prominently with student-authored work on specific topics. In the low-SES classrooms, worksheets were the primary form of print material, and few examples of extended student writing were present. Bracey also noted that low-SES school libraries had 40% fewer books available and seldom added to their numbers during the school year.

Classroom Applications

Teachers need to ensure that the opportunity for reading a variety of print materials is available for their students regardless of grade level or content area. Research indicates that the more students read, the better their skills develop, and yet reading the standard classroom text often leaves students bored and unengaged, particularly if the text is outdated by student standards. Teachers need to use school librarians, the Internet, other teachers, parents, community members, and the students themselves to provide a wide range of print material beyond the basic textbook.

Many local newspapers have programs for free newspaper delivery to local classrooms. Often included with these papers are curricular activities that teachers can use or adapt to their own curricular needs. Many newspaper articles are short and provide a more motivating context for class content. Content and relevant "real-world" application for it will be more easily accessible for the struggling reader. Even comics and editorial cartoons provide opportunities for students to derive meaning from printed material.

Poetry and short stories abound on the Internet and can often be the perfect vehicle to introduce students to the elements of fiction in their own personal writing. Rhyme, rhythm, plot development, and characterization can all be addressed in context and act as a springboard for students as emerging authors.

Although worksheets may have their place in reinforcing rote memory skills, teachers would be wise to avoid relying on them as their number one way of infusing print material into their students' school day. Worksheets should be used as reinforcement rather than core curriculum. By providing a variety of print material, teachers can give students the opportunity to explore extended texts in meaningful ways.

Precautions and Possible Pitfalls

 It is important that teachers remain mindful of school and district policies regarding materials that can be used in the classroom. Some districts allow anything, and others have strict guidelines. Some districts have well-defined boundaries for acceptability of materials. It is very important that teachers make themselves aware of these policies prior to introducing controversial materials to their classrooms. Teachers should screen the materials they bring to the classroom to ensure they are appropriate for the students and the curriculum.

Source

Bracey, G. W. (2001). Does higher tech require higher skills? *Phi Delta Kappan, 82*(9), 715–717.

 Strategy 78: Use scaffolding to improve reading comprehension.

What the Research Says

Clark and Graves (2005) maintained that scaffolding plays a vital role in developing a student's reading comprehension. They define *scaffolding* as a temporary supportive structure that teachers create to assist students in accomplishing a task they probably could not have completed alone, and it is grounded in Vygotsky's social constructivist view of learning in which a child's development first appears in collaboration with an adult. According to Clark and Graves, what makes scaffolding an effective teaching technique is that it helps keep a task whole, while students learn to understand and manage the individual parts without being too overwhelmed with the whole.

Classroom Applications

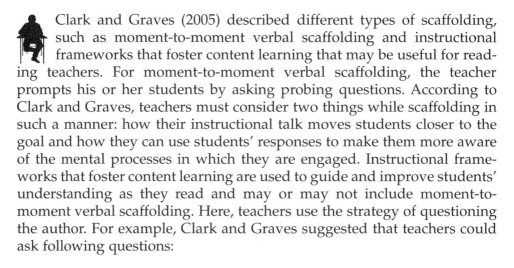 Clark and Graves (2005) described different types of scaffolding, such as moment-to-moment verbal scaffolding and instructional frameworks that foster content learning that may be useful for reading teachers. For moment-to-moment verbal scaffolding, the teacher prompts his or her students by asking probing questions. According to Clark and Graves, teachers must consider two things while scaffolding in such a manner: how their instructional talk moves students closer to the goal and how they can use students' responses to make them more aware of the mental processes in which they are engaged. Instructional frameworks that foster content learning are used to guide and improve students' understanding as they read and may or may not include moment-to-moment verbal scaffolding. Here, teachers use the strategy of questioning the author. For example, Clark and Graves suggested that teachers could ask following questions:

- What do you think the author means by that?
- How does that connect with what the author has already told us?
- How did the author work that out for us?
- Did the author explain it clearly?
- What's missing?
- What do we need to find out?

Precautions and Possible Pitfalls

Teachers should be aware that, during the planning phase of scaffolding, they must consider all their students' strengths and weaknesses and who will be doing the reading, the reading selection itself, and the purpose of the reading. It is important that the teacher create some pre-reading, during-reading, and post-reading activities designed to assist this particular group of students in reaching those purposes; otherwise the activity may not be as effective as it could be. In addition, teachers should be able to provide enough support for students to succeed, but not so much that they do all the work—not an easy balance to maintain.

Source

Clark, K., & Graves, M. (2005). Scaffolding students' comprehension of text. *The Reading Teacher, 58*, 570–580.

> **Strategy 79: Remember that deficits in reading ability are often associated with a complex range of issues.**

What the Research Says

Pellittera, Dealy, Frasano, and Kugler (2006) examined the construct of emotional intelligence (EI) as a framework for understanding the emotional processes students with reading difficulties experience in the school or classroom context. Their research considered emotional factors and specific elements such as interpersonal interactions of peer groups, opportunities for developing emotional learning, and the dynamic affective–aesthetic responses of the individual students during the reading process. The article examined the underlying affective processes as they relate to cognition, motivation, and social functioning.

The authors (Pellittera et al., 2006) stated that a student's social and academic difficulties can be explained by the breakdown of these emotional processes. Students can experience difficulties in understanding social interaction with peers because of poor perception of emotional cues and failing to access emotional knowledge in school social situations. These factors affect performance in literacy instruction. Further, the authors stated that constructs related to emotional intelligence examined in reading disability literature are understood to impact a student's academic functioning.

From a human ecological perspective, Pellittera et al. (2006) described the particular social–emotional and learning needs of students with reading disabilities that must be considered in creating an optimal personal learning environment fit. The authors listed the systems that most directly impact the emotional dimensions of the student with reading disabilities:

- the psychological environment of the school and the classroom,
- the policies that determine the student's class placement, curriculum, and activities, and
- the structure of the student's interpersonal peer relations.

In their introduction Pellittera et al. (2006) described the research of Gredler (1997), who stated that "individuals tend to interpret stress reactions and tension as indicators of vulnerability to performance. . . . Therefore the only way to alter personal efficacy is to reduce stress and negative emotional tendencies during a difficult task" (Gredler, 1997, p. 290). Pellittera et al. (2006) also listed specific emotionally intelligent interventions and discussed their implementation in the school environment.

Classroom Applications

The overall culture of the school and the classroom can produce an environment that is so emotionally stressful that certain students become emotionally paralyzed or so academically dysfunctional that achievement is the last thing they want to strive for. Their behavior turns inward, often aimed at protecting their self-esteem, managing tensions within the learning or teaching environment, and coping with the frustration of academic cognitive tasks. Many students with reading problems have experienced excessive failure and have negative reactions and emotions connected to academic triggers and the teacher's instructional efforts in the school setting.

A major goal of intervention regarding these factors is to create an emotionally positive classroom environment that reduces the students' general anxieties and increases their positive associations with the school and classroom. The emotional environment of the school and the classroom are created by the interpersonal interactions between students and the adults within the setting. Teachers need to develop emotional awareness in themselves and begin to create a more intelligent classroom environment. Smiles, a pleasant tone of voice, and the use of encouraging words are a beginning. Removing negative stresses should be a curricular priority.

On a different level, a more systemic intervention considers the emotional needs of the students when scheduling classes and class activities. In some counseling situations, placement of students can include selecting educational environments that buffer threats to self-esteem and foster a student's willingness to take risks. Teacher matching can also be considered. Teachers have a responsibility to set and monitor group dynamics and the emotional tone of the classroom interactions. When a teacher values empathy, emotional sensitivity, and self-awareness in a learning environment, he or she can alter peer group dynamics and derogatory behavior within a classroom. Peer rejection and a student's failure at social adjustments are associated with academic performance within literacy strategies.

In addition, peer or cross-age tutoring arrangements pairing older struggling readers with younger struggling readers often set up a positive dynamic for both participants. With preparation, such arrangements provide a sense of competence for the older student that improves self-esteem, self-efficacy, and a positive emotional experience regarding reading.

Individually, the written text needs to become a source of motivation to read and a positive stimulus with positive affective associations. This is the big goal. Teachers need to help students become comfortable with not knowing all the words rather than experiencing reading mistakes as a sign that they are always wrong. Teachers also need to structure activities that are challenging yet still provide students with positive and successful experiences. From an emotional intelligence perspective, teachers can use reader-response activities to help the students examine their own emotions and develop the ability to reflect on their own responses to learning activities. In this way, reading sessions can be used as a vehicle for personal social insight and self-awareness. Further, deciphering the text provides teaching and learning opportunities for young readers to begin to see themselves and their beliefs and feelings more clearly.

Planning for the emotion dynamics of the learning environment is essential. The emotional realm affects and influences the learning environment of struggling readers and learners in general. By becoming aware of and regulating the emotional reactions of students in literacy activities, teachers can increase not only fluency and mechanics but also the motivation to engage in reading materials both inside and outside the classroom. Teachers should remember that every academic task has an emotional component.

Precautions and Possible Pitfalls

It's not unusual to find that underachieving older students are resistant to strategies teachers might employ. A few students have had so many negative experiences and interactions with teachers and peers that school has become a painful place. The many attempts teachers have made to "reach" them over the years may have hardened them. Chances are, many teachers have tried to reach out to them, and now they anticipate efforts and are ready to resist. There are no easy answers for dealing with these students. Sometimes time and sincerity are the most effective qualities in building trust.

Sources

Gredler, M. E. (1997). *Learning and instruction: Theory into practice* (3rd ed.). Upper Saddle River, NJ: Merrill.

Pellittera, J., Dealy, M., Frasano, C., & Kugler, J. (2006). Emotionally intelligent interventions for students with reading disabilities. *Reading & Writing Quarterly, 22*, 155–171.

Strategy 80: Explore what it means to be literate.

What the Research Says

Rasinski and Padak (2004) stated that scholars appear to have reached consensus that a balanced approach to reading instruction reflects the greatest promise for improving literacy instruction. In their view, the "balanced approach" includes instructional components in phonics or word decoding, fluency, and comprehension. While they agreed with the approach, they felt the issue of balance in literacy is much more complex than current instructional models and literature may suggest. They argued that a more comprehensive consideration of literacy instruction is needed. To be comprehensive, literacy needs to be integrated within the literacy curriculum itself. It must be integrated into all facets of the classroom and school's learning environment. Further, literacy instruction needs to be integrated with both the home and community environment. The authors stated that literacy instruction is more than just balancing classroom strategies; balance and comprehensiveness go hand in hand in all aspects of the students' lives.

Classroom Applications

Balanced literacy curriculum and instruction are, by consensus, very hot topics in literacy education. Balanced reading instruction has many meanings, and many versions of such programs exist. To many teachers, the term *balanced reading instruction* describes attempts to establish equity between literacy instruction mechanics (such as phonics, spelling, and comprehension strategies) and the more holistic strategies involving process writing, literature-based instruction, and reader reflection for meaning. To others, including the media, it means teaching that combines phonics instruction, phonemic awareness strategies, and spelling. Fitzgerald (1999) defined balanced reading instruction as a philosophical perspective that includes three wide categories of beliefs: (1) that children should possess certain global abilities, such as understanding and responding to what they read; (2) that children should have certain local abilities, such as word identification routines and strategies; and (3) that children should have a love of reading or a knowledge of reading.

As appealing as the balanced approach to literacy may be after years of discussions about reading instruction, we need to remember that the concept of balance is considerably more complex than it appears at first glance, especially for the classroom teacher. The balanced approach concept may be simple and appear obvious, giving students everything that has been demonstrated to work, but in reality it involves much more than disparate approaches to instruction. While dedicating 30 minutes to word decoding and phonics balanced against equal time devoted to guided reading may be appealing, this approach may not produce the desired results. In sixth grade, for example, giving more attention to guided reading and less to phonics and decoding, yet teaching both, may be more beneficial. In middle school, it might be more appropriate to spend time negotiating meaning and comprehension. In high school, contrasting and comparing similar readings in a reflection paper may be appropriate for measuring comprehension.

It's clear that the truth is in the details when considering what the real meaning of "balanced" is. Beyond the surface of consensus on balanced reading curriculum is a huge range of options that teachers need to consider. Maybe the term *comprehensive literacy curriculum* better describes the complex and interrelated nature of the types of literacy philosophy we should strive for within a balanced approach. Consider how a balanced philosophy, as a working strategy, could be applied within the following important instructional considerations.

School/Community/Home: Balanced Literacy Throughout the Day and the Year

Most examples of balanced curriculum consider literacy only within the boundaries of the classroom, school, and school year. We all know students spend the largest part of their day and year outside of the classroom. In a comprehensive program, educators need to take into account the home and support the parents and the community give year-round in helping students learn to read and write.

It's no secret that parents are most involved with their children in their early years: the preschool years before formal school begins and during the elementary school years. If we want parents involved in secondary schools, we need to develop a pattern of involvement and target parents during these time frames. Learning to read before school begins requires parent involvement. Preschool children develop basic literacy concepts and conventions and especially phonemic relationships before formal school begins. Common sense tells us that this gives children an advantage once school begins.

The exact role parents and community play can vary; however, the obvious example is parents reading to their children. This is just the beginning in developing a home–school component. The home needs to support literacy instruction at school, and the school needs to support literacy instruction at home. Teachers need to recommend activities that tie into school content, literacy skills, and strategies that are part of the school instruction. Again, Rasinski and Padak (2004) found that parents appreciate specific and concrete suggestions from teachers. For example, parents can work with local libraries to help students get library cards. Teachers need to be fairly specific and direct in communicating advice for the home environment. This is especially true over the long periods of time during holidays and summer. Literacy activities can be practiced at home, and teachers can encourage parents to model reading and writing behaviors as well as sending literacy tips home. These might include book list suggestions. The bottom line is to help parents and students connect what goes on in school and what goes on in the community and home.

Balanced Instruction Within Instructional Cooperative Learning Groups

What does balance within cooperative grouping practices look like? Most would agree that one-on-one or small-group strategies offer teachers the most direct means of targeting instruction at the specific needs of students. However, is it a good idea to keep struggling learners grouped together for a long time? Won't these students begin to feel a sense of failure or lack of self-esteem by being segregated from the more advanced students? Also, when students are not the focus of the teacher's attention, they might not be fully engaged in productive reading activity.

How does whole-group instruction work? Most teachers aim instructional strategies toward the middle of the academic range. Students at either end of the achievement spectrum receive work that is either too easy or very frustrating. Some students are presented with content they are not ready to learn, and some already know the content. Also, quiet students in large classes often are ignored, and teachers sometimes assume they understand the lesson while their understanding may be only superficial.

Most would agree that, in general, cooperative small-group instruction provides the students with the greatest opportunity for achievement. A balanced literacy approach would seem to call for small-group instruction with the smallest teacher–student ratio possible. During other times of the day, maybe in other content areas, teachers can have students work individually, in pairs, in heterogeneous small groups, and in whole groups. Balance can be achieved, and the variety of teacher and student contacts can be maximized.

Balanced Instruction in Reading Genre and Text Types

What does a balanced approach to choice of reading genres or texts types look like? In most school settings, narrative fiction, or stories, tends to be the norm. Literacy practices today call for expanding the range of what is considered reading or literacy activities. The variety of other text genres that students can read and use as a model for writing is huge and getting bigger. Magazines, scripts, newspapers, picture books, electronic texts, and multimedia all can be sources of curriculum. At the far end of the spectrum, you can include charts, tables, graphs, signs, and maps.

Most would agree that in a balanced program, nonfiction, informational texts, and poetry should be included along with narrative fiction. Is this too restrictive? The big questions to ask are what texts should be used in reading instruction and why. What does balanced and comprehensive look like?

The Affective Domain

Beyond just setting up learning environments to teach students to read and write lies the greater goal of helping students become lifelong readers and writers. This goal suggests a definite affective component to literacy instruction. Nurturing the lifelong reading and writing potential in students is more than just mastering a set of skills within curriculum and assessment. Students who like to read and write will read and write more and will develop fluency and intellectual growth as a result of increased literacy.

In addition to helping students master skills, a truly balanced approach must develop students' desire to read and write and a love of the written word that continues well beyond the classroom. Sometimes this component is missing from school literacy programs. Find time to model your own positive reading experiences and facilitate reading and writing in ways that enable students to see they are learning skills to create a richer and more satisfying life for themselves.

Balanced Instruction for a Wide Range of Learners in the Same Classroom

All teachers, at all grade levels, know that students are not equal in the literacy skills they bring to the instructional environment. A truly equitable program requires a differentiated approach, and a critical element of such an approach is time. Students who struggle need more time than those students who have fewer difficulties. Struggling readers read fewer words than students who do not experience difficulty. If they are not given more help and time, they will never catch up with the more advanced readers. Equal time on task for all does not mean fairness. Check out various models of reading recovery programs and you will find examples of how creative educators try to accommodate struggling readers.

Balanced Literacy Instruction in the Content Areas Across the School Day

In many instructional settings, reading time significantly outweighs writing instruction time. In a truly balanced and comprehensive approach, reading and writing should carry equal weight. In addition, in secondary school content areas, reading and writing should be balanced within content delivery. Teachers are often so concerned with covering their specific content that writing and reading are not considered true curriculum. Rasinski and Padak (2004) called for reading and writing to be taught in an integrated fashion. They believed the best way to become a good writer is to read a lot, and the best way to become a good reader is to read a lot. They went on to say that all reading assignments should have a writing component and all writing assignments should have a reading component.

In the content areas, teachers develop a habit of teaching and lecturing around the reading. They view literacy instruction as a barrier to the transfer of content and would often rather "tell" the students what they need to know. Reading and writing should be developed in the curriculum as ways to explore the content. In a balanced and comprehensive approach, students consistently use reading and writing to explore and discover in the content areas. Teachers need to foster the development of confidence in students to glean information from and comprehend what they read. They will need these skills beyond the classroom when a teacher is not there to help them.

Precautions and Possible Pitfalls

Literacy is not accomplished just within school. The schools are often involved with the students only during schools hours, and the resources students have access to generally are available equally. Once they leave the school, the playing field for learning becomes uneven. Students go home to very different environments and areas of the community. Resources are not equally distributed, and some students have advantages that others don't.

Be careful to not call attention to students who appear more resourceful at the expense of those who don't have access to the same resources. The beautiful Internet information that one student brought to class may put the other students, without computer and Internet access at home, at a disadvantage. Some parents foster literacy in their children and others may not. Environment plays a big part in how prepared students are when they walk into class. Teachers shouldn't make students pay emotionally for a situation they can't control.

Sources

Cassidy, J., & Cassidy, D. (2004). Literacy trends and issues today: An on-going study. *Reading and Writing Quarterly, 20,* 11–28.

Fitzgerald, J. (1999). What is this thing called "balance." *The Reading Teacher, 53,* 100–107.

Rasinski, T., & Padak, N. (2004). Beyond consensus—beyond balance: Toward a comprehensive literacy curriculum. *Reading and Writing Quarterly, 20,* 91–102.

Strategy 81: Select literacy instructional design principles that have been documented.

What the Research Says

Because of the difficulty many struggling middle school students have with science content area texts, Carnine and Carnine (2004) examined and discussed six aspects of instructional design incorporating literacy strategies. The goal was to integrate middle school science content and reading skills to increase levels of students' success. The investigation examined an approach that featured carefully selected vocabulary, word reading instruction, oral and silent reading with reading fluency practice as needed, and explicit instruction on comprehension strategies, such as retelling, concept mapping, and summarization.

Classroom Applications

Carnine and Carnine's (2004) article is not research in the classic sense, but it described a somewhat novel approach to teaching middle school students in a content area incorporating specific reading strategies from reading research literature. The following summarizes and critiques some of those activities.

1. Students need good fluency before they can begin to concentrate on comprehension. In classes with a large number of struggling readers, oral reading fluency is highly correlated with and a predictor of reading comprehension. The fluency-building activities and strategies recommended here involve re-reading sections of previously read passages in order to build fluency. One of the best things about this technique is that students are able to graph their correct word-per-minute rate and see their improvement. Much of the time, progress in literacy activities is hard to see, but this technique helps provide real, positive feedback visually. It may require a teacher to copy or retype and number passages from books previously read for students to use in this fluency exercise. Next, the cumulative number of words is noted in the left-hand column for each line. It is then simple for a student to keep track of the number of words read in one or two minutes. This is one of the most motivating activities that students can use to chart their own progress.

2. Students often have a difficult time and are confused and frustrated by the amount of new vocabulary and content thrown at them in school grade-level textbooks. It's hard to get the core or

basic concepts in the midst of all the details stuffed into chapters. To strive for better comprehension, teachers should try to carefully select key words, pre-teach them, and review them. Teachers may need to decode and help the students pronounce these words. Select multisyllabic words that students may have trouble with. Also begin to teach and define the meaning of affixes typical in such content areas as the sciences. These are all things that can be done before reading assignments.

3. For comprehension strategies, try a "partner retell activity." Partner reading begins with the goal of identifying the main idea and relating the details, actively engaging the pair of readers in the reading process. Partners trade the roles of "reteller" and "listener" in short 30- to 60-second, face-to-face read-alouds. The reteller recalls the main idea of his or her partner, who listens and relates to the reteller. The next step is to have the pair focus on finding one or two details in the text that tell more about, support, or further define the main idea. In the end, the teacher can reinforce and confirm the important details or do a quick check on the activity with discussions and questioning. All this serves as a foundation for other activities to follow, such as some type of written work like content mapping.

4. The following are all part of an example of a scaffolding approach to teaching students to construct graphic organizers of the text they have read. This complex sequence of steps uses scaffolding to shift from teacher direction and control to student creation and then to student self-direction and control. This can be accomplished over time, within a variety of instructional units.

Show and explain to students a variety of traditional examples of graphic organizers, such as flowcharts, concept maps, and matrices, some developed by professionals and others by students.

Inform students about what graphic organizers are and when, why, and how various types of them should be used. Jones, Pierce, and Hunter (1988/1989) provide information on why and how to create graphic organizers to comprehend text; their article includes illustrations of a spider map, a continuum–scale, a series of events chain, a compare–contrast matrix, a problem–solution outline, a network tree, a fishbone map, and a human interaction outline.

As a classroom or homework assignment, give students a partially completed graphic organizer to structure. Give them feedback on their work. Have students complete empty graph organizers entirely on their own, and give them feedback on their work. Organize groups of students to create their own graphic organizers. Give students specific feedback on their construction and evaluation of graphic organizers, such as the following:

The graphics are neat and easy to read.

Ideas are expressed clearly.

The content is organized clearly and logically.

Labels or other strategies (colors, lines) are used to guide the reader's comprehension.

Main or core ideas are the focus, not the details.

The entire organizer is visually appealing.

The reader doesn't have to turn the page to read all the words.

Once the groups complete their graphic organizers, have each group exhibit theirs to the other groups. Have all groups critique the graphic organizers of all other groups, giving the creators feedback based on the rubric used. Supplement as necessary.

As a homework assignment, have students develop graphic organizers completely on their own, using rubric criteria. Encourage students to give one another feedback during the process.

Finally, have students work independently to create graphic organizers without support from others, either students or teachers.

Precautions and Possible Pitfalls

 In this era of testing content area, teachers are under increasing pressure to transfer content information that students need to succeed on the tests. State frameworks and standards are defining specific class curricula more than ever. Some teachers decide to teach around reading problems and transfer the required information using other means.

Many times teachers will see adding a literacy component as a threat to the limited time they have to teach their content. "Struggling readers" as a group include students who simply can't read (decode) text and others who are able to read but lack the necessary comprehension skills to reach grade-level expectations. The key for teachers is to incorporate strategies and instructional designs that address reading problems while, at the same time, facilitating content mandates.

Scaffolding is one of those teacher skills that will take time to develop. With experience teachers can learn what type of support to provide and when to remove it. They need to make sure scaffolding attempts are truly within students' zone of proximal development. If the instruction is too easy, the work becomes busy work. If it is too hard, no amount of scaffolding will help them perform independently, and they will become frustrated.

Sources

Carnine, L., & Carnine, D. (2004). The interaction of reading skills and science content knowledge when teaching struggling secondary students. *Reading & Writing Quarterly, 20,* 203–218.

Jones, B. F., Pierce, J., & Hunter, B. (1988/1989). Teaching students to construct graphic representations. *Educational Leadership, 46*(4), 20–25.

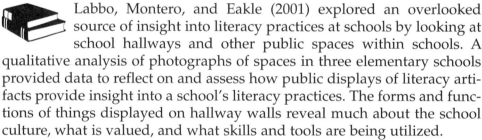

Strategy 82: Display a variety of literacies as they provide insights into how literacy is practiced and valued.

What the Research Says

Labbo, Montero, and Eakle (2001) explored an overlooked source of insight into literacy practices at schools by looking at school hallways and other public spaces within schools. A qualitative analysis of photographs of spaces in three elementary schools provided data to reflect on and assess how public displays of literacy artifacts provide insight into a school's literacy practices. The forms and functions of things displayed on hallway walls reveal much about the school culture, what is valued, and what skills and tools are being utilized.

In this study, over a course of two weeks, the researchers took photos of all objects on the walls in three elementary schools. One rural, one suburban/urban, and one suburban school served as data sources. This was followed by a systematic analysis of the content of the photos. The researchers identified a number of categories of literacy artifacts.

- *Sense of community/identity:* Literacy work products designed to foster pride, positive self-image, and a sense of school or community spirit
- *Curriculum/content area work:* Literacy work products, individual or group, produced to illustrate the children's best efforts within a content discipline
- *Writing products:* Displayed writing products including research reports, group compositions, poetry, and responses to literature
- *Author focus:* Commercially produced posters and bulletin boards designed to promote reading or to provide information about authors

- *Functional signs:* Basic signs providing directions, behavioral
  expectations, legal notices, or designations of how facilities are used

Conversely, the researchers also considered what was missing from the walls and what they thought should be included. They commented on materials and equipment left in hallways that were not intended for display and how that contributed to a view of the school environment.

Finally, after the study, they felt that little attention was being paid to the nature and the types of things that are posted in public display spaces in the school. They commented that very little of the space available was devoted to promoting multimedia literacies. It is their conviction that school public spaces can be additional valuable learning spaces to reflect and support multimedia literacy, especially if the school's cultural norms bend to accommodate time for pausing, wondering, reflecting, inquiring, and generally just noticing what's on the walls.

Classroom Applications

Few teachers have given much thought to media representations exhibited in the hallways and common public areas of the school or their functions. Items displayed in the hallways are a reflection of the media tools and communication strategies that are taught, used, and valued within the school's culture. How does this hallway evidence reflect on the multimedia literacy-based activities being integrated into classroom learning environments alongside the more traditional print-based literacies? One of the most interesting statistics in the Labbo et al. (2001) study indicated that only 11% of the items displayed reflected use of computer-related tools.

The larger question for educators is how these public display areas can better be used to support students' active learning and foster development of new twenty-first-century media communications and other literacies. Following are a few ideas to consider.

- *Display the learning process, not just the final product.* By focusing
  exclusively on the polished finished product, educators send a
  mixed message to students. Viewers' and children's learning could
  be enhanced by including a poster or photo essay describing the
  process needed to produce the final product.
- *Display multimedia computer-related work, not just paper and pencil
  products.* If using computer time for skill-and-drill software
  applications, try expanding the uses to include Web page design,
  multimedia presentations, computer art applications, photo
  manipulations, on-screen video production, multimedia slide
  shows, and other technology-driven media tools to "read" and
  "write" various symbolic forms of information (e.g., music,

graphics, sound effects). Think about displaying a computer screen in some way that can be seen in the public areas.

- *Don't use these spaces for storage.* Using public space for purposes that are not instructional suggests overcrowded conditions or a lack of caring.
- *Don't leave wall space empty, or schools will look sterile and institutional, not like friendly places where young people can be stimulated to engage in learning.* Try word walls of key instructional words, summaries of school events and participation, calendars or other concepts of time, activity lists, and theme-based bulletin boards designed to display the best student work. Display materials that invite celebration and provide a literacy or communication activity challenge to those creating the display.
- *Set standards for spelling, grammar, and appearance of all exhibited work.*

Precautions and Possible Pitfalls

Public spaces within schools are limited resources. Encourage all members of the school community to utilize the space. Don't overlook student groups that traditionally do not engage in these types of activities. Participation in public exhibits builds the school community and engages students in ownership of the school experience. It also creates a learning environment that values student work and pride.

Source

Labbo, L. D., Montero, M. K., & Eakle, A. L. (2001). Learning how to read what's displayed on school hallway walls—and what's not. *Reading Online, 5*(3). Retrieved April 4, 2006, from http://www.readingonline.org/newliteracies/lit_index.asp?HREF=labbo/index.html

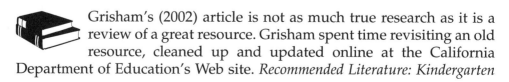

Strategy 83: Read Recommended Literature: Kindergarten Through Grade Twelve *on the California Department of Education's Web site.*

What the Research Says

Grisham's (2002) article is not as much true research as it is a review of a great resource. Grisham spent time revisiting an old resource, cleaned up and updated online at the California Department of Education's Web site. *Recommended Literature: Kindergarten*

Through Grade Twelve (http://www.cde.ca.gov/ci/rl/ll/) was published first in 1989 at the height of literature-based reading programs in California. The original publication contained a list of children's books recommended for specific grade levels, categorized as "core" books to be used as whole-class readings, "recreational" for independent reading, and "extended" reading to build on core books. It was published again two years later in an annotated version with a short synopsis of each book on the list.

According to Grisham (2002), California teachers generally found these resources to be highly useful for developing literacy strategies at the time, and school administrators found them indispensable as a reference for book adoptions for each grade level. As literacy instruction moved toward more skill-based programs, the recommended literature list was not updated. However, in 2002, new technology produced an updated list online, and the Web-based version has lots of features not found in the print version.

Classroom Applications

 Recommended Literature: Kindergarten Through Grade Twelve is located on the California Department of Education's Web site at http://www.cde.ca.gov/ci/rl/ll/. The following is a direct copy of the links and services they offer:

Recommended Literature: Kindergarten Through Grade Twelve is a collection of outstanding literature for children and adolescents. The recommended titles reflect the quality and the complexity of the types of material students should be reading at school and outside of class.

Search List: Search the online database for titles using specific criteria.

Search Categories: Explanation of the search categories used in the online database.

Literary Genres: Explanation of the genres used in the online database.

Classifications: Explanation of the classifications used in the online database.

Awards: Explanation of and links to the home sites of the awards noted in the online database.

Connections to Standards: Gives background of content standards and how titles in the online database are linked to them.

Cultural Designations: Explanation of the cultural designations used in the online database.

District Selection Policies: Information about selection policies and Web resources.

Previous Literature Lists: Links to lists of authors and titles of previously published literature lists.

Frequently Asked Questions (FAQs): Answers to the questions most commonly asked.

Acknowledgments: A list of the many individuals who worked on this project.

The site is easy to navigate and is almost a one-stop Web site for literature searches. The search features and the links to book award sites are highlights of the site and a great resource for all educators. The powerful search engine breaks down the search by grade level, language, culture, awards, and a few other categories to really narrow search boundaries. The Awards link searches many book award Web sites that are updated, and most also have links to past years' awards. These are two of the site's best features. The California Department of Education has created an exceptional resource for the classroom teacher and others involved in literacy education.

Precautions and Possible Pitfalls

 There are none. There is very little not to like about this Internet site. The only potential problem is that it might stop teachers from looking for other resources.

Source

Grisham, D. L. (2002). Recommended literature: A new children's literature resource. *Reading Online, 5*(9). Retrieved February 28, 2006, from http://www.readingonline.org/

8

Developing a Professional Identity

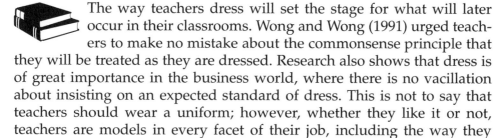

Strategy 84: Create the right perception through professional attire.

What the Research Says

The way teachers dress will set the stage for what will later occur in their classrooms. Wong and Wong (1991) urged teachers to make no mistake about the commonsense principle that they will be treated as they are dressed. Research also shows that dress is of great importance in the business world, where there is no vacillation about insisting on an expected standard of dress. This is not to say that teachers should wear a uniform; however, whether they like it or not, teachers are models in every facet of their job, including the way they dress. As children become older, they become increasingly able to remember, and then practice, that which they see modeled.

Eden (2001) stated that parents, students, and administrators have a stereotypical image of a "good" teacher. This includes body language, motion, and speaking style. When parents find the teachers' dress inappropriate, they react.

Classroom Applications

A teacher seeking a job would never go to an interview in anything other than the most professional attire. In fact, most administrators say a candidate's attire influences their decision in the development of an interview process. However, once teachers are hired, particularly if they are young or close in age to the students, they may resort to casual attire. This choice of dress can sometimes even look very similar to the clothing the students are wearing. Some beginning teachers have the notion they should dress so the students will like them and show their "withitness."

Students don't need to like their teachers, but they do need to respect them. Teachers are role models and should be concerned about their dress for several reasons. First, the way a teacher is dressed makes a statement about who that person is. Secretly, teachers' dress also sends a message about their expectations. Second, if teachers are to be considered professionals, they must dress like professionals. Certainly a person's manner of dress has great significance in the business world, where there seems to be no doubt about an expected standard of dress. This is not to say teachers should have uniformity in the way they dress. However, certain common-sense standards seem clear. It is not necessary to dress in one's "Sunday best," but a shirt and tie for men and slacks or a skirt with a blouse or sweater for women can help create a positive image. Women should leave the very short skirts, low-cut blouses, shorts, and tight stretch pants at home. A thoughtful, reasonable, and well-planned wardrobe is all that is necessary. The message to students will help establish credibility and contribute to an effective learning environment.

As a new teacher, the challenges are great. By making dress work for teachers rather than against them, the signals are clear—those who want respect for themselves and their profession must dress accordingly.

Precautions and Possible Pitfalls

Given the fact that most schools do not have a dress code for teachers, and because of the legal implications of the possible infringement on personal liberties, it is difficult to enforce professional dress for teachers. Frequently teachers will cite low pay as one of the reasons they don't dress more professionally. However, one has only to look at school secretaries and support staff (who usually make much less than teachers) to see a standard of professional dress. Conversely, if the principal dresses as casually, sloppily, or provocatively as some teachers do, their credibility and respect from teachers and the community might be suspect. Beginning teachers, especially if they are young, can benefit from every possible advantage. Dressing in a professional, businesslike manner won't make someone a better teacher, but it will set the stage for what will subsequently happen in the classroom.

Sources

Eden, E. (2001). Who controls teachers? Overt and covert controls in schools. *Educational Management Administration & Leadership, 29*(1), 97–111.

Siefert, K., & Hoffnung, R. (1991). *Child and adolescent development.* Boston: Houghton Mifflin.

Wong, H., & Wong, R. (1991). *The first days of school.* Sunnyvale, CA: Harry K. Wong.

Strategy 85: Explore and discover the natural teaching styles within.

What the Research Says

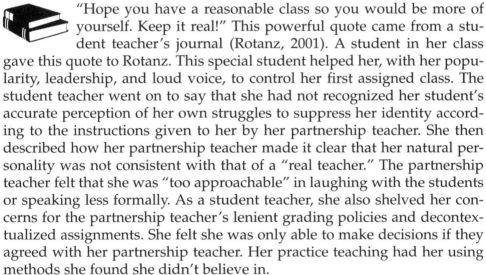

"Hope you have a reasonable class so you would be more of yourself. Keep it real!" This powerful quote came from a student teacher's journal (Rotanz, 2001). A student in her class gave this quote to Rotanz. This special student helped her, with her popularity, leadership, and loud voice, to control her first assigned class. The student teacher went on to say that she had not recognized her student's accurate perception of her own struggles to suppress her identity according to the instructions given to her by her partnership teacher. She then described how her partnership teacher made it clear that her natural personality was not consistent with that of a "real teacher." The partnership teacher felt that she was "too approachable" in laughing with the students or speaking less formally. As a student teacher, she also shelved her concerns for the partnership teacher's lenient grading policies and decontextualized assignments. She felt she was only able to make decisions if they agreed with her partnership teacher. Her practice teaching had her using methods she found she didn't believe in.

While the Rotanz (2001) article was not classic research in a formal sense, it does illustrate the dilemma in which many new teachers find themselves. Rotanz used her reflective journal entries to conclude that student teaching can be a very divisive activity as those who are there for support can actually stymie new teachers' development in finding out who they are as teachers. She went on to point out situations that contributed to her negative feeling and emotional reactions to her relationship with her partnership teacher.

Experiences such as the one Rotanz described in her article act to demoralize a new teacher who looks to his or her partnership teacher or university preparation as golden. She also went on to reflect about the lack of respect most teachers at her site had for her university training. She came to realize that the reality of the site and a real classroom was something she wasn't really prepared for. She also realized that the very people who were there for support hindered her development as a teacher and student collaborator.

Classroom Applications

Rotanz (2001) pointed out a situation and dilemma that many student teachers and some new teachers encounter. The true point of student teaching is to work with guides who help find and protect teachers from gross mistakes. Teachers aren't there to clone themselves after the style or the work of others. It is more of an exploration and blending of tactics that fits individual professional style. Teachers new to the profession often don't know they have had a bad experience as a student teacher until it is over. The key here is to work for a placement based on some mutual compatibility. Sometimes college or university education teachers know the schools in their area and can suggest specific ones based on what they know about the candidate and the school. If a candidate is lucky, they can suggest a principal and maybe even a teacher within their content area.

Take time to reflect on teaching and learning methods, styles, and techniques that make sense and try to find placements that help hone the best guess at how teachers want to plan instruction and teach.

What the Research Says

Neal Glasgow recalls:

My first placement put me in an art room with a master teacher who expected me to use lessons that she created and had been using for years. I didn't create anything new in projects or assessments. I couldn't do what she did some of the time or do it as well as she did most of the time. I felt horrible because everything I did was subpar. She wanted all her classes to experience the same projects and instructional strategies. Therefore, I was stuck and missed out on half of the experiences new teachers are supposed to have, such as creating learning and teaching pathways. What do you do for a backup plan when the ideal placement doesn't come along or turns sour? Quick communication works best here.

I could have avoided this placement if I hadn't blindly accepted it. Mitigate and compromise with those responsible for supervision. Find out what their expectations are and whether you share them. Often their letters of recommendation carry weight, and you want a good one, so performance is important. A good supporting teacher is a guide on the side and mentor, not a blueprint to copy. After teaching for a while, I came to the conclusion that it takes three trips through a lesson or project to really get it down. It also differs with the student mix you get. My master teacher's expectations were beyond my reach, and my placement was a recipe for failure.

However, my university supervisor recognized the mistake and supported me through the experience. He said he would make sure no other new teachers would be placed with my master teacher. However, it did some damage to my ego and development as a teacher. I still see my second master teacher 25 years later. She let me plan and deliver my own lessons and find myself. She laughed at my mistakes, offered suggestions on how I could improve my lessons and strategies, and became a good friend.

Source

Rotanz, L. (2001). Breaking free of the puppeteer: Perspectives on one practice teacher's experience. *High School Journal, 84*(3), 19–25.

> ### Strategy 86: *Take time to recognize and remedy stressful situations.*

What the Research Says

 Many studies have been performed over the years that have documented high levels of stress and burnout in schoolteachers. Sources of teacher stress may include time demands, large class sizes, mountains of paperwork, difficulties with misbehaving students, financial constraints, and lack of educational supplies.

Teacher stress and burnout is a consideration for many educators (and it certainly should be for the general population, as we face huge teacher shortages in the areas of mathematics, science, and special education nationwide). The stress some teachers face can lead to physical and emotional exhaustion. The consequences can include less job satisfaction, lessened student–teacher rapport, and decreased teacher effectiveness in meeting the needs of students.

Liston, Whitcomb, and Borko (2006) examined the emotional factors that affect first-year teachers and debated where teachers should get the support for the emotional roller-coaster they will experience as beginning teachers. They looked at support mechanisms and offered suggestions on how new teachers should be supported by both the hiring school or district and their teacher education program. Intrator (2006) looked at a range of issues faced by novice teachers, especially what it means for young teachers to take care of their health and spirit amid the stress that marks the first years of teaching.

Classroom Applications

Liston et al. (2006) characterized the struggles of first-year teachers related to the emotional intensity and stress of the beginning of a career. The stress related to jumping from theory and purely intellectual constructs to everyday classroom practice presents a shocking reality for new teachers. The workload is daunting, even with a favorable schedule. Preparing standards-based curriculum that is new, untried, and many times unfamiliar, coupled with standardized testing accountability, can be very intimidating. Added to the task list are meetings, assigning grades for the first time, marking papers, and responding to parents. Unlike experienced teachers, beginning teachers have not adopted consistent approaches to routine tasks so they can concentrate on more deserving matters. There is also a specific amount of uncertainty, and beginners often feel a sense of overwhelming complexity to their overall workload. Teachers make many small decisions daily and manage a range of dilemmas, and beginning teachers spend more energy dealing with them than veterans. To add to all this, after a few months, disillusionment can set in.

New teachers usually choose teaching on the basis of personal visions of the value of education, strong ideals and beliefs about the nature and rewards of teaching, and the role they will play in students' lives. New teachers find the rewards they expect are not easily realized in today's classrooms. A gap develops between vision and real-world practice. To add to all of this, teachers have to defend their practices and decisions and represent the teaching profession as well.

In spite of all the negative points above, there are emotionally charged moments when new teachers build relationships with students and students authentically engage and get it or have an "aha moment." These moments can often balance out the negative and let teachers know that they really can have an impact. These small moments of success and feelings of satisfaction are related to a sense of efficacy which in turn relate to a teacher's effectiveness and commitment to teaching.

There is no doubt that the first years of teaching are often extremely challenging. With increased demands for more accountability as measured by standardized testing, less parental involvement, and more time demands being placed on teachers, the need for teachers to take care of themselves has never been greater. Teachers must make time for themselves to deal with the everyday stresses of teaching. The idea must be one of working smarter, not harder. If teachers let themselves become physically and emotionally exhausted, oftentimes cynicism and other factors related to burnout and attrition follow.

Frequently, new teachers complain that if only there were more hours in the day to get things accomplished, they wouldn't be so stressed; however, the answer is not to find more hours in a day, but instead to organize the hours they already have in a way that is both healthy and productive. One way to help decrease stress is to connect with a mentor or colleague in the same department or building who can help with organizing and planning. The new teacher cannot be afraid to share concerns or ask for help. He or she can receive advice and suggestions from exemplary veterans so there is not a continual reinventing of the wheel. The beginning teacher can get help in prioritizing and organizing what needs to be done.

It is not necessary to grade every single paper that comes across the teacher's desk. Sometimes a checkmark on the assignment or activity to note that it was completed is sufficient. Computer software grading systems, which also allow the teacher to enter grades, print out individual student reports, and post class grades, can be a tremendous timesaver.

The teacher who wants to work until caught up should buy a sofabed, set it up in the classroom, and have the phone number of Pizza Hut on speed dial, as the in-basket will never be empty. Veteran teachers know not to plan large assignments near the end of grading periods so as not to pull all-nighters grading student work. The new teacher should also definitely think about a "no late work" policy before school starts to avoid having an additional pile of paperwork to grade right before report cards are due.

Economic concerns may be remedied by asking for help. Many schools are receiving help from parent and community groups that supplement educational resources with wish lists or mini-grants ranging from the basics such as construction paper, whiteboard markers, and tissues to class sets of dictionaries, supplemental texts, and DVD players. As a new teacher, it is critical to explore these additional resources.

Another key factor to help reduce stress is to develop and teach (just like any other lesson) the rules and procedures for maintaining classroom behavior. Too often, new teachers are heard to say that they don't have time to teach rules and procedures because the class must be to Chapter 37 by March. The reality is that if classroom rules and procedures are not in place and effective, there will be little actual learning taking place. The result will be increased frustration for both the teacher and the students.

Not taking the time to teach rules and procedures could also force a teacher to buy antacids in the large economy size to keep in a desk drawer.

Eating a well-balanced diet, getting a good night's sleep, and exercising are all known to be essential for good health and can be extremely helpful in reducing stress. However, sometimes as a new teacher, taking care of oneself is the first area to be compromised. A daily multivitamin can help when a well-balanced diet is not always possible.

Just as teachers make time to grade and prepare lesson plans, so too should they make time for exercise. Reducing stress can be as simple as taking a brisk walk around the block, attending a yoga class, or working out at the gym. The effects of exercise can give teachers time for reflection, clear their minds, and help them to reorganize priorities.

Teachers cannot teach students well if they're demoralized and over-whelmed. If beginning teachers have no strategies for retaining their enthusiasm, rejuvenating their spirit, or rebounding from the days that go sour, children will suffer. High-impact teaching needs energy, presence, and skills at full power.

Precautions and Possible Pitfalls

Stress and burnout in teaching are usually not the result of one event; rather, they are the continual process in which environmental forces threaten a teacher's well-being. Stress can also be exacerbated by unrealistic demands the teachers place on themselves. It is unrealistic for any new teacher to expect to perform at the level of an experienced teacher. It is, therefore, crucial to teacher success to be able to share concerns with others. Using mentors can help by giving new teachers an outlet for expression while capitalizing on opportunities to learn what they are doing right and give them support when problems arise. Mentors can also share their own struggles and frustrations as new teachers and offer solutions by sharing the ways they overcame their problems.

The first years of teaching are a time for the beginning teacher to develop both as a person and as a professional. With almost half of new teachers leaving the profession in the first three years, it is imperative to give every manner of support possible in helping reduce stress and burnout.

Sources

Coates, T. J., & Thorsen, C. E. (1976). Teacher anxiety: A review with recommendations. *Review of Educational Research, 46,* 159–184.

Intrator, S. M. (2006). Beginning teachers and the emotional drama of the classroom. *Journal of Teacher Education, 57*(3), 232–239.

Kyriacou, C. (1987). Teacher stress and burnout: An international review. *Educational Research, 29,* 146–152.

Kyriacou, C., & Sutcliffe, J. (1987). Teacher stress: Prevalence, sources, and symptoms. *British Journal of Educational Psychology, 48,* 159–167.

Liston, D., Whitcomb, J., & Borko, H. (2006). Too little or too much: Teacher preparation and the first years of teaching. *Journal of Teacher Education, 57*(4), 351–358.

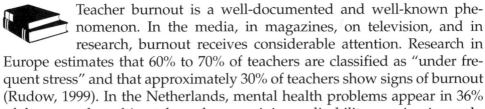

Strategy 87: Avoid burnout by choosing mentors carefully.

What the Research Says

 Teacher burnout is a well-documented and well-known phenomenon. In the media, in magazines, on television, and in research, burnout receives considerable attention. Research in Europe estimates that 60% to 70% of teachers are classified as "under frequent stress" and that approximately 30% of teachers show signs of burnout (Rudow, 1999). In the Netherlands, mental health problems appear in 36% of the cases that ultimately end up receiving a disability pension in work-incapacitated teachers (USZO, 1998). In addition, in comparison to others who do "people work," such as mental health workers and other health professionals, teachers appear to be at high risk for burnout. Teachers report more burnout symptoms than other workers in social professions.

In this study (USZO, 1998), it was hypothesized that a teacher's perceived superiority would be reduced among individuals high in burnout, especially with respect to positive behaviors. To carry the idea further, it was hypothesized that individuals high in burnout would be able to maintain a negative sense of superiority (feeling less bad than others). One hundred twenty secondary school teachers were asked to generate information about feeling inferior and superior in relationship to others. To no surprise to the researchers, only positive superiority was reduced among teachers high in burnout. They felt less good, but also less bad than others.

In summary, this research indicates that teacher burnout is accompanied by a lack of perceived superiority with respect to positive behaviors that may have a range of consequences for both teachers and their classroom environments. Teachers in a state of burnout do feel superior on negative behaviors, and this contributes to the maintenance or repair of feeling a lack of superiority. Thus, burnouts may use their colleagues' flaws and failures to boost their own self-esteem and to possibly prevent a decline in their performance as a teacher. Maslach and Jackson (1981) defined burnout in a multidimensional fashion characterized by three qualities.

1. *Emotional exhaustion:* A depletion of emotional resources or feeling empty or worn out.

2. *Depersonalization:* Characterized by negative and cynical attitudes toward students.
3. *A reduced sense of personal accomplishment:* Individuals in burnout assess their accomplishments in negative terms.

The research concluded that burnout contributed to lower student achievement as students were perceptive and very aware of the burned-out teacher's state of mind. Other interesting comments included reflection that school culture fosters burnout when administration enforces clearly defined, narrow, measurable goals on teachers for academic achievement. Schools without these strict goals seem to give teachers more opportunity for experimenting with new teaching and learning methods that foster a more collaborative and supportive relationship with administration, thus seeing fewer symptoms of burnout.

Classroom Applications

New teachers should be aware of the phenomenon of burnout and its related symptoms. The first recommendation is for new teachers (or any teacher new to a district or school) to quickly size up the professional environment they encounter and avoid forming professional relationships with teachers who offer limited support, resources, or negativity due to potential burnout.

Nothing is less rewarding than to find a beginning teacher on a committee or in a working situation in a school where it is "not cool" to be professionally enthusiastic about the job. The concept of teachers as professionals has always been debated (usually outside the teaching profession). In these days of prescribed curriculum and standardized tests, curriculum choices become less and less the responsibility of the teacher. Where teachers do have control is in the area of how curriculum is taught. In the heterogeneous mix of today's classroom, determining *how* is much more important than ever. Because of this, good teachers are required to be more professionally savvy than ever.

As a new teacher, don't compromise your professional enthusiasm to better fit in. Seek out other like-minded thinkers to avoid the symptoms of burnout presented in the research. There is a term, *communal orientation*, that refers to individuals who care for and are concerned about other people. Nurses who care for their patients or have concern for them tend to experience less burnout. Overlay the same idea onto the student–teacher relationship. The one characteristic of burnout over which teachers exhibit little control is in an inequitable relationship where teachers invest more care than the recipients of the care (the students). Teachers need to find ways to understand and cope with this.

Following are some ideas that can contribute to a new teacher's sense of professional responsibility.

- Spend more time talking with colleagues about ideas, not students.
- Decentralize and focus more on students' needs than on how the teacher is perceived by students and others. (This takes time!)
- The new teacher can become involved and offer services on school or district curriculum writing projects or other projects.
- Teachers should have a working knowledge of county or statewide educational issues or programs they might want to become involved with, both in their content area and in education in general.
- Become involved with students in nonclassroom activities (sports, clubs, etc.).

Precautions and Possible Pitfalls

All teachers occasionally feel some of the symptoms of burnout. A professional perspective is something that is created and developed, and it continually needs maintenance. One of the warnings Rudow (1999) gave was that teachers feeling symptoms of burnout should not try to remedy the situation by working harder. They felt that by working harder, teachers just added to their feeling of frustration. The idea is to not work harder, but to work smarter and more efficiently. Find strategies to reduce the mundane and focus on the more creative and satisfying aspects of the teaching profession.

Sources

Brenninkmeijer, V., Vanyperen, N. W., & Buunk, B. P. (2001). I am not a better teacher, but others are doing worse: Burnout and perceptions of superiority among teachers. *Social Psychology of Education, 4*, 259–274.

Maslach, C., & Jackson, S. (1981). The measurement of experienced burnout. *Journal of Occupational Behavior, 2*, 99–113.

Rudow, B. (1999). Stress and burnout in the teaching profession: European studies, issues, and research perspectives. In R. Vandenberghe & A. M. Huberman (Eds.), *Understanding and preventing teacher burnout: A sourcebook of international research and practice* (pp. 38–58). New York: Cambridge University Press.

Uitvoeringsinstelling Sociale Zekerheid voor Overheid en Onderwijs (USZO) [Benefits Agency for the Public Service and Education Sector]. (1998). *Statistiek arbeidsongeschiktheid, Onderwijs* [Statistics incapacity for work, education]. The Netherlands: Author.

> **Strategy 88: Use conflict and tension as an opportunity for personal growth and change.**

What the Research Says

New teachers vary in their ability to perceive, grapple with, and resolve the normal conflicts and tensions that exist in the teaching and classroom environment. As identified in the research (Beach & Pearson, 1998), some new teachers avoid or minimize conflicts and tensions by conforming to the system or authority figure in the workplace. Others are so overwhelmed that they find conflicts and tensions unmanageable, leading to a sense of loss of control, resignation, and futility, or wanting escape from the system. A review of 16 studies (Beach & Pearson, 1998) on the effectiveness of programs fostering beginning teachers' reflections found that preservice and student teachers' reflections were primarily technical or practical, with little evidence of substantial reflection (Hatton & Smith, 1995). During early student teaching experiences, focus is usually concentrated on conflicts and tensions in developing basic teaching techniques. Later in student teaching and into their first year of teaching, they shift out of their more egocentric modes of teaching, learning, and relationships to focus more on their students and their reaction to their teaching. In this study (Beach & Pearson, 1998), 28 students enrolled in a 15-month postbaccalaureate teaching program were required to reflect on their clinical experiences in journals and small-group interactions.

Four basic types of conflicts and tensions were categorized.

- *Curriculum and instruction*—conflicts and tensions between planned instruction and actual events, or between their perceptions and student perceptions of relevancy, or between beliefs about their own teaching and curricular choices and school- or department-mandated curriculum and pedagogy.
- *Interpersonal relationships*—conflicts and tensions with and among students, other teaching colleagues, and administrators. This category could also relate to a sense of personal isolation.
- *Self-concept or role*—personal conflicts and tensions regarding the need to be accepted and well liked, the role ambiguity of transition from student to teacher, and the further definition of self.
- *Contextual and institutional*—conflicts and tensions related to the expectations of the institutions in which they work, teach, and learn. This generally involves acclimation and socialization to the culture of school and teaching.

The same research (Beach & Pearson, 1998) also identified three levels of strategies for coping with conflicts and tensions.

- *Avoid/denial:* In the beginning, new teachers frequently describe their dealings with conflicts and tensions in highly positive terms. Some assume problems will diminish with time, so they avoid coping.
- *Immediate solutions:* New teachers frequently generate short-term, quick-fix solutions. They defer tensions and conflicts between the cooperating teachers or students to the back burner. They only deal with issues when they are forced to.
- *Incorporation:* New teachers accept their conflicts and tensions as a necessary part of growth and incorporate positive changes and alteration of class and management structures to better avoid conflicts or create clear, workable mitigation plans for students. Informal professional support structures are created and integrated into interpersonal relationships with colleagues and administrators.

Classroom Applications

While some new teachers have assigned mentors or are part of statewide induction programs, many are left to work their way through the first few years of teaching in isolation. If structured support is not available to teachers, it is important to seek out exemplary experienced colleagues to network with, provide observations, and give feedback of teaching practice. Teachers need these observations to be evidence-based (teacher called on ten male students and one female student; desks were arranged in groups of four, etc.). The observations can be useful in giving feedback about a teacher's practice and allowing opportunities for teachers to grow and improve without the added stress of an administrator present or having it tied to a teacher's evaluation. Communication is key for teachers. Having an experienced teacher with whom to brainstorm ideas or strategies, or sometimes just plain vent to, can be a real help. The more comfortable a teacher is with others observing and giving feedback, the more opportunities there are for real growth.

Precautions and Possible Pitfalls

Good teaching is a continuous and exciting journey. If teachers think they will finally have it all down pat one day, they are mistaken. Unfortunately, it is still true that new teachers often are placed in a position of trial by fire. They are given assignments that more experienced teachers would never be given. It is common to have to teach in more than one room or teach a variety of classes, forcing the new teacher to prepare for multiple settings, disciplines, and ability levels. It is hard to give advice for situations like this. In induction programs such as the Beginning Teacher Support and Assessment (BTSA) Induction Program in California, there is support for new teachers to limit the number of preparations, classroom changes, and involvement on multiple committees and coaching assignments through the first two years. It is ironic that the most inexperienced teachers are often given the most challenging assignments. Good planning and communication with all stakeholders helps.

Sources

Beach, R., & Pearson, D. (1998). Changes in preservice teachers' perceptions of conflict and tension. *Teaching and Teacher Education, 14*(3), 337–351.

Hatton, N., & Smith, D. (1995). Reflection in teacher education: Towards definition and implementation. *Teaching and Teacher Education, 11*(10), 33–49.

Strategy 89: Exchange ideas with colleagues as a means of professional development.

What the Research Says

Professional development has often consisted of short workshops and inservices for teachers based on needs perceived by administrators and district office personnel. Professional development is something that is often done for or to teachers instead of with or by them. All too frequently this professional development may not enhance a teacher's classroom practice.

In a study exploring a group of teachers attending monthly meetings (McCotter, 2001), researchers found that it was possible to provide new and meaningful ways of support and collegiality enabling continuous professional growth and development.

Members met monthly to provide support and feedback to one another. Support was expressed in several ways: having the opportunity to ask questions and pursue feedback, the sharing of similar experiences, suggesting solutions or strategies, or just voicing support either verbally or nonverbally. The most important characteristics of these monthly meetings consisted of a "what is said in here, stays in here" pledge, group and individual reflection and critique, seeking feedback, and all-important collaboration. Group members felt this type of professional development helped them to reflect on their practice and experiences and, more important, had relevance and purpose for their classroom practice.

Classroom Applications

Clearly a focus in education today is providing meaningful professional development for all stakeholders. Because beginning teachers have needs and concerns that experienced veteran teachers may not have, it is important for them to feel supported and have their problems taken seriously. Many teacher induction programs are now providing professional development specifically designed for their beginning teachers. These programs are based on needs assessments given to new teachers and on surveying teachers with a few years' experience under their belt to determine what kind of professional development would have been helpful in the first year or so of teaching. Based on this feedback, districts are tailoring programs to meet specific needs.

Many new teachers feel totally intimidated around their experienced colleagues and might be cautious, if not downright reluctant, to discuss problems or concerns for fear of being perceived as weak or not in control. When new teachers can get together in a group and share problems and concerns with their peers, they realize they are not the only ones experiencing these questions or problems. The support can be as simple as giving practical suggestions for solving situations in the classroom to encouraging new teachers to step outside their comfort zone and try a new teaching strategy. The collegial communities that emerge from this ongoing support and collaboration can be lifesavers to a struggling teacher.

The use of reflective conversations with fellow beginning teachers, as well as a mentor trained in the art of reflective conversation, can also be of great benefit. This reflection should be more than just thinking back on a problem or lesson; it should operate with the purpose of changing one's practice and enhancing students' learning. By engaging in these conversations in a nonthreatening environment, beginning teachers have the opportunity to perceive themselves through students' eyes.

The importance of collaboration with colleagues cannot be overlooked. It is one of the most important components of good professional development for beginning teachers. If teachers new to the profession can share meaningful discussions involving a sharing of knowledge and focus on teachers' communities of practice, then as they progress from novice to experienced, confident veteran, the collaboration may well continue throughout their professional careers. The benefits to new teachers, both personally and professionally, cannot be ignored.

Precautions and Possible Pitfalls

New teachers should be aware that professional development is not a one-size-fits-all proposition. So much advice (some good, some bad) may be thrown at them during their first few years that they need to take care not to become jaded or overwhelmed. They would also do well to distance themselves from the veteran complainers who may see all professional development opportunities as a waste of time. These are the teachers who have taught the same way for the last 25 years, haven't had a new idea or instructional strategy in that time, and can't understand why kids today aren't "getting it." Coming out of teacher education programs, teachers thinking they are equipped with all the tools and knowledge they will ever need in the classroom will be sadly disappointed. Effective and successful teachers will discover they not only participate in, but also seek out, professional development opportunities to continually evaluate and strive to improve their practice.

Sources

McCotter, S. S. (2001). Collaborative groups as professional development. *Teaching and Teacher Education, 17*(6), 685–704.

McLaughlin, H. J. (1996). The nature and nurture of reflection. In K. Watson, C. Modgil, & S. Modgil (Eds.), *Teachers, teacher education and training* (pp. 182–189). New York: Cassell.

 Strategy 90: Surround yourself with mentors.

What the Research Says

It is no secret that the first year of teaching can, at best, be trying. Many studies have concluded that the theory of a teacher in training encounters little that resembles the reality that a new teacher faces with a class of 35 students. Two conditions that can contribute to first-year difficulties are the physical and social isolation that many new teachers experience (Lortie, 1975).

Smith and Ingersoll (2004) examined whether mentoring and induction programs had a positive effect on the retention of beginning teachers. They reviewed data from a national school and staffing survey. They found that beginning teachers who were provided with mentors from the same subject field and who participated in collective induction activities such as planning and collaboration with other teachers were less likely to move to other schools and less likely to leave the teaching profession after the first few years of teaching.

Classroom Applications

Smith and Ingersoll (2004) cited the overall turnover rate among beginning teachers in 1999–2000 to be 29%, with 15% changing schools at the end of the first year and 14% leaving teaching altogether. Beginning teachers at private schools were less likely to change schools but twice as likely to leave teaching at the end of the first year. Most states now have some type of mentoring programs available to new teachers.

Smith and Ingersoll (2004) examined the qualities of induction programs and identified a number of activities that contributed to higher retention. Important elements identified were mentorship programs, collaborations and planning time with other teachers, seminars for new teachers, and regular communication with administration or department chairs. The researchers found that the most important factors were to have a mentor or mentors in the same field and to have common planning time with other teachers from the same discipline.

It is critical for new teachers to surround themselves with exemplary experienced colleagues. In most schools, almost without exception, teachers work in settings where the sociocultural context, if not the actual physical structure, encourages little interaction among adults and can contribute to feelings of isolation and frustration. By developing a relationship with a mentor and establishing regularly scheduled times to meet and talk, the new teacher will learn to cope with the myriad problems that may be encountered and will have the opportunity to learn and grow professionally. Data from California's BTSA (Beginning Teacher Support and Assessment) Induction Program indicates that ongoing collaboration and reflections between the new teachers and their mentors help new teachers gain insights, perspectives, and deeper understandings of the context and complexity of teaching while giving them the support and encouragement they so desperately need.

Precautions and Possible Pitfalls

It is critical to the success of the new teacher–mentor relationship to have mentors who are carefully selected, well trained, and accessible. Mentors need to be trained in the art of reflective conversation and really *listening* to the new teacher's concerns. What the new teacher doesn't need is a mentor who will just offer to fix the problem.

Sometimes experienced teachers are more eager to offer solutions, often based on their own personal experience, rather than asking questions that help guide the problem-solving process. This technique does little to help new teachers build confidence in their own problem-solving strategies.

Having a mentor who really listens and is accessible is immensely important. Beginning teachers need to be careful of aligning with veteran teachers who are negative. This is usually someone who has been in the profession a long time, is counting the days to retirement, and has been teaching the same way for 20 years. This person is usually the one who hasn't attended a professional growth opportunity in years, feels students are an imposition, and will be eager to find a willing ear to bend.

Sources

Lortie, D. C. (1975). *Schoolteacher: A sociological study.* Chicago: University of Chicago.

Smith, T. M., & Ingersoll, R. M. (2004). What are the effects of induction and mentoring on beginning teacher turnover? *American Educational Research Journal,* 41(3), 681–714.

> ### Strategy 91: Look behind the scenes when assessing the teaching styles of others.

What the Research Says

 Once leaving the confines of a college or university classroom, new teachers are often confronted with a range of teaching styles that they may not be familiar with. This can be a confusing period, as many times the college or university programs have defined teaching styles and techniques that are deemed the "correct" way to teach and may be very different from what a new teacher is confronted with in the real world.

Black and Davern (1998) described scenarios where new teachers were confronted with confusing classroom situations that became so distracting the new teacher failed to see the innovative aspects of the particular classroom. The article went further to describe a communication breakdown that begins with new teachers failing to ask host teachers questions that would have helped them to see the "method behind the madness" in what they were observing and experiencing, usually for the first time.

For example, it is very common to see problem-based pedagogy or discovery learning techniques in classrooms these days. Kids are out of their seats, working in teams, and the noise level can be high. To a novice, it can look like nothing constructive is taking place, yet to a veteran teacher, it is a controlled and orchestrated teaching and learning environment.

Various teaching strategies can be seen in such classrooms, such as cooperative grouping, sophisticated teaming skills, mutual learning, learning self-regulatory skills, self-pacing, and competitive strategies. Yes, students are out of their seats and not all the students seem to be engaged, but the majority of them are. Having students sitting quietly in their desks doesn't ensure everyone is on task either.

University supervisors critiqued the scenarios that were used in the research to show how novice teachers could easily misread valid learning and teaching strategies.

Classroom Applications

Careful analysis of the overall character of a class activity, lesson, or strategy can help a novice teacher focus on the details. Teachers shouldn't let first impressions define what is going on. List questions, analyze them, and be ready to discuss them with the classroom teacher. Critiquing teaching practices is a skill in itself and needs to be learned. Without appearing judgmental, ask the teacher or teachers involved why he or she chose a specific teaching strategy. Once novice teachers are aware of new perspectives, they can learn from them and to apply them to their instructional practices. Ultimately, it is important to make distinctions between those practices that new teachers will use and incorporate into their repertoire and those they would not.

Strategies for successful observations include the following:

- Listen carefully to the concerns of the teacher being observed. Practice presenting a message to them that indicates interest and the desire to discuss issues freely, nonjudgmentally, constructively, and openly.
- Model respect and appreciation for the challenges that school staff experience. Go behind the instructional scenes and ask what the teacher educator needed to do before the observation and what resources were needed to get to that point in time with the students.
- Explore the teacher's perceptions of the needs of the class to help validate what is happening in the classroom. Explore the strengths and weaknesses of the strategies used.
- Articulate teaching practices and philosophies to veteran teachers. Practice skillful ways of raising difficult subjects. Realize that differences are inevitable within any staff. Nurture the spirit of independent thought and learn to diplomatically raise differences regarding practices and philosophies. Develop a critical analytic ability and reflective skills to help identify, explore, and articulate ideas.

Precautions and Possible Pitfalls

⚠ Some veteran teachers may not be as receptive to questioning. Teachers shouldn't take it personally. Hopefully all contacts will be positive and useful. As with any profession, there is a range of competency among teachers, and not every contact made will click. Also, teachers are not "good" or "bad" all the time. They have good and bad days and successful and not-so-successful lessons. Classes of students can also have bad days where nothing seems to work. Proms, dances, Fridays, Mondays, sporting events, weather, and a range of other factors can affect a specific lesson or observation on any given day.

Source

Black, A., & Davern, L. (1998). When a pre-service teacher meets the classroom team (managing conflicts of teacher strategies). *Educational Leadership, 55*(5), 52–55.

9

Fostering a Positive Relationship With Families and Community

 Strategy 92: Treat parents as part of the solution.

What the Research Says

Students want their parents to be involved in their education. A high level of parental involvement in children's education generally leads to a high level of academic achievement. Parents frequently are involved with their children's education while children are in elementary school, but often stop being involved once children are in high school. One study looked at 748 urban elementary and secondary school students (Grade 5, $N = 257$; Grade 7, $N = 257$; Grade 9, $N = 144$; and Grade 11, $N = 90$) and their requests for and attitudes about their families' involvement in their education. Of these, 449 were Black, 129 were Hispanic, and 121 were White. The study compared high- and low-achieving students in mathematics and English (or reading for elementary school students). It also examined whether there were ethnic differences in students' feelings about family involvement. Students in all grades requested parental assistance with schoolwork and had positive attitudes about using their parents as educational resources, although elementary students made more requests and had more positive attitudes than secondary school students. Both high- and low-achieving students showed interest in parental involvement. However, at the elementary school level, high-achieving Hispanic students in mathematics had more favorable attitudes than did lower-achieving Hispanic students in mathematics. Black and Hispanic students were generally more interested in parental involvement than were White students.

Classroom Applications

Teachers should reach out to parents to enhance their involvement and develop a partnership in their children's education. Many parents are unaware that they have the ability to have an impact on their children's education even if they are not well educated themselves. Teachers can explain and illustrate for parents how a parent can function as an educational manager or teacher. Some ways the parent can act as manager are as follows:

- Provide time, a quiet place, and adequate light for studying. Help the child determine the best time and place to work.
- Each night, ask if there is a homework assignment, and ask to see it when it has been completed.
- Each night, ask about what happened in school.
- Have a dictionary accessible and encourage the child to use it.
- Find out when tests are to be given, and make sure the child has a good night's sleep before and a good breakfast the day of the test.
- Visit the school to discuss the child's progress and to find out what can be done at home.
- Communicate positive attitudes and expectations about the child's school performance.
- Avoid letting a child's household responsibilities assume more importance than schoolwork.

Teachers can prepare a handout for parents so they have some idea about what they can do at home to support this partnership.

Precautions and Possible Pitfalls

If parents do not speak English well, they may be reluctant to communicate with teachers. In such cases, if the teacher cannot speak the parent's language, a community volunteer might act as a school advocate and resource, or someone from the school might be able to translate a letter or handout for parents into the parents' native language.

Sources

Hartman-Haas, H. J. (1983). *Family educational interaction: Focus on the child.* Paper presented at the annual meeting of the American Educational Research Association, Montreal, Canada.

Hartman-Haas, H. J. (1984). *Family involvement tips for teachers.* Division of Research Evaluation and Testing Research Bulletin (pp. 1–12). Newark, NJ: Newark Board of Education.

Strategy 93: Literacy programs work best when they involve the whole family.

What the Research Says

Weinstein (1998) synthesized research related to literacy and family involvement and suggested parents' practices influence the school achievement of their children when it comes to reading and writing. Weinstein (1998) indicated that literacy programs in schools can be strengthened when they involve at least two generations of a family and that these relationships affect literacy use and development. She pointed out that studies of language use among Mexican Americans (Delgado-Gaitan, 1987), Navajos (McLaughlin, 1992), and Cambodians (Hornberger, 1996), for example, showed how language and literacy use reflect the cultural patterns of values and beliefs and may or may not be shared by schoolteachers and others. As immigrant children develop their English language ability, they can positively affect their parents' literacy development. The goals of a family program would be to improve children's achievement by promoting parental involvement.

Classroom Applications

This is a unique opportunity for teachers to bring the community into the classroom, encouraging the parents to visit their literacy lessons and participate in discussions and language-development activities. A major objective of a family literacy program is to improve reading skills (Weinstein, 1998), and this can be achieved when the teacher provides a variety of reading activities, such as teaching families to imitate behaviors of families in the homes of successful readers, like reading aloud to children and asking them specific questions. The children can also reverse this process by reading aloud to their parents when they return home from school. This becomes a two-way instruction program with parents sometimes teaching their children and the children sometimes teaching their parents. In this way, generations can reach out to each other.

One example of such activities in action is getting the different generations of one family together in the classroom to discuss their family, backgrounds, beliefs, and values and how these compare with what they see in their community. The teacher can help prepare for this by gathering information about the family's cultural background from magazines and books. For example, if the children are from a country in South America, the teacher can access photos of the family's country of origin from *National Geographic* and other sources and videos about life in that country and then get the elders to describe the photos and explain the videos to the children in the class. In this way, both generations get practice in a range of literacy skills while passing knowledge from one generation to another.

The class can produce a booklet on the culture in focus and/or develop a Web page on various aspects of that family's life, such as a family tree. This project-based work can link the classroom to the wider community and better involve parents and their children in developing literacy skills, although the focus is not on language learning.

Precautions and Possible Pitfalls

The main problem in setting up intergenerational literacy programs is selling their worth to both generations. The parents need to be informed about the benefits, especially the language and literacy benefits, of participating in such a nonlinguistic project. The children need to be informed about the benefits of the two-way language instruction program that lie behind such a method. When the teacher informs both sides about the benefits of this two-way intergenerational method, the family project can progress smoothly.

Sources

Delgado-Gaitan, C. (1987). Mexican adult literacy: New directions for immigrants. In S. R. Goldman & K. Trueba (Eds.), *Becoming literate in English as a second language* (pp. 9–32). Norwood, NJ: Ablex.

Hornberger, N. (1996). Mother-tongue literacy in the Cambodian community of Philadelphia. *International Journal of the Sociology of Language, 119*, 69–86.

McLaughlin, D. (1992). *When literacy empowers: Navajo language in print.* Albuquerque: University of New Mexico Press.

Weinstein, G. (1998). *Family and intergenerational literacy in multilingual communities.* ERIC Q&A. Washington, DC: National Center for ESL Literacy Education.

Strategy 94: Learn what teacher education programs don't teach about parent conferences.

What the Research Says

A questionnaire was developed to determine preservice program requirements relative to information and skills for parent–teacher conferences. Of the 136 teacher education institutions that were questioned, 124 institutions responded. The percentages of those that frequently required preparation for parent–teacher conferencing are listed as follows:

- Elementary: 59%
- Early childhood education: 57%
- Special education: 44%
- K–12/All levels: 42%

Nineteen percent of the responding institutions provided and required a separate course for parent–teacher conferences. Seventy-five percent indicated that these skills are taught in a methods course context. Seventy percent included parent–teacher conferencing content and skills in field-based experiences.

Despite renewed emphasis on parental involvement, preservice programs did not consistently identify parent–teacher conferencing skills as a major objective. Field-based experiences address the topic but appear hindered by school policies in actual conferences.

Classroom Applications

Many new teachers do not feel prepared for parent–teacher conferencing, and they are not alone. Many veteran teachers avoid them and are not comfortable in these situations. Experience is the best teacher. If a beginning teacher does not receive a background and a basic understanding of parent–teacher communication techniques, he or she may need to look for other sources of information on effective strategies. Learning on the job by acquiring information from colleagues can be helpful. Teachers can also search academic literature, where there is an extensive knowledge base.

Parents come to the table with their own agenda, and the teacher is usually there to react to their concerns. Occasionally, a teacher can react positively to their concerns about the student. Most of the time, teachers are in a position that requires them to mitigate and litigate the student–teacher or student–curriculum–pedagogy relationship. Occasionally, the teacher is called to defend his or her practices. Following is a list of suggestions that can help.

- Collect phone numbers (including work phone numbers) and addresses, and put the information on file cards. This lets students and parents know the teacher is willing to be proactive in communicating with home. If a student's last name is different from his or her parents, making sure the correct last name is used can be critically important in establishing rapport from the beginning of the conversation. Identify early which parent the students would like the teacher to communicate with.

- Let parents know how they can best reach the teacher—through telephone calls, e-mail, or other strategies. Teachers can send the information home by mail or announce it during open house. The smart teacher will create a returnable parent acknowledgment of receiving the information and reward the student!

- If appropriate, the teacher can make calls during school hours with the student present. After the teacher has spoken to the parents, parents often want to talk to their son or daughter. This works well with behavior problems. Students usually want to avoid these situations. Once a new teacher does this, the rest of his or her class will quickly get the message that parental relationships are important to the classroom teacher.

- Teachers should acknowledge potential trouble early and be proactive. The teacher can avoid getting calls by making calls home first. It's common for the first call to be made to someone in administration. Often, a call at the first sign of trouble can clear up misunderstandings early.

- It is important to realize that the classroom experience the student takes home is filtered through the mind of that student. Teachers need to itemize and break down the potential issues ahead of time and prepare a response. Acknowledge the concerns the parents bring and prepare to redefine them. It is helpful to remember that the teacher and the parents are on the same side, as collaborators in the students' education.

- As a "new teacher on the block" try to talk to counselors, administrators, or other teachers familiar with the students or student before making calls or conferencing with parents. Sometimes even veteran teachers need help in dealing with certain parents. Teachers shouldn't put themselves in a position to be ambushed. If a teacher is really worried, it is perfectly fine to have a counselor or administrator familiar with the parents present and let the parents know they will be there.

- Sometimes it might be better for a teacher to let others familiar with the parents and students make the call. The teacher can then set up a conference if necessary. A teacher shouldn't see this as a sign of weakness; it can be the best strategy. A vote of confidence directed toward the teacher by a trusted counselor or administrator can get around the school's community quickly and begin to build the new teacher's reputation as a caring and effective teacher and communicator. This can be a really necessary strategy for non-English-speaking parents!

● Once in a parent–teacher conference, the teacher should start the conference by listening carefully to what the parents have to say. Having itemized grades, lessons, handouts, student work, and so on will help. The teacher can then break down parent concerns and carefully address each one individually. Being organized and prepared with potential solutions to the problems a teacher expects to hear ahead of time can reap rewards in increased communication and rapport with parents.

● Letting supervisors know ahead of time about problems that could spill over into their laps allows teachers and supervisors to work on strategies together. Giving the supervisor copies of relevant materials (classroom policies, copies of tests, etc.) in advance so they are brought up to speed can help make the new teacher's job easier.

Precautions and Possible Pitfalls

Many times parent conferences turn out to be hugely successful. However, they can also turn sour. Occasionally parents simply will not be there for the teacher or for their son or daughter. They may not have control over their relationship with their child themselves. It is sad to say that phone calls home and parent conferences may be a lost cause in some cases. Counselors can often alert the teacher to situations where conferencing won't help. A teacher could end up listening to the parent's problems and never really resolve the issues with their student. In these cases, the teacher will need to follow through on the paperwork the school or district requires, such as sending home notifications. However, sometimes teachers may need to accept the fact that they are on their own and need to come up with strategies that won't include the parents.

Sources

Henderson, M. V., Hunt, S. N., & Day, R. (1993). Parent-teacher conferencing skills and pre-service programs. *Education, 114*(1), 71–73.

Rabbitt, C. (1984). The parent/teacher conference: Trauma or teamwork. *Phi Delta Kappan, 59,* 471–472.

Strategy 95: Be aware that there is more than one model of emotional intelligence.

What the Research Says

Cobb and Mayer (2000) pointed out in their research review article on social and emotional intelligence that educators looking to incorporate emotional intelligence into their classrooms and schools should be aware that there are at least two models of emotional intelligence curricular approaches out there. Cobb and Mayer stressed that each model that makes its way into schools needs to be empirically defensible, measurable, and clear enough to serve as a basis for curriculum development.

Cobb and Mayer (2000) divided emotional intelligence into two models. The first, the ability model, defines emotional intelligence as a set of abilities and makes claims about the importance of emotional information and the potential uses of reasoning well with the information. The second is referred to as the "mixed model." It mixes emotional intelligence as ability along with social competencies, traits, and behaviors and makes great claims about the success this type of intelligence can lead to.

Cobb and Mayer (2000) went on to review how these two ideas have been experimented with in schools, methods of measuring and quantifying these ideas, and offering ideas on how schools can work with the different notions of social and emotional and intelligences. Cobb and Mayer believed the model that emphasizes emotional knowledge and reasoning only may have advantages because it has the potential to reach more students.

Classroom Applications

According to Cobb and Mayer (2000), emotional intelligence emerged or re-emerged into popular culture and education in Daniel Goleman's 1995 bestselling book, *Emotional Intelligence*. The book characterized emotional intelligence as a mix of skill sets or intelligence such as awareness of emotions, traits described as persistence, zeal, and good behavior. Goleman collectively called these emotional intelligence behaviors "character." Cobb and Mayer went on to say the public received the idea of emotional intelligence enthusiastically. It seemed to de-emphasize the importance of general IQ and held the promise of a more level academic playing field for those whose cognitive abilities might be challenging. It also offered educators the opportunity to integrate a student's reasoning from both the head and heart. Schools could now develop a student's emotional competencies that would result in a "caring community" or a place where students felt cared about and respected and could feel more bonded with their classmates.

To find out more about what curricular choices teachers have, especially for younger students, try looking at the Collaborative for Academic, Social, and Emotional Learning at http://www.casel.org. This site offers the most complete selection of resources for teachers.

Precautions and Possible Pitfalls

The research and science on social and emotional intelligence lag behind popular media reports and most opinions on the topics. The topics have only been in the national spotlight since the mid-1990s, and it's hard to find definitive school practices that have the strong research behind them. While some of the theory has caught on in education, it feels like the business world has really embraced the concepts. The lack of research should not deter teachers from considering the theories and how they might see their potential in their classroom or school.

Source

Cobb, C. D., & Mayer, J. D. (2000). Emotional intelligence: What the research says. *Educational Leadership, 58*(3), 14–18.

> *Strategy 96: Rearrange elements of the school day instruction to maximize social and emotional teaching and learning opportunities.*

What the Research Says

Bonaiuto, Johnson, and Poliner (2005) looked at five elementary schools in the Needham Public School District (5,000 students) in Massachusetts to examine the results of a social and emotional intelligence curriculum. The district had implemented an evidence-based social and emotional learning program five years earlier, stressing skills, but it found that it was not changing behavior. The district adopted the program to affect negative behaviors such as bullying and harassment in addition to drug and alcohol abuse and violence.

Earlier research by the Collaboration for Academic Social and Emotional Learning (CASEL, http://www.casel.org/) found that students developed and established knowledge about social and emotional decision making. However, the researchers wanted to know if the program changed student behavior in the classroom, on the playground, or on the weekends. Researchers heard from teachers, playground supervisors, and parents that students did not consistently apply skills (self-management, decision making, social communication, and problem solving) targeted by the adopted program.

Researchers concluded that teaching social and emotional skills was only one part of changing behavior and that teachers still needed to find ways for students to practice those skills throughout the day. In response, the schools developed a number of strategies to encourage students to apply their skills and social and emotional literacy.

In Needham Public Schools, teachers made a conscious effort to rethink their practices, routines, and general daily school organization. Embedding social and emotional literacy skills in routine daily practices made a big difference. They still teach explicit social and emotional skills but now provide opportunities to see the skills modeled, to practice the skills, and to apply them in everyday and new situations. In the school setting, students are also able to receive feedback and reinforcement. Researchers found that teaching the skills alone didn't affect behavior without additional modification of the way teaching and learning occurred in the schools.

Classroom Applications

 Following are a few of the strategies the Needham School District targeted.

- *Gatherings—Getting students together.* Schools worked and restructured to provide regular opportunities to gather students to help them form connections with teachers and one another. They found that people behave better when they feel known and welcomed rather than invisible and alienated. Gatherings take the form of morning meetings, circles, or advisory groups. They provide opportunities for students to get to know one another better. Groups greet each other, share, participate in activities, and receive news and make announcements. Students plan very active leadership roles in these activities. These gatherings provide structured opportunities to get to know one another, feel welcome, have a voice in classroom culture, practice social skills, and take ownership.
- *Cooperative groups.* Cooperative learning has been around in various forms for years. Teachers in this study made a distinction between group work and cooperative learning. Within the paradigm of social intelligence, cooperative learning provides an authentic setting to learn and practice social intelligence skills. Skills are taught, practiced, and assessed as part of the group's

activity. A grading and performance rubric as well as activity objectives can define listening, positive encouragement, leadership, sharing, reflecting skills, and content objectives. Teachers can develop checklists of behaviors observing group dynamics and can share their observations with the students.

- *Social routines and schedules.* Schools examined their school routines to find opportunities for students to practice their skills in a safe and reinforcing environment. They first reversed lunch and recess so recess comes before lunch. Students could expend energy and eat in less of a rush when not looking forward to recess. They also changed or adjusted age-appropriate games, and better defined playground rules and consequences used by recess teachers and those used by classroom teachers. Adults came to consensus on recess, and recess structure became one that could be taught to the students.

Middle school teachers believed the 45-minute periods led to a rushed and disorganized school day, which impeded social and emotional learning. They modified schedules to take advantage of longer blocks of time to better form relationships and provide learning opportunities. Teachers observed that students were calmer and more focused. Even students who doubted their ability to sit for 90 minutes found they liked longer periods more than shorter periods.

The changes that were made in the Needham study to learning and teaching structures, routines, and practice produced big payoffs. Combining and embedding the social and emotional skills into the curriculum takes thought and planning. Teachers can always teach the skills like they would subject-matter content, but that's not enough to get kids to adopt them as new behaviors. Teachers need to do more to get them to apply those skills in their daily world and reality. It requires attention to the learning environment as well.

Precautions and Possible Pitfalls

 Teachers need to keep parents in the loop. Lessons learned at school need to be reinforced at home. Design and develop a parent component to the social and emotional curriculum. The students are only with teachers four to six hours out of the day.

Source

Bonaiuto, S., Johnson, G., & Poliner, R. (2005). Learning throughout the day. *Educational Leadership, 63*(1), 59–63.

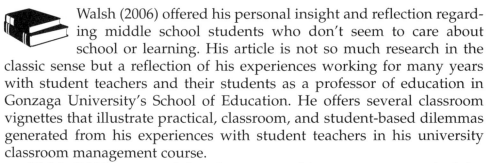

Strategy 97: Develop individual strategies for students who "don't do" school.

What the Research Says

Walsh (2006) offered his personal insight and reflection regarding middle school students who don't seem to care about school or learning. His article is not so much research in the classic sense but a reflection of his experiences working for many years with student teachers and their students as a professor of education in Gonzaga University's School of Education. He offers several classroom vignettes that illustrate practical, classroom, and student-based dilemmas generated from his experiences with student teachers in his university classroom management course.

Walsh (2006) proposed that there are positive engagement principles to address the challenges teachers face with reluctant learners. Basically, they are:

- Get to know students so that they can experience an informed and interested role model.
- Take time to talk to students even as they push teachers away.
- Don't take student antagonism and inaction personally by taking a step back; instead, build trust and use positive regard.

Walsh elaborated on these principles and suggested that the complex nature of most reluctant learners requires a teacher to develop an array of adaptive teaching behaviors to re-engage these students in the learning and teaching paradigm.

Classroom Applications

Most teachers come from a background of being successful students and have a hard time understanding why some students just don't "do" school very well. They often internalize or personalize the resistance that students exhibit or their rebuffs to the teacher's efforts.

For most teachers, depersonalizing student responses to their efforts is a challenging task with a steep learning curve. Teachers need to develop the skills and insight to look beyond the resistance and see what lies beneath it and not see resistance as a personal attack on their class, subject, personality, or teaching style. Beginning teachers and some veteran teachers often respond to these types of students with disappointment and anger. Teachers often look to punishment, coercion, or avoidance as solutions to their dilemma with the student. Students are usually not very responsive to these approaches.

In contrast to punishment, avoidance, and coercion, developing strategies to get to know students, taking time to talk to them, and not taking antagonism, resistance, and stubbornness personally, a teacher can avoid being trapped emotionally as they try to get into the head of the kid who doesn't seem willing to "do" school. In this way, a teacher can objectively set in motion a range of adaptive strategies to meet the needs of the situation regarding a turned-off, discouraged, or disenfranchised student. The teacher's goal is winning over reluctant learners and showing them the individual steps they can take toward a more successful relationship with teaching and learning.

Most teachers get plenty of guidance on how to set standards, be firm and in control, and be consistent. These are great attributes but are only a piece of the classroom management puzzle. These attributes are safe and predictable but don't directly address the various models of disengagement, apathy, defiance, or other ingrained and practiced defenses. Every disengaged student is a complicated problem that requires more than high standards, firm control, and consistency. Walsh (2006) suggested the following positive engagement principles: (1) get to know students, (2) take time to talk to students, and (3) don't take the student's antagonism and inaction personally. These concepts are elaborated on in the following paragraphs.

Gathering Student Information

Polished teachers subconsciously observe, listen to, study, and generally size up their students. They form mental file folders of information guiding their choices about where students should sit, who might work best together, who will do homework and who won't, and what strategies might motivate them to authentically engage in learning. They "read" their students, learning how best to accommodate their needs and what might not work. They are able to enter their students' world, see their personal agendas and develop working strategies to engage all students. Many of these skills come with experience. How can novice teachers begin to acquire these skills?

Novice teachers can use forms, surveys, questioning, inventories, or other teachers to get to know who they are teaching and managing. Parent questionnaires can gather insight into their perspectives, and student questionnaires can provide interesting inventories, feelings, attitudes, and values regarding subject matter, preferred learning styles, and learning difficulties.

Teachers can also ask students for suggestions of assessment preferences, instructional strategies, and evaluation and grading procedures. Many older students can tell teachers how they learn best.

Writing samples and simple reading activities can help a teacher assess skill levels early in the class. Assessing study skills can provide a clear view into homework habits and general academic skills and motivation. A few simple homework assignments can begin to show patterns of performance.

For help in these areas, try support4learning for assessment tools at http://www.support4learning.org.uk/education/learning_styles.cfm and Study Guides and Strategies at http://www.studygs.net/.

Student–Teacher Discourse

There is often a burnout factor at work here for veteran teachers. Many times teachers come up with cliché statements out of frustration. Phrases like "Work with the ones who care and want to be there" and "You can't save them all" help frustrated teachers create distance between themselves and a challenging student. Usually an unengaged student is really indirectly saying something else with their attitude. They are saying that they feel they can't do the work today, they are distracted or don't care today, they're depressed, or they don't have the skills or background to do the work. They may write down anything to get through the assignment, say "I don't know," when asked a question, or present some other type of passive compliance in the classroom. Passive compliance can turn to more decisive resistance when pushed. Older students often have seen and successfully resisted many teachers' efforts and have become very good at staying disengaged. The first rule is to not be provoked into escalating the situation or tension between the teacher and the student. Timing in dealing with effective communication is important. All this disengagement and resistance can manifest itself with individuals, small groups of students, or in whole classes, depending on group dynamics and peer interaction.

Many of these types of students have much more experience provoking inexperienced teachers than the teacher has trying to diagnose the primary cause of their disengagement. Some students are experts at getting teachers to back off to a safe distance. The problem with being at a safe distance is that teachers cut off avenues of communication. At this point, be careful not to look to intimidation, coercion (grades), avoidance, or punishment (referrals, etc.) as tactics. Teachers may contain the problem, but this approach won't solve it or make it more manageable.

Emmer, Evertson, and Worsham (2003) offered three communication techniques to help persistently unengaged students. They are: (1) communicate without attacking the student or students, which is called *Constructive Assertiveness*; (2) solicit and affirm students' viewpoints by active listening and positive processing, which is called *Empathic Responding*; and (3) resolve conflict through mutual agreement, which is called *Problem Solving*.

All three strategies offer teachers concrete practical steps or techniques to continue student–teacher dialogue. They encourage teachers to keep the lines of communication open by clearly communicating their concerns, listening to students' perspectives, and mitigating or negotiating mutual satisfying solutions to classroom friction.

Teachers need to avoid personalizing student behavior, inaction, antagonism, angst, or drama. Teachers have to remember that students all have a social agenda and a social and emotional curriculum to work through as they move through the school system and mature. Mood swings and social crises are all part of the job. Students are learning how to have relationships, maintain friendships, date, and deal with their parents—all while taking classes.

It is sad to say that the most unlovable students are often the ones who need love the most, and they are the most difficult to deal with. Also, often students think they are more in charge of school situations than the teacher. Most of the time a student's actions say more about their maturity and social skills than the teacher's teaching. Teachers can develop a practice of defining the space between themselves and the students. When confronted with a challenging situation, Walsh (2006) suggested that teachers use the following three interrelated steps, adapted from his article and summarized here.

Take a Step Back—where the teacher disengages before responding and stays composed in the midst of emotionally charged confrontations. Taking a step back means de-escalating the emotion that is normally present during tense conversations. Teachers often see 150 or more often unpredictable students a day, and by stepping back, they are allowing themselves time to read a situation and avoid the instinct to engage in power struggles that usually get a teacher nowhere. Teachers feel the need to be in charge and dominate verbal exchanges. Winning these battles often does nothing to increase student engagement.

Build Trust—taking the high road by continuing to talk and ask questions during prolonged conflicts. Don't give up on reluctant students. They find all types of ways to push teachers away and resist engagement. Continue to reach out to the most challenging students. Effort over time will tell the student that teachers are for real. Over time teachers will begin to build trust, and even the most resistant student will begin to see the teacher as safe, approachable, and nonthreatening. Remember, many of these students have only been approached by teachers with punishment, coercion, or intimidation strategies.

Use Positive Regard—respecting and affirming students while dealing with their antagonism and inaction. Walsh (2006) said these actions help teachers override their natural "fight or flight" instincts when engaging students who seem to always say, "I don't care." There are points in any classroom discourse when a student will cross the line with defiance, disrespect, or harassment and destroy the learning and teaching environment for everyone. A teacher's authority should always be respected, and at these times, teachers have to act quickly and decisively. Teachers need to stay focused on the behavior and the inappropriate nature of the confrontation. A teacher who treats students with respect during these tense moments, even while the students are exhibiting horrible behavior and are being disrespectful themselves, leave the situation open to future dialogue. Sometimes teachers lose sight of the fact that they write their rules and consequences for usually only one or two students in the class. Ninety-five percent of the rest behave and engage without much effort on the teacher's part. Take time to see the positive, and don't be overwhelmed by the temporary negative interactions and situations one or two students can create. Staying positive will help the entire class stay focused and reduce the power that negative attacks bring.

Many new teachers (and at times, some veteran teachers) are emotionally vulnerable to students who resist learning and don't "do" school. Many behaviors and responses to school situations are deeply ingrained in students who often have not had many positive academic or personal experiences with teachers. The basic strategies listed above arm teachers with professional behaviors to help them begin the identification and acquisition of their own style of dealing with the resistant student. They give teachers alternatives to the anger, punishment, coercion, and avoidance that Walsh (2006) described as the responses that many beginning teachers exhibit. Remember there is a story behind every behavior a student exhibits, and it's up to the teacher to depersonalize and find a way to make sense of the underlying pathology and respond appropriately and effectively to become a positive force in every student's life.

Precautions and Possible Pitfalls

The need for patience is important here. Reading students and classroom situations are part art and part science. Acquiring skills in these areas requires practice, reflection, and adjustments that come only with time and experience. There are so many factors that influence student behaviors that it's very difficult to have the right response all the time. All teachers have their ups and downs trying to manage learning environments. However, the more teachers work at it, the better they become!

Sources

Emmer, E. T., Evertson, C. M., & Worsham, M. E. (2003). *Classroom management for secondary teachers* (6th ed.). Boston: Allyn & Bacon.

Walsh, F. (2006). A middle school dilemma: Dealing with "I don't care." *American Secondary Education, 35*(1), 5–15.

Strategy 98: *Reflect on what teens have to say about their experience with adolescence.*

What the Research Says

Cavanaugh, Girod, and Padales (2005) collected 464 short essays written by teenagers about issues specific to the experience of today's adolescents. Teens chose from 13 different writing prompts derived from an extensive literature review that reflected issues found in adolescent development. The essays were written directly to teachers to give voice to teens about adolescent experiences, dreams, and concerns.

The examination of the distributions of essays written to specific prompts suggested higher than expected interest in communicating to educators about issues of motivation and engagement in teaching. The researchers' qualitative analysis suggested six themes along three axes of tension that included fearfulness and risk taking, boredom and stress, and frivolity and responsibility. The researchers believed that these themes suggested clear lessons for teachers and teacher educators working in today's classrooms.

Classroom Applications

Teachers need to look at the results of this study and begin a personal discussion and reflection on how educators can better structure a student's school and classroom experience to alleviate some of the distractions that teens feel inhibit their academic, psychological, and physical well-being.

Nineteen percent of the teens in the study chose to write to the theme of fear. Fear essays seem to break into different categories: fear for the future (war, terrorism, etc.), fear of being poor, or fear of abusing drugs or alcohol; fear for their physical safety, including gang violence, bullying, etc.; and fear of relationship issues such as intimacy within relationships, concerns about abandonment by friends or family; and fear about positive relationships with peers, teachers, and parents.

Risk taking or risky behavior concerned 72% of the participants. Risk was divided into physical risks, such as drugs and alcohol, driving, violent or dangerous play, fighting, bullying, and unsafe sexual behavior, and social–emotional risks in relationships or academic settings.

Cavanaugh et al. (2005) concluded that, taken together, the themes of fear and risk taking suggested that teens are at the same time unsure of themselves and their place in the world while also compelled to explore, reach out, and test and clarify the boundaries of their social–emotional and physical space. They live their lives in conflict between fear and caution, pushing away yet needing comfort. They are eager to lead their lives but generally are unsure of themselves, their personal boundaries, and their comfort zones. It's key to be able to talk to students in positive ways about risk-taking behavior and the role it plays in establishing identity. Forward-thinking teachers can seek ways to provide appropriate and healthy risk-taking opportunities in schools and classrooms so teens feel less willing to look for more dangerous opportunities outside of school. For some students, simply playing a team sport is a very risk-taking behavior.

Regarding the theme of boredom, it recurred through 49 essays. Thirty-seven essays used words like "bored," "uninteresting," and "not exciting." Boring and uninspiring teachers were written about by teens in 141 essays. Only 42 students wrote about positive experiences. The terms "disinteresting," "dull," and "generally apathetic in their work" were found as descriptors of teachers and their teaching methods.

In contrast, 89 student essays featured thoughts on stress in their lives. The stress fell into two large categories. First, stress was reported from social and relationship situations in 31 essays. These stressful events included fights with parents, conflict with teachers, peer conflicts, and pressures from boyfriends and girlfriends. Parental and peer pressure over a variety of sources and stressors dominated this category.

The second category of stress came from schools. Workload issues, expectations of academic excellence, and pressures related to postsecondary expectations were cited most.

Overall, a large number of essays described a teen life of boredom and stress occurring at the same time. School was cited as the overwhelming stressor and cause of both conditions. Teachers can work at accommodating teens who often desperately want to study something that is interesting to them. Consider the notion of opened-ended curriculum and multiple learning pathways where projects and activities offer teens choices in how and what they want to learn within a larger curricular topic. Assessment can also provide options for how students want to demonstrate to what degree they have mastered the goals and curricular standards. These techniques might alter the perception that teachers are dull, boring, or uninspired.

The themes of frivolity (17%, or 77 essays) and responsibility (25%, or 112 essays) made up the last of the six themes. Frivolity topics provided relatively shallow accounts of adolescent values, concerns, and aspirations. Most adults would classify these essays as frivolous or shallow. Teens described the value of their cars, music collections, appearance, clothing, or athletic ability. Some expressed sadness about valuing these items and appearance over deeper qualities such as personality and empathy. Social success in many peer groups, however, is based on seemingly shallow attributes. Shallow or frivolous concerns often act as the social currency of the teen culture.

Others described responsibility as a major problem in their lives. In many cases it was addressed as a theme that governed their lives. Employment and caring for brothers and sisters or aging relatives were mentioned as responsibilities beyond those of students, athletes, and peer leaders. Often essays painted a picture of anything but the stereotypical life of a carefree teen. It helps if one refrains from taking an adult perspective and instead takes a teen's view of these values.

Following are suggestions that Cavanaugh et al. (2005) offered to address the concerns related in the essays. They were written for a mixed audience, not just teachers. Some deal with issues usually mediated and organized by administrators. Read them from a unique perspective and take what can be used in a given situation.

- Reward affect, interest, and motivation in the classroom, not just traditional achievement. Prepare new teachers with effective strategies for engendering motivation and engagement while simultaneously teaching powerful and important content.
- Better educate teachers about adolescent issues. Teacher education must employ case methods in the study of adolescent issues rather than traditional, theory-driven studies in educational psychology and development.
- Better prepare teachers to use counseling skills and assume a counseling stance with teens who may need social and emotional support, in addition to academic support. As teachers often have stronger relationships with teens than counselors, teachers must know how to support and advocate for teens in need.
- Allow for positive risk taking in schools. Risk taking is healthy, powerfully engaging, and arguably developmentally positive. Teachers should explore methods for positive risk taking in the classroom such as through role-playing, goal setting, and taking and defending a personal opinion.
- Encourage longer-lasting relationships between teachers and students. Explore creative ways to schedule more consistent contact between teachers and students. Although this appears to be a policy issue in schools themselves, teachers can certainly learn to advocate for scheduling reorganization.
- Discard the disrespectful image of the carefree teen and recognize that many teens are working hard and desperately want to be successful both academically and socially. Through simulation and case methods, teacher education should help teachers expose their existing dispositions and stereotypes of teens.
- Allow for independent inquiry and self-exploration. Teacher education must help teachers learn to use inquiry and self-exploration in the classroom while simultaneously moving toward identified content standards and benchmarks.

- Reorganize or reinfuse schools with an ethic of caring. Teacher education must orient teachers to the social and emotional work involved in teaching and the moral and ethical roles that teachers must play in the education of youth.

Surprisingly, these types of arrangements and relationships were part of every one-room school in the country at one time. They continue to exist in many elementary schools but have become more difficult to find in middle and high schools.

Precautions and Possible Pitfalls

Do not lose track of the fact that mental stability, peace of mind, and overall mental health manifest themselves in more mental energy for academic endeavors. Students who are often trapped by some of the feelings and thoughts described here don't have the mental energy to be at their best when distracted. Teachers can create a caring and safe environment to maximize the academic potential that each student brings to class.

Source

Cavanaugh, S., Girod, M., & Padales, M. (2005). By teens, for teachers: A descriptive study of adolescence. *American Secondary Education, 33*(2), 4–19.

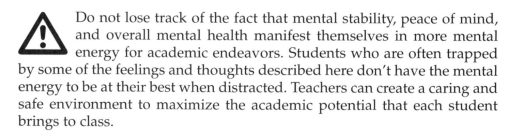

Strategy 99: Consider engaging parents in the mutual monitoring of their students' work in mathematics.

What the Research Says

Sirvani (2007) examined the effects of parental involvement on mathematics achievement in four high school Algebra I classes taught by a single teacher. Two classes acted as control groups, and two others were the experimental groups. A total of 52 freshmen (33 males and 19 females) participated, including 55% African American, 35% Hispanic, and 10% White, with 90% qualifying for reduced price or free lunch.

The parents of the students in the experimental classes received monitoring sheets twice a week that contained scores on homework and test grades. The parents of the control groups received nothing extra. Simply, students in the experimental groups outperformed the students in the control groups. When the results were examined regarding gender differences, parental involvement did not affect student achievement differently. Lower-achieving students in the experimental group significantly outperformed other such students in the control group.

Classroom Applications

This study gathered data from Algebra I classes in high school. In many high schools, students in Algebra I classes are already a year behind in the math class sequence. Algebra I competency is also the math level that many high school exit exams target for assessment. Many students find Algebra I a major obstacle in their path toward mathematics literacy and struggle from Algebra I on or develop some type of math phobia from their experience.

Many parents want to help their children but can do so only if they are aware of the academic problems their children face. According to this study (Sirvani, 2007) teachers could improve their students' scores and performance in mathematics courses by including parents in the learning and teaching equation. Also, if implemented, a parent involvement program can build a more positive relationship with parents overall, which is always a good thing for schools.

Precautions and Possible Pitfalls

Teachers should be aware that once students leave the classroom, the teaching and learning playing field becomes uneven. Many households and families are not prepared or willing to help their child. A class of math students will be divided between families willing to provide the time and resources to help and those who won't or who have limited resources. There is no easy solution to this problem. A teacher might need to identify the more needy students and dedicate more time and resources to make up for the lack of family participation.

Finally, it should be obvious the study cited here has limitations. First the study sampled basically only two ethnic groups, African Americans and Hispanics. Second, the sample size was small. Also, Algebra I students in high schools don't represent students in other math disciplines. It's hard to predict if the results of this study can be universally applied. Finally, progress reports and report cards were sent home during the study, and the study did not use any statistical instruments to eliminate the effects of these variables.

Source

Sirvani, H. (2007). The effect of teacher communication with parent on students' mathematics achievement. *American Secondary Education, 36*(1), 31–46.

Strategy 100: Encourage students to participate in service learning opportunities.

What the Research Says

Research on service learning by Simons and Cleary (2006) focused on four specific areas: (1) the impact of service learning on students' academic learning and personal and social development; (2) the benefits of service learning for student and community recipients; (3) an evaluation of interdisciplinary service learning; and (4) an evaluation of multicultural service learning programs.

In this context, the term *service learning* refers to a pedagogical method that intentionally integrates learning with service, and within this framework, service and learning goals are of equal weight. Each enhances the other for all participants. This pedagogical method requires students to apply theoretical knowledge to real-world situations, and at the same time, they connect the service experience to the course content through reflection.

Simons and Cleary (2006) looked at 142 students enrolled in undergraduate psychology courses at a teaching university during the fall of 2002. Ninety-five percent of the students self-selected to participate in service learning opportunities in local elementary schools, afterschool programs, or community learning programs. Forty-eight percent continued in the service activities after the required hours, and 75% reported that they would engage in future service learning. Data analysis showed that these students improved in diversity and political awareness, community self-efficacy, and civic engagement. The study suggests that service learning contributes to students' academic learning and personal and social development through social–emotional processes. Social–emotional learning contributes to service learning, and at the same time, service learning provides students with opportunities to demonstrate values and skills derived from social–emotional learning such as respect and responsibility.

Classroom Applications

Many studies have examined the impact of service learning, but the Simons and Cleary (2006) study was the first to use exploratory methods designed to demonstrate that participation affects academic learning and personal and social development. It also supported the notion that short-term community involvement commitments often transitioned to long-term commitments to community service. All these findings may be of particular interest for teachers and administrators.

First, many secondary schools have various programs incorporating some form of service learning. Also, many colleges and universities value and encourage secondary students to participate in service learning or other volunteer situations. These types of community participation programs are routinely valued by both parents and students as part of their college or university application and acceptance process.

Schools should try to expand and facilitate these types of arrangements and opportunities for students. However, individual teachers can help their students by making systematic efforts to connect classroom instruction to service learning either by encouraging individual students or creating all-class projects. For example, one high school routinely sends groups of biology students into neighboring elementary schools to teach science concepts and laboratory experiences. A high school Spanish teacher near the California–Mexico border has adopted an orphanage and routinely organizes fund-raising and the collection of useful clothing and other materials to be donated to the orphanage. This goes on all year and has expanded to include other teachers and classes.

A simple Internet search using the term *service learning* offered many, many sites that specialize in facilitating these types of relationships. The studies clearly show the value of these arrangements, and they are only limited by the teacher's willingness to make them happen.

Precautions and Possible Pitfalls

Liability and protecting students are always big considerations when organizing these types of relationships. If teachers are interested in incorporating service learning into the classroom, they need to include parents and administrators in the process. While many arrangements are possible, they all need to fall into the comfort zone of parents, schools, and school districts. Don't try to create these relationships alone!

Source

Simons, L., & Cleary, B. (2006). The influence of service learning on students' personal and social development. *College Teaching, 54*(4), 307–319.

Strategy 101: Make an extra effort to recruit minority and culturally diverse parents.

What the Research Says

Each day America's schools face greater diversity than at any time since the turn of the twentieth century. During the past two decades, schools have taken in great numbers of students from Laos, Cambodia, Vietnam, and the Philippines. With families from Mexico, Central America, and the Caribbean, along with immigrants from China and Korea, all coming to the United States seeking more favorable job options, politically stable environments, and educational opportunities for their children, America's schools have never been more diverse. In the Los Angeles Unified School District (the second largest in the United States), students speak some 80 different languages.

Studies of Latino immigrant families repeatedly show that the parents are highly interested in their children's education (Goldenberg & Gallimore, 1995). These parents, although they may be unfamiliar and uncomfortable with the American educational system, display a strong desire to see their children succeed and want to contribute to this success. Research with parents of minority and low-income students suggests they would like to be much more involved than they currently are in supporting their children's schools (Metropolitan Life, 1987). Studies including African American parents report the same high interest, but find that many of these parents lack the confidence that is necessary to support involvement (Chavkin & Williams, 1993).

Classroom Applications

The face of America's teacher is typically female, White, and monolingual. This reality poses some interesting challenges for involving parents of minority and culturally diverse parents in the education of their students.

The beginning teacher may feel somewhat apprehensive in recruiting parents of minority and culturally diverse students to be resources in the classroom. This reluctance is based on a concern about language difficulties, possible cultural differences, or simply inexperience on the part of the new teacher. And yet, because of our changing population, the beginning teacher should expect a diverse population of students. The challenges now facing teachers in these diverse settings may require the need for social understanding that goes beyond the aspects of culture often approached in teacher education multicultural classes. Challenges include the proper handling of major holidays, religious customs, dress, and food.

Even veteran teachers express a need for more intensive kinds of insight into the social ideals, values, and behavioral standards of each culture. They also require a more firm understanding of these standards and the cultural approaches to child rearing and schooling, first in the parent's own culture and then in the cultures these parents have passed down to their children.

Many new teachers focus on critical thinking and Socratic questioning techniques, which emphasize a student's active class participation (usually verbal). If students are from a cultural background that stresses quiet respect in school, they may need to be coaxed into becoming more active participants in their own learning. Teachers can speak with parents on why active participation is important to their child's education. Teachers can also provide alternative opportunities, such as allowing students to write journal entries or interact in small-group discussions.

Following are some suggestions that new teachers can use to make their classrooms more culture-friendly and to promote students' values of helping and sharing.

- Select two classroom monitors representing different cultures, and encourage them to work together.
- Allow students to help each other study vocabulary (students with greater English proficiency help those with a lesser ability).
- Allow students to work in small groups to preview their homework assignments, discussing possible strategies for problems and ensuring that everyone understands the assignment. This also helps students whose parents may not be able to read the assignment in English.
- Use choral reading as well as individual reading.
- Have more than one "student of the week" so that the attention is shared.
- Share cleanup of the whole room at once, rather than having each group clean up an activity center before the children move to another (observed in a kindergarten classroom).
- Emphasize joint ownership of classroom crayons and other materials rather than doling out a box per child.

Precautions and Possible Pitfalls

Parents of culturally diverse students can be an untapped resource in today's classrooms. Care should be taken to keep parents informed through communication (either written or verbal) in the parent's native language if their English is not proficient. Teachers must also be aware that just because they send home information in the parents' native language, the parents may still not be able to read or write in that language. It is not uncommon to find parents who have had no formal education. The more information teachers can have about their students, their family, and their cultural identity, the more teachers can best work with parents in supporting students' learning.

Sources

Chavkin, N. F., & Williams, D. L. (1993). Minority parents and the elementary school. In N. F. Chavkin (Ed.), *Families and schools in a pluralistic society* (pp. 73–83). New York: State University of New York Press.

Goldenberg, C., & Gallimore, R. (1995). Immigrant Latino parents' values and beliefs about their children's education: Continuities and discontinuities across cultures and generations. In P. Pintrich & M. Maehr (Eds.), *Advances in achievement motivation* (Vol. 9, pp. 183–228). Greenwich, CT: JAI Press.

Metropolitan Life. (1987). *Strengthening links between home and school.* Long Island City, NY: Author.

Trumbull, E., Greenfield, P. M., Rothstein-Fisch, C., & Quiroz, B. (2001). *Bridging cultures between home and school: A guide for teachers.* Mahwah, NJ: Lawrence Erlbaum Associates.

Index

CORWIN PRESS